THE INTERNET, ORGANIZATIONAL CHANGE, AND LABOR

The challenge of virtualization

David C. Jacobs and Joel Samuel Yudken

Routledge
Taylor & Francis Group

LONDON AND NEW YORK

First published 2003
by Routledge
11 New Fetter Lane, London EC4P 4EE

Simultaneously published in the USA and Canada
by Routledge
29 West 35th Street, New York, NY 10001

Routledge is an imprint of the Taylor & Francis Group

© 2003 David C. Jacobs and Joel Samuel Yudken

Typeset in Palatino by Wearset Ltd, Boldon, Tyne and Wear
Printed and bound in Great Britain by TJ International,
Padstow, Cornwall

British Library Cataloguing in Publication Data
A catalogue record for this book is available from the British
Library

Library of Congress Cataloging in Publication Data
Jacobs, David.
The internet, organizational change, and labor : the challenge of
virtualization / David Jacobs, Joel Yudken.
p. cm.
Includes bibliographical references (p.   ) and index.
1. Labor supply–Effect of automation on. 2. Internet–Economic
aspects. 3. Organizational change. I. Yudken, Joel. II. Title.
HD6331.J334 2003
303.48'33–dc21
2002156618

ISBN 0-415-26998-9 (hbk) ✔
ISBN 0-415-26999-7 (pbk)

THE INTERNET,
ORGANIZATIONAL CHANGE,
AND LABOR

The Internet and computer networks are dramatically reshaping the workplace as we devote more time both at work and at home to using the Internet. We are better informed and can work more efficiently, yet there is anxiety about the security of our jobs. *The Internet, Organizational Change, and Labor* examines what is happening to jobs, organizations, and unions in the age of the Internet, revealing both the opportunities and dangers for workers in the digital age.

This book explores the Internet's impact on organizations and labor from an interdisciplinary perspective. It looks at how the new digital technologies affect the number and quality of jobs, shape cultural change, and influence the prospects for union revival. Overall, it concludes that the Internet reduces transaction costs and thereby aids profit-making, but also assists workers, consumers, and citizens in challenging business practices.

This is a balanced analysis of the Internet aided workplace. Unlike many enthusiasts of e-commerce, this book identifies dangers in the Internet-driven enterprise, such as contingent employment, employee monitoring, and job loss. It also explores the potential benefits for employees, proposing possible strategies for reforming the economy.

David C. Jacobs is Professor of Economics and Management at Hood College in Frederick, Maryland, USA. He is co-editor of *The Future of the Safety Net: Social Insurance and Employee Benefits* for the Industrial Relations Research Association.

Joel Samuel Yudken, Ph.D. is Sectoral Economist and Technology Policy Analyst in the Public Policy Department of the American Federation of Labor and Congress of Industrial Organizations (AFL-CIO).

CONTENTS

CONTENTS

ACKNOWLEDGMENTS

The authors thank *The Philosophy and Public Policy Quarterly* and *Perspectives on Work* for publishing some of our ideas in an early stage. Thanks also to the faculty at the University of Auckland and Massey University for sponsoring seminars at which David Jacobs presented related papers. Additional thanks to Christine Owens, Director of Public Policy, AFL-CIO for her indulgence and support of Joel Yudken in carrying out this project. Last but not least, we want to express our appreciation to our families for their continuous support, and above all, their great patience, especially during the final, demanding months of completing the book.

INTRODUCTION

The Internet and allied information technologies are reshaping the workplace in myriad ways. While this reality is widely acknowledged, hyperbolic rhetoric clouds public understanding. Some talk loosely of revolutionary change and a new era of high tech entrepreneurialism. Many observers display an uncritical optimism about markets and new technology. They see the Internet as further perfection of a triumphant capitalism, cutting costs, and building profits. They wax enthusiastic about the speed of data on broadband and the leaps in processor power and are as yet unchastened by the losses on NASDAQ.

The exaggerated good news is frequently promulgated in the American business school, where neoclassical and technological orthodoxy typically reign. In the late 1990s, the Dean of a prominent Washington, DC business school praised the "dot-com" as the inspiration for all school activities. Students registered in droves for Managing Information System (MIS) courses. While student interest has topped out, many business school faculty remain cheerleaders for e-commerce, seldom inquiring as to the treatment of stakeholders. E-businesses are ordinarily viewed from the vantage point of managers alone. Only in a minority of schools is MIS reconsidered from the perspective of labor and other social movements. UK Informations System scholar Steve Walker is one of those who argue the need for a "social movement informatics" (Walker 2002).

In the chapters to follow, we will describe important dynamics in the Internet-driven workplace. We cannot present a complete picture, but we will draw inferences from cases through the application of an institutionalist lens, by which we mean an analysis sensitive to underlying power relationships in the operation of markets.

We do not accept the rigid assumptions of neoclassical economics. The real world is not characterized by perfect competition, actors do not have perfect information, and labor does not have perfect mobility. The effects of the Internet cannot be understood if self-adjusting markets are assumed. We are very much influenced by the pragmatist philosophy of

1

John Dewey and his emphasis on social consequences (including the fate of the least advantaged) as the measure of institutional policies. We question the neoclassical interpretation of labor as a commodity, as a means for economic activity, rather than as the end of such activity.

Among other things, the Internet facilitates the global mobility of capital. Investors can shift their assets and lenders can move their capital instantly over national borders. This is one form of information that flows freely on the Internet. The Internet renders communication nearly instantaneous and reduces the marginal cost of transmitting information. It permits the coordination of internationally dispersed workplaces. It has produced the so-called "virtual workplace," in which employees perform and coordinate much of their work online.

The Internet has altered the economies of organizing and protest. Web protests have compelled recalcitrant employers to acknowledge worker abuses. Similarly, the Internet has permitted citizens to broadcast protests of government actions, to evade the limitations of government media, and to reach a global audience.

Multiple examples demonstrate the impact of the Internet as an instrument of protest. The 1999 derailment of OECD negotiations over the Multilateral Agreement on Investments was widely attributed to an e-mail campaign. Protesters at the 1999 Seattle meeting to launch the World Trade Center evaded police through wireless e-mail and a "global positioning system." Zapatista rebels in Mexico have pursued what Rand Corporation analysts call a "netwar" against the government, emerging from a women's organizing project of the left-oriented 1990s' e-mail provider, the Institute for Global Communications. Arquilla and Ronfeldt (1998) define netwar as a campaign by an ideologically coherent issue network to mobilize information in the pursuit of its program and to change the opponent's understanding of the world. What remains to be seen is whether Internet-based protest organizations have the capacity to endure (Castells 2001: 138).

The Internet provides impetus to network structures, that is, informal organizations based on lateral relations among employees, consumers, and others. These parallel structures are fluid and not easily contained within formal hierarchies. They are capable of challenging much more powerful organizations because of the flexibility with which they can deploy and coordinate their supporters. The military origins of the Internet required a system that would provide redundant paths of communication, reducing vulnerability to attack. The preference of many programmers for collaboration based on freely available code continues to shape the development of the Internet. The resulting architecture is as hospitable to grassroots movements as business processes.

Amazon.com illustrates both the potential and perils of Internet-driven change in the workplace. Consumers benefit from convenience and economy. They are able to order books (and now many other products) without spending money for postage or stationery, without expending energy in travel to a bookstore or on the phone, etc. Search, travel, and order costs are minimized. Employees are relatively uninvolved with the products for sale, of which there are too many for any individual to master. There are few limits to what might be sold, and consumers and employees may be anywhere on the planet.

Amazon manages a vast warehouse system but economizes in the efficient management of its assets. The web-site encourages repeat purchases by recommending books to consumers. Book reviews abound; some were found to be ads in disguise placed by the publisher. Despite Amazon denials, the computer technology has permitted "dynamic pricing," prices adjusted in accord with customers' personal data (Anonymous 2000).

The excitement of a new venture initially appealed to the employees, and C.E.O. Jeff Bezos capitalized on this by his "Day 1" rhetoric. However, Amazon has sent many of its jobs offshore to reduce costs and disgruntled employees have begun to use the Internet to organize a virtual union to protest their treatment.

Economizing, sociologizing, and praxis

Amazon is well known as an e-commerce enterprise, but the Internet is also reshaping pre-existing enterprise, even the central firms of the manufacturing economy. General Motors, Ford, DaimlerChrysler, Renault, and Nissan are developing a joint web platform, "Covisint," to manage relations with suppliers, with the goal of effecting economies through continuous auctions among bidders. The auto companies will have enhanced power to push parts' prices downwards, and suppliers will seek to reduce labor costs (Lucore 2002).

The experience of Amazon and other virtual enterprises suggests a tentative model for Internet processes. Three dynamics can be inferred. First, the Internet contributes to "economizing," the pursuit of efficiency through markets. The virtual workplace has lower costs to commend it, although they may come at workers' expense. Employers choose to utilize the Internet to reduce communication costs, to facilitate outsourcing, and to manage a disparate set of contingent employees (all of which actions are focused on cost minimization). The Internet encourages disintermediation within enterprises, that is, the elimination of costly intermediate operations standing between management and the individual employee. Economizing treats employees and suppliers largely as means for profit-making rather than ends in themselves.

Second, the Internet is a vehicle through which unions and other social movements pursue what Daniel Bell (1973) called the "sociologizing mode," "the effort to judge a society's needs in a more conscious fashion ... on the basis of some explicit conception of the 'public interest.'" Unions and Non-Governmental Organizations practice this mode. An example is WashTech, the online association for high-tech workers at Amazon and Microsoft. While it has not won representation rights, it has built an active online community and has scored some successes through litigation, pressure tactics, and by educating its membership. (Another way of looking at this process is to observe that the Internet "socializes" disputes in that it involves society in judgment and resolution.) Here, Internet technology permits employees and other stakeholders to constitute themselves as ends rather than means in social and economic change.

Third, the Internet places expert knowledge at the disposal of any worker and facilitates the production and distribution of goods without the necessary intervention of management or middlemen. The personal computer has the capacity to engage in a form of online production. For example, college faculty are already experimenting with electronic journals which liberate them from reliance on commercial publishers. Stepping beyond Bell's analysis, let us call this additional option the "praxis" effect. This remains more promise more than reality, but it is implied within the emerging field of computer-supported cooperative work and participatory design. In praxis, employees become the authors of production, ends rather than means.

Three recent books relating to the Internet and the workplace illuminate aspects of the economizing, sociologizing, and praxis dynamics. Erran Carmel, author of *Global Software Teams* (1999), describes software companies' coordination of developers linked internationally by the Internet. While Carmel believes that cost reduction (economizing) often motivates the outsourcing of software development, he argues that the benefits accrue widely across borders. Lawyer and activist Nathan Newman, author of *Net Loss* (2002a), examines the Internet as a forum for debate and struggle as to the outlines of the global economy. He submits that the Internet will play a critical (sociologizing) role in providing countervailing power to unions and non-government organizations. In other writing, Newman (2000) stresses the value of the Internet as a platform for the collaborative development of software (praxis). Finally, journalist Maggie Jackson, author of *What's Happening to Home* (2002) warns of the threats to privacy and household in life online. Software developer, writer, and union activist alike must be alert to the tyranny of the home office. While these accounts of the Internet differ significantly in focus, together they illuminate economizing, sociologizing, praxis as dimensions of the Internet-driven workplace (see Jacobs (2002)).

In an interview, Nathan Newman described his own precedent-setting use of e-mail for organizing and protest purposes in the early 1990s:

4

My work using email for organizing started really in 1994. It was not really specifically campus organizing but it heavily involv[ed] students because they had the highest density of Internet access at that point. In 1992–1993 I had seen some of the potential of the Internet for organizing during a strike of graduate students at UC-Berkeley where email became a prime tool for organizing and actually ... for challenging the control of information by the union executive board. When Prop[osition] 187 was passed in 1994 [denying legal rights to California immigrants], I was working with a Bay Area immigrant rights group and I offered to set up an email list to help discussion and pull in new folks who were online into the movement.

While my initial announcement of the list was for Bay Area residents, hundreds of people from across the country joined within days, and with a Bay Area rally planned for December 11, 1994, groups on campuses across the country adopted the day for rallies as well. Within three weeks, a national movement of protests on immigrant rights in the wake of Prop 13 had been organized. I'm not sure if these were the first protests organized purely by email but I haven't found documentation of others yet. *The Nation* and *USA Today* soon wrote up the protests as part of the new use of the Internet for political work and my email list 187resist became a key information exchange not just for students but for nonprofits and political organizations involved with immigrant rights across the country. It was soon supplemented by a parallel list on affirmative action and one on labor issues (Newman 2000b).

Newman has been both theorist and practitioner with respect to the development of Internet strategies to enhance the power and labor and other social movements.

Information processing

Information is the subset of human knowledge that is necessary for the coordination of work processes and the generation of a product in an organization. Tushman and Nadler's (1978) information-processing model demonstrates that organizations differ in the way that they use information. Mechanistic structures limit the discretion of most employees, provide them with limited information, and require that they implement rigid rules (Burns and Stalker 1961). Organic structures depend upon widely shared information and invest most employees with the authority to make decisions. Mechanistic organizations function well in predictable environments and organic structures are well suited to volatile markets and rapid technological change. Intensified global competition and technological change now render mechanistic organizations less adequate in many if not most situations. On the other hand, the Internet and computer networks in general enhance the information-processing capacity of organizations and promote impetus to organic structures. In their most developed form, organic structures become the instrument, the means, of all the individuals who labor within them, and these individuals become the ends of the organization.

Industrial relations systems

John Dunlop's enormously influential *Industrial Relations Systems* (1993), cited technology as an important factor influencing the web of rules under which workers and managers interacted in the varied nations of the world. Dunlop (ibid., p. 61) listed these dimensions of technical context: fixed or variable workplace, relation of workplace to residence, stable or variable workforce and operations, size of the work group, job content, relation to machines or customers, and the scheduled hours and shifts of the workplace.

The Internet alters the technical context of the workplace in these ways. It introduces a variable and movable workplace, sometimes at home or elsewhere on the globe, increases flexibility as to the size and arrangement of the workforce, alters job content, and modifies the relationships of workers and machines. Dunlop's analysis, however, ultimately gives us little with which to evaluate the scope of Internet-associated changes. Dunlop takes as given the hierarchy of the modern corporation and finds inexorable global movement toward American models. His assumption of linear development and convergence toward the United States industrial relations system (also evident in *Industrialism and Industrial Man* (Kerr *et al.* 1960)) obscures the choices of the actors, including technological choices. All this may dull his insights as to the Internet impacts on the workplace, especially if the Internet stimulates significant reform of corporate hierarchies and renders more practical highly organic models of organizations.

History of technology

Harry Braverman (1974), Harley Shaiken (1986), and other "labor process scholars" have explained how technology may deprive workers of control or deepen their command over the details of production. For example, Shaiken noted the multiplicity of choices in the use of numerical control: to substitute for skilled machinist labor or as an aid to the skilled machinist. The Internet can be used in ways that advance the interests of workers, perhaps through sociologizing and praxis, or managers, through economizing.

Economists and social philosophers have long debated the effects of

6

technology. Adam Smith argued that technical advancement accelerated the division of labor, increased output, and resulted in an upward spiral of wealth. On the other hand, David Ricardo warned that investment in technology inevitably came at the expense of workers' income (given a fixed wage fund). Marx believed that technology necessarily displaces labor; this is the value it has for the capitalist (even as declining consumption depresses the economy). These classic views of technology fail to anticipate the complex impacts of the Internet as it potentially brings creative power to individuals and groups, enabling a vast realm of desktop production, at the same time that it promotes efficiencies in business-to-business (and consumer) transactions. While Adam Smith stressed the prosperity deriving from the division of labor, and Frederick Taylor later campaigned for the simplification of work, Internet and allied personal computer technologies may vertically enrich and horizontally integrate work (Heilbroner 1972).

In the following pages, we explore the Internet's impact on organizations and the workplace from complementary perspectives. On the one hand, Joel Yudken investigates the "Emerging Virtual Economy" in Part I, which consists of five chapters emphasizing history and economics. Yudken considers the new digital technologies as they are reflected in popular culture and as they engender popular hopes and fears in Chapter 1 entitled "Between utopia and dystopia." Chapter 2, "One, two, many industrial revolutions" asks whether digital technologies constitute a new "industrial revolution" paralleling electrification and automation. Yudken's third chapter, "The Wizard of Oz and the jobs dilemma," provides some preliminary speculation about the impact of the new technologies on the number and quality of jobs. In Chapter 4, "E-business and the virtual organization," Yudken surveys varied models of e-commerce as they are put to the test in the current environment, while Chapter 5, "Jobs in the virtual economy" considers workers' and unions' prospects as e-commerce evolves.

David Jacobs contributes Part II, "The Internet, social intelligence, and labor," consisting of three chapters emphasizing philosophy and politics. Jacobs examines the underlying reality of labor's plight in so-called "free markets," virtual or otherwise, in Chapter 6, "Labor problems." Chapter 7, "Social intelligence, open source, and craft" explains how the Internet derives its logic from and contributes to the social character of knowledge and innovation. Finally, Chapter 8, "Internet unionism and labor-friendly enterprise" speculates on how the Internet might be employed in the interests of workers, in the development of unions and reform of the economy.

We agree that the prospects for workers in the emerging economy depend in part on labor's response to the challenges the new technologies provide. That is, how will workers and their unions respond to the challenge of "virtualization" – the structural, organizational and technological complement of economic globalization, the expansion of international financial and trade flows and the integration of national economies?

Virtualization refers to much more than the spread of new information technologies. It also encompasses the globalized diffusion of new or modified versions of existing organizational forms – such as lean production – into productive activity, enabled, mediated and aided by these technologies. Confronted with these organizational transformations and the larger economic and social forces driving them, will workers remain "factors of production," merely the means for profit-making by others, or will they become authors, actors, and ends in themselves?

References

Anonymous (2000) "Dynamic Pricing on the Web is Proving Difficult," *Marketing Week*, October 26: 43.

Arquilla, J. and Ronfeldt, D. (1998) "Preparing for Information-Age Conflict: Part 1, Conceptual and Organizational Dimensions," *Information, Communication, and Society*, 1(1): 1–22.

Bell, D. (1973) *The Coming of Post-Industrial Society*, New York: Basic Books.

Braverman, H. (1974) *Labor and Monopoly Capital: The Degradation of Work in the Twentieth Century*, New York: Monthly Review Press.

Burns, T. and Stalker, G. M. (1961) *The Management of Innovation*, London: Tavistock Publications.

Carmel, E. (1999) *Global Software Teams*, New York: Prentice Hall.

Castells, I. (2001) *The Internet Galaxy: Reflections on the Internet, Business, and Society*, New York: Oxford University Press.

Dunlop, J. T. (1993) *Industrial Relations Systems*, Cambridge, MA: Harvard Business School Press.

Heilbroner, R. L. (1972) *The Worldly Philosophers; The Lives, Times, and Ideas of the Great Economic Thinkers*, New York: Simon and Schuster.

Jackson, M. (2002) *What's Happening to Home: Balancing Work, Life and Refuge in the Information Age*, New York: Sorin.

Jacobs, D. (2002) "The Internet and the Workplace: Introduction to a Technological Revolution," *Perspectives on Work*, 6(2): 4–5.

Kerr, C., *et al.* (1960) *Industrialism and Industrial Man; The Problems of Labor and Management in Economic Growth*, Cambridge, MA: Harvard University Press.

Lucore, R. E. (2002) "Challenges and Opportunities: Unions Confront the New Information Technologies," *Labor Studies Journal*, 23(2): 201–214.

Newman, N. (2000) "Storming the Gates," *American Prospect*. online: http://www.prospect.org/print/V11/10/newman-n.html (accessed 1 April 2003).

Newman, N. (2002a) *Net Loss: Internet Prophets, Private Profits, and the Costs to Community*, State College, PA: Pennsylvania State University Press.

Newman, N. (2002b) "Internet Organizing," e-mail (10 October 2002).

Schumpeter, J. A. (1947) *Capitalism, Socialism, and Democracy*, New York: Harper Torch Book.

Shaiken, H. (1986) *Work Transformed: Automation and Labor in the Computer Age*, Lexington, MA: Lexington Books.

Tushman, M. L. and Nadler, D. A. (1978) "Information Processing as an Integrating Framework in Organization Design," *Academy of Management Review*, 3: 613–621.

Walker, S. (2002) "Social Movement Informatics," e-mail, 18 October.

Part I

THE EMERGING VIRTUAL ECONOMY

1

BETWEEN UTOPIA AND DYSTOPIA

Virtual organizations

Player Piano is Kurt Vonnegut's classic satire about a world dominated by a supercomputer and where people have been replaced by machines. One of the characters, Katherine Finch, asks the novel's protagonist, Dr. Paul Proteus, if he thinks there will be "a Third Industrial Revolution."

Proteus responds, "In a way, I guess the third one's been going on for some time, if you mean thinking machines ... machines that devaluate human thinking. Some of the big computers like EPICAC do that all right, in specialized fields."

Katherine considered thoughtfully. "First the muscle work, then the routine work, then, maybe, the real brainwork." Proteus, who was just beginning to have doubts about a society in which he was both leader and beneficiary, answers, "I hope I'm not around long enough to see the final step" (Vonnegut 1972: 2).

Written in 1952, *Player Piano* expressed fears already emerging in the early post-war period that the industrial "revolution" brought about by computer automation would displace and deskill large numbers of workers. While Vonnegut's dystopian vision has not been realized, at least not yet, its central theme has been echoed many times in the ensuing decades.

Many believe that we are in the throes of a new industrial revolution, driven by continuous, complementary advances, and convergence, in microelectronics, computing, telecommunications, and related technologies. For the first time we may have the ability to substitute computing for mental labor on a significant scale. Virtually all computers in the 1950s were large, stand-alone machines, sometimes filling up entire rooms. The linking of multiple machines together for interactive data communications was at a very early stage. Today's typical PC, which can fit on a desk or even on a person's lap, is orders of magnitude faster, more powerful, and more versatile than the massive, vacuum tube-based computers in existence at the time *Player Piano* was written. In addition, most computers today are joined together in complex, high-speed digital telecommunications networks spanning the globe. It is conceivable, therefore, that today's advanced computing and networking capabilities have the *potential* to transform the organization and nature of work far beyond that envisioned by Vonnegut.

Indeed, the "virtual organizations" proposed by some "e-business" enthusiasts would leave businesses stripped back to their core areas of expertise and competence, outsourcing all support functions and business operations to external providers (Atwood and Parker 1998). Others go further, envisioning "lights-out factories," or plants with no workers, whose operations would be regulated, coordinated and managed both by computerized automatic control systems, employing artificial intelligence, and by remote control from corporate headquarters via the Internet. At the same time, these installations' computers would communicate and conduct transactions with those of contractors and suppliers around the globe via the Internet, with little human intermediation (Port 2001).

These visions are still far from being realized even with today's powerful technologies, and certainly were not realizable using technologies of even a decade ago. Nevertheless, the same economic and technological logic underlying earlier efforts to automate industrial processes (since the first steam-driven machines replaced human power in textile mills during the early nineteenth century) continues to motivate present-day efforts to automate productive activities, perhaps moving us closer to the "virtual" business models portrayed above. Most efforts to replace or substitute machines for human power and skills derive in large part from the managerial quest to reduce labor costs and achieve ever greater control over work processes.

The "ideal" of the completely automated factory has a long history, but today's technologies make this goal much more achievable than ever before. A United Auto Workers union official has acknowledged that Internet-commerce applications employed on a large scale by the big automakers could have significant impacts on autoworker jobs. He was not completely convinced, however, that these impacts would be any more significant than those inflicted on his union's members by earlier waves of automation and "innovative" organizational practices, such as "lean" manufacturing, in the auto industry during the 1970s and 1980s.[1]

Some scholars are skeptical about the importance of the Internet as a productivity-enhancing tool, especially compared to earlier periods of major technological change since the Industrial Revolution (Gordon 2000). The so-called "dot.com" bust in 2000 has greatly dampened the hype that fueled the "dot.com" boom of the last half of the 1990s. But the Internet is not just a fad; its economic and cultural impacts are just beginning to be felt. Some writers argue that the dot.com bust actually may have paved the way for a new cycle of information technology (IT) inno-vations, this time led by entrepreneurial firms with sound business strat-egies aimed at making a profit (Levy 2002). Newer technologies, such as broadband and wireless, are expected to broaden the use and impact of the Internet.

In fact, both home and business Internet use is still on the rise. According to a recent US Department of Commerce study, more than half of the United States is now online, and the rate of growth of Internet use in the nation is currently 2 million new Internet users per month (DOC ESA/NTIA 2002). The economic impact of the Internet, however, is rooted in how it is used both in the workplace and for commerce. Although the percentage of adults who use computers at work rose modestly from 51.6 percent to 56.6 percent between October 1997 to Sep-tember 2001, the share using the Internet and/or e-mail at work grew significantly from 17.6 percent to 41.7 percent. The 13 months between August 2000 and September 2001 saw an especially large jump of approximately 15 percent of adult employees using in Internet/e-mail use at work (DOC EST/NTIA 2002: 57).

Meanwhile, business-to-business (B-to-B) electronic commerce (e-commerce), continues to far outstrip business-to-consumer (B-to-C) online purchasing, the basis of most dot.com enterprises, in terms of share of total economic activity, although both types of e-commerce con-tinue to grow in all industry sectors.

In the following chapters we examine how growth in the use of the Internet and advanced computer network technologies in economic activity could affect jobs, skills, and labor markets in the "new economy" of the twenty-first century. This is a more complicated question than it appears on the surface. By undertaking this assessment we enter into a long-standing, often contentious, debate about how technological change has affected work organizations and jobs since the Industrial Revolution. Both "utopian" and "dystopian" themes shape the views of witnesses to periods of rapid industrial and technological change. The "utopians" claim that the technical and organizational innovations accompanying industrialization create great new wealth, more and better jobs, and easier living (Greenbaum 1995: 33). The dystopian view emphasizes the displacement, degradation, and deskilling of work – not to mention a despoiled environment, uprooted communities, and diminished quality of life – associated with rapid industrial change.

The dramatic growth of the Internet has been no exception in terms of provoking hyperbole. The Internet and new "information age" technol-ogies have been hailed as ushering in, in the words of former President Bill Clinton, "an economic transformation as profound as that that led us into the industrial revolution" (NYT 2000). The emerging economy built around the high-tech revolution and globalization has variously been called the New Economy, the Internet Economy, and in a 1998 *Business Week* (1998) special report, "The 21st Century Economy." Information technologies have been called in publications and brochures "the engine of global growth in the 21st century" and the "dominant force in a global economy." The IT revolution has been credited with the uninterrupted economic growth of the 1990s, which has been called the longest economic expansion in US history. Kevin Kelly, author of *New Rules for a New Economy: 10 Radical Strategies for a Connected World* goes further, asserting that we are in for a long period of "ultraprosperity" (Kelly 1999).

In a slightly more sober assessment, though still deeply optimistic about the IT revolution, the *Business Week* report recognizes that although "the gains from new technologies will boost the economy well into the century ... [T]he path to the 21st Century Economy will be a bumpy one" (*Business Week* 1998). "Each innovative surge creates economic and social ills," it continues, "from recessions to stock-market crashes to widespread job losses – and this one won't be different." In the end, however, it contends that "that's the price a nation must pay to achieve the benefits of dynamic change." Despite these bumps, information technology will continue to drive substantial productivity gains across the economy and faster economic growth than "most economists expect." It will foster higher education levels, an expansion of wages across the board and a shrinking wage gap. The standard of living for the next generation will rise, and baby boomers will be able to retire in comfort (ibid.).

At the end of the 1990s, many government and business leaders talked glowingly of the social and economic transformational nature of information technology, especially of Internet or electronic commerce (e-commerce) – the conducting of economic transactions via digital electronic networks. In an address to an International Labor Organization (ILO) conference in 1999 in Geneva, Switzerland, President Clinton called the digital revolution

> a profound, powerful and democratizing force. It can empower people and nations, enabling the wise and far-sighted to develop more quickly and with less damage to the environment. It can enable us to work together across the world as easily as if we were working just across the hall.
>
> (Clinton 1999)

In remarks presented at a conference on the "Digital Economy" in 1999, Clinton's Secretary William M. Daley touted e-commerce's enormous potential "to change the way we work, the way we shop, the way we get our news, and the way we conduct business." He added:

It is creating businesses that would not exist without it. It is creating whole new forms of businesses.... E-commerce is much more than a service sector tool. It is becoming a basic element for most manufacturing operations – from design, to development, to product, and to distribution. To paraphrase [Intel CEO] Andy Grove, there won't be Internet companies and non-Internet companies. A company will either be an Internet company or it won't be a company at all.[2]

Even when recognizing potential downsides of this movement, e-commerce proponents' primary concerns are with how to remove the obstacles in the way of the Internet achieving its full economic potential. A document prepared for the 1998 Organization for Economic Co-operation and Development (OECD) Ministerial Conference on electronic commerce in Ottawa, Canada, exclaims that "[g]lobal electronic commerce has potentially far-reaching economic and social implications for the nature of work, daily life, business-to-business relationships, and the role of governments" (OECD 1998: 1). It touts the "'borderless' nature of the information and communications technologies underlying global electric commerce," which is "creating a new economic order changing the ways people participate in society as citizens, consumers, workers and governments." In a report prepared on the social and economic implications of the Internet and electronic commerce, the OECD acknowledges that some social and economic displacement is likely in this "new economic order." Nevertheless, the primary objective of the OECD meetings on e-commerce has been to facilitate the "successful adaptation and spread of global electronic commerce ... to foster a stable and predictable environment which facilitates its growth and maximizes its economic and social potential" (OECD 1999).

There are pessimistic, even dystopian, views of the "Information Age," as well. In a period of only about half a decade, the Internet has become a ubiquitous feature in popular culture. It frequently makes its appearance as a prop in movies and television, usually as a piece of modern everyday life, but often also as a tool used by spies and law enforcement officers, not to mention by drug dealers, thieves, and assorted evildoers. In movies like *The Net* or *Minority Report* we see a darker, more ominous side of the Internet. Here, its potential for increasing the ability of powerful institutions (government, the military, corporations) to monitor and control our behavior is the story.

The plots of these movies are essentially a variation on the "Big Brother" theme in George Orwell's *1984*. Long before either television or the Internet became ubiquitous features of contemporary life, Orwell's classic book predicted interactive television systems capable of monitoring every person's actions placed in every private and public space. Today, misuse of the Internet can be a threat to civil liberties.

A more contemporary dystopian vision is developed in the movie, *The Matrix*. In the not too distant future, a class of electronically networked intelligent machines goes to war with the humans, who in desperation destroy much of the natural environment, blocking out the sun – the primary source of energy and electricity for both. The machines adapt by enslaving the humans, virtually turning them into human "batteries," all linked to a vast "neural interactive simulation" network – a.k.a. the "Matrix" (hence the movie's name). The humans are bred in tubes, and from babyhood kept immobile, held in place by wires plugged into their brains and bodies. In their minds, however, they live in a virtual reality – a "computer-generated dream world" – believing from their earliest memories that they are growing up and living in the late twentieth-century world, rather than the actual future era, roughly 200 years later, where they serve as nothing more than the machines' energy supply. The action of the movie revolves around the efforts of the human protagonists to unplug themselves, and begin to unplug others, from both networks, and learn to fight back both in real time and space and in the virtual reality.

Aside from the visceral thrills provided by the numerous intense, computer-aided action sequences, clearly designed to attract moviegoers, we can extract an important message from the movie about technology and human existence in the modern age.[3] On the one hand, *The Matrix* is one more in a long list of tales about human-made technological artifacts (e.g., Mary Shelley's *Frankenstein*, Hal in Arthur C. Clarke's *2001*) getting out of control and wreaking havoc, although it probably is closer to the genre of books and movies typified by George Orwell's *1984* and Fritz Lang's *Metropolis*. It touches on several themes associated with pervasive, deep-rooted fears about life in the modern technological, computerized, Internet age: machines replacing and enslaving humans; a machine-culture displacing if not destroying traditional, simpler, more "organic" and healthier ways of life; powerful, pervasive, impersonal forces, operating globally, fueled and enabled by modern technologies (computers, microprocessors, Internet, biotechnology, etc.), and controlling and shaping our lives; the same impersonal, authoritarian forces increasingly limiting our choices and actions, while impinging on every aspect of our private lives at home and at work, *à la* Big Brother; and technology defiling the environment, undermining communities and destroying or deskilling our jobs.

A ray of hope – and an important lesson – is provided by the tiny band of humans who have freed themselves from the machines. On the one hand, humans created the machines and the conditions that led to environmental calamity and subsequent enslavement. On the other, they can unplug their machines, and unplug themselves. As the main protagonist "Neo" finally realizes, the "reality" created by machines is only made up of digital patterns of "1s" and "0s," that is, it is just a product of programming. They have the power to reprogram and rework technology to free themselves and create a better way of life – the search for "Zion" in the film.

Perhaps because use of the Internet has spread so rapidly in the workplace, the home, the library, and everywhere, its potential dark side has not elicited much public concern. Nevertheless, there are serious public policy issues, which many public interest groups and civil rights organizations have been trying to address. These issues include basic consumer protections, consumer and worker privacy, affordable public access to Internet and telecommunications services (especially in the emerging broadband data communications and media markets), diversity of information sources and viewpoints (despite media consolidation), etc. For the most part, the public interest groups' efforts reflect a general acceptance of the potentially beneficial aspects of Internet technologies. Their primary objective is to protect consumers from unwarranted abuse of these technologies by governments and large corporations. Many also seek to overcome the influence of powerful corporate entities in the new digital media and communications markets, to ensure ordinary working families and, especially the economically disadvantaged, have adequate access to the economic and social benefits that these technologies offer.

Jobs and workplace impacts of the new generation of digital technologies (the Internet, wireless, broadband) have not yet generated as great a concern as the consumer impacts, though certain issues, such as increasing threats to employee privacy in the workplace (e.g., electronic monitoring), have been receiving more attention. Perhaps the most sweeping and alarming picture of what the "Information Age" might mean for work and jobs in the future, is Jeremy Rifkin's 1995 book, *The End of Work*. Rifkin argues that the global economy is experiencing a transformation as significant as the Industrial Revolution. Characterizing this change is a shift from "mass labor" to highly skilled "elite labor" accompanied by increasing automation in the production of goods and services. Sophisticated computers, robots, telecommunications, and other information technologies, he claims, are rapidly replacing human beings in every sector and industry. He foresees near-workerless factories and virtual companies which will displace most traditional forms of jobs. Occupations destined for extinction include factory workers, secretaries, receptionists, clerical workers, sales clerks, bank tellers, telephone operators, librarians, wholesalers, and middle managers. The creation of new high-tech positions in the growing "elite knowledge sector" – high skilled technicians, computer programmers, engineers, and professional workers – will never be enough to absorb the millions of workers who lose their jobs to automation, as it penetrates into every aspect of the production process (see Rifkin 1995a, 1995b).

Rifkin made this prophecy at the very beginning of the Internet revolution, but it is strongly reminiscent of Vonnegut's dark satirical portrayal of a world where computers replaced people, written over 50 years ago. Thus, we are brought full circle in our consideration of whether computers and automation will lead us toward a better way of life or toward some kind of dystopian existence. The reality probably will be somewhat less bleak than Vonnegut's and Rifkin's pessimistic visions. But there also is reason to be skeptical about the many rosy scenarios put forward about the Internet revolution. Successive waves of mechanization and automation since the Industrial Revolution have profoundly altered the nature of jobs and the structure of labor markets. It still may be an exaggeration to claim, as a National Governors' Association (NGA) report does, that "[i]nformation, technology, communications, and intellectual capital, rather than energy and raw materials, power today's businesses," and that "[k]nowledge skills, and technology, not natural resources and primary metals, are the major inputs to today's products." It is not an overstatement to say that the Internet economy "has major implications for the nation's citizens, businesses, and governments." The NGA study cautions, however, that in the "new economy," job security will decline; technological advances will create new occupations in some industries while eliminating them in others. It adds that:

> To survive and even thrive in this churning job environment, workers will need to acquire new skills and be prepared to constantly reinvent themselves. The wage gap between skilled and unskilled workers will continue to widen. Those who enhance their skills will experience wage growth; those who do not will experience wage stagnation or even real wage decline.
>
> (NGA 1999)

In short, whether an individual interprets the Internet era as utopia or as dystopia depends upon where he or she is situated in the emerging labor markets of the so-called New Economy, the balance of experienced advantages and disadvantages. New technology does not inevitably displace or deskill jobs. The NGA study notes that the opposite, the creation of new jobs and development of new skills, can occur. By the same token, we cannot *a priori* presume that new technology *necessarily* will generate a net increase in new, higher-skilled jobs, which usually are assumed to accompany productivity gains, as technology boosters often claim. The actual impacts of new technology on workplaces, labor markets, and jobs are highly contingent on multiple technical, social, economic, political, and institutional factors ignored in the simplistic models of techno-optimists and techno-pessimists, alike.

References

Atwood, R. and Parker, A. (1998) "History: The Evolution of Electronic Commerce," *Financial Times*, 14 July.

Business Week (1998) "The 21st Century Economy," *Business Week*, 24–31 August, 58ff.

Clinton, W. J. (1999) "Address by William J. Clinton, President of the United States to the International Labor Conference, Geneva, Switzerland, June 16, 1999," *ILO Focus*, Summer/Fall, 7–8.

Gordon, R. J. (2000) *Does the "New Economy" Measure Up to the Great Inventions of the Past?* Working Paper 7833, Cambridge, MA: National Bureau of Economic Research, August.

Greenbaum, J. (1995) *Windows on the Workplace: Computers, Jobs and the Organization of Office Work in the Late Twentieth Century*, New York: Monthly Review Press.

Kelly, K. (1999) "The Good News Is, You'll Be A Millionaire Soon, The Bad News Is, So Will Everybody Else," *Wired*, September, 151–154.

Levy, S. (2002) "Silicon Valley Reboots," *Newsweek*, 24 March, 42–50.

National Governors' Association (NGA) (1999) *Remaining Vibrant in the New Economy: State Policies for the Twenty-First Century*, Washington, DC, 7 September. Online: (www.nga.org/NewEconomy/overview.asp).

New York Times (NYT) (2000) "Clinton Sees Computer Economy as Key to World Prosperity" (2000) *The New York Times On The Web* (http://www.nytimes.com/yr/mo/day/news/financial05cnd-clinton-econ.html) 5 April.

Organization for Economic Co-operation and Development (OECD) (1999) *The Economic and Social Impact of Electronic Commerce: Preliminary Research Agenda*, Paris: OECD.

Organization for Economic Co-operation and Development (OECD) (1998) "Provisional Agenda," OECD Ministerial Conference, *A Borderless World: Realising the Potential of Global Electronic Commerce*, Ottawa, Canada, 7–9 October.

Port, O. (2001) "Brave New Factory: From the Line to Supply Chain, All Goes on Autopilot," *BusinessWeek Online* (www.businessweek.com/premium/content/01_30/b3742096.htm) 23 July.

Rifkin, J. (1995a) *The End of Work: The Decline of the Global Labor Force and the Dawn of the Post-Market Era*, New York: Tarcher/Putnam.

Rifkin, J. (1995b) "Vanishing Jobs," *Mother Jones*, (http:www.motherjones.com/mother_jones/SO95/toc.html) September–October.

US Department of Commerce, Economics and Statistics Administration and National Telecommunications and Information Administration (DOC ESA/NTIA) (2002) *A Nation Online: How Americans Are Expanding Their Use of the Internet*, Washington, DC, February.

Vonnegut, K. Jr. ([1952]1972) *Player Piano*. Avon/Bard, New York.

2

ONE, TWO, MANY INDUSTRIAL REVOLUTIONS

The notion of the "New Economy" has been hit hard since the "dot.com" bubble burst in early 2000. NASDAQ, the high-tech stock index, shortly after soaring to slightly over 5,000 in the first quarter of 2000, dropped precipitously in the second and the third quarters of 2000, continuing its downward trend through 2002 to roughly one-fifth its peak value. But the problem ran deeper than the failure of most dot.coms to make a profit. The hype around the Internet during the late 1990s included a widely accepted statistic that Internet traffic was doubling every three months. Analysts estimate that Internet traffic actually grew at a rate closer to 100 percent a year. This is still hefty by most standards, but nowhere near the volume that led more than a dozen companies to build expensive fiber-optic networks, most of which remain unused. Millions of miles of fiber-optic lines were buried beneath streets and oceans, but only an estimated 2.7 percent of this capacity is actually being used. Much of the remaining fiber could lie dormant forever. Meanwhile, the resulting fiber glut caused bandwidth prices to plummet by an average of 65 percent, forcing most of the long-haul data-transmission companies to file for Chapter 11 bankruptcy protection (Dreazen 2002).

Hence two major areas of technological innovation, the Internet and advanced telecommunications – hailed as ushering in a new Industrial Revolution, and indeed did help fuel the remarkable economic boom of the late 1990s – in the end seemed to be instrumental in triggering a recession and one of the worst stock market crashes in Wall Street history. This clearly is a case of technological advance getting ahead of the marketplace; earlier examples include computer microprocessors outpacing the demand for computing power and agricultural advances driving down farmers' pricing power (Berman 2002). But it also illustrates how even the most conservative and savvy investors can confuse hype with reality in the face of seemingly ground-breaking technological innovations with huge economic potential.

A new industrial revolution?

Not everyone has bought into the notion of a "New Economy," and many critics undoubtedly feel vindicated by the collapse of the dot.com-telecom speculative bubble. Some academics, such as Northwestern University economist Robert J. Gordon (2000, 2002), challenge the contention that the Internet/information technology revolution is as historically significant as the nineteenth-century Industrial Revolution, which profoundly altered the material basis of our economy and society (Castells 1996: 30). Gordon further argues that the economic growth ostensibly generated by the advent of the Internet, underlying what became known as the "New Economy," does not measure up to the so-called Second Industrial Revolution associated with the "great inventions" of the late nineteenth and early twentieth centuries.

In particular, Gordon identifies the inventions of electricity, the internal combustion engine, petroleum and chemicals, a cluster of communication and entertainment technologies (the telegraph, telephone, movies, radio, and television), and indoor plumbing, all developed roughly between 1860–1900, which "set off sixty years between roughly 1913 and 1972 during which multi-factor productivity growth grew more rapidly than before or since, and during which everyday life was entirely transformed" (Gordon 2000: 4). It was this period, not the first Industrial Revolution, Gordon claims, "that created the golden age of productivity growth" (ibid.: 18).

Gordon's critique is part of a debate among economists over the extent that information and communications technology (ICT) has contributed to productivity growth in the US economy over the past two decades, especially the productivity growth revival and accompanying economic boom in the United States between 1995–2000.[1] While much of this debate is highly technical – it largely revolves around statistical measurement problems – it has significant analytical and policy importance. Productivity growth is not the only important measure of economic transformation, but it is widely viewed as a primary factor in the generation of economic growth. As such, it is considered a good indicator of ICT's impact on the economy – large improvements in productivity growth indicate significant changes in the economy as a whole, small changes suggest smaller economic impacts. Since the 1980s, the "productivity paradox," expressed by Robert M. Solow's well-known quip, that "we can see the computer age everywhere but in the productivity statistics," defined much of the debate. If ICT was transforming the economy, why didn't it appear in the productivity growth data?

Since 1999, a consensus has grown that ICT was in fact responsible for the remarkable productivity growth since 1995; the "productivity paradox" was largely if not completely explained. The debate has now shifted to how significant this growth has been for the economy as a whole, and not just a few sectors. Gordon notes that the gains in productivity growth[2] were mostly confined to the ICT-producing industries (computer hardware, including peripherals, and telecommunications equipment) and the ICT-using durable goods sector. The ICT impacts on non-durable goods ICT-using industries, and the service-related industries, in particular, have been more ambiguous. Gordon claims that there have been virtually no spill-over effects from productivity gains in the ICT-producing and ICT-using durable goods sectors into the remaining 88 percent of the economy, concluding that "the New Economy has been remarkably unfruitful as a creator of productivity growth" (Gordon 2000: 46).

Gordon's thesis is both interesting and problematic at the same time. On the one hand, Gordon reminds us – if the dot.com crash didn't do the job – that perspective, especially historical perspective, is useful for tempering the over-hyped claims of the New Economy. The Internet may or may not, after all, be one of the greatest inventions of all time. It may not in the end be fostering an industrial revolution rivaling those of the nineteenth century. And the New Economy may not in fact be such a radical break from the "old" economy. In deflating the hype surrounding the Internet and the continuing evolution of information and communications technologies, Gordon enables a more realistic assessment of the economic and social implications of the Internet.

On the other hand, comparing the Internet with nineteenth-century "great inventions" is an apples and oranges comparison. The historical contexts for the different technological "revolutions" were so different as to make such comparisons largely meaningless. Nobody questions the huge magnitude of the transformation from a feudal agricultural economy, where artisanal crafts workshops were the primary units of material goods production, to mid-twentieth-century industrial society based on mass production, consumption, and communications, where the standard-of-living of middle-income families probably was in many respects higher than that of the eighteenth-century upper classes. The scale of these changes probably exceeds that of the changes in modern society wrought by the New Economy. After all, we are just evolving from an already highly developed, industrialized twentieth-century world to one that is more highly developed, in the twenty-first-century world. Whether the latter transformation some day surpasses the early Industrial Revolutions, and qualifies as a bona fide industrial revolution, only future historians may be able to judge.

It is useful to understand the historical linkages and trajectories of technological change since the Industrial Revolution to put into perspective the changes wrought by the still evolving Internet and related ICT industries of the New Economy. But it does not make sense to dismiss the Internet, as Gordon does, as being nothing more than a derivative, or subsidiary, of the earlier invention of electricity (Gordon 2000: 47; 2002: 30). It would be equally silly, for instance, to claim that electricity – and subsequently the Internet – is nothing more than a byproduct of the pioneering research on electromagnetism by James Clerk Maxwell in 1873, or Michael Faraday even earlier in the eighteenth century, which provided the intellectual foundations for all electricity-based industries (Mowery and Rosenberg 1989: 23).

Scientific and technological advances are cumulative. The innovations of one era build upon the advances and innovations of earlier periods. The diffusion of innovations also depends upon what economists call *complementarities* with numerous other innovations developed both contemporaneously and in earlier periods. The technological exploitation of electricity, for example, would not have been possible without a large number of complementary technological inventions and advances, such as the dynamo for electricity generation, techniques for electric power transmission over long distances, a small and efficient electric motor for use in factories and in homes, and a range of metal alloys with special characteristics. Many of the these innovations, in turn, required advances in metallurgy, which enabled the development of techniques to produce precision components (such as turbines) made of inexpensive, high quality, steel alloys capable of sustaining high temperatures and pressures (Mowery and Rosenberg 1989: 25). But the production of cheap steel and metal products required an efficient and abundant source of energy, namely coal (coke), which replaced wood (charcoal) as the primary fuel used in blast furnaces in the eighteenth and nineteenth centuries (Rosenberg 1982: 84). Taking Gordon's argument to its logical extreme, therefore, the Internet and just about any important invention in history could be reduced to subsidiary inventions of the human mastery of fire (which probably used wood as fuel).

Although the Internet may not be as important an invention as electricity, there is compelling evidence that it is having significant economic and social impacts, which are likely to grow in the future. Even Gordon acknowledges the extraordinary diffusion of the Internet, which has been more rapid than any invention since television in the late 1940s and early 1950s, with more than 50 percent of US households connected to the Internet by the end of 2000 (Gordon 2002: 27). Other economists provide evidence that ICT has had a measurable impact on the productivity of non-durable goods (i.e., services) ICT-using sectors. For example, Brookings Institution economists James E. Triplett and Barry P. Bosworth (2002) note that the service industries are the most ICT-intensive industries, and show that ICT has made a substantial contribution to service sector labor productivity growth. Bart van Ark, Robert Inklaar and Robert H. McGuckin similarly write that the diffusion of ICT has been a prime contributor to productivity growth outside the ICT-producing sectors, and that, in particular, "service sectors are among the main bene-ficiaries of increased investment in ICT, leading to faster growth in labor productivity and in many cases even in more total factor productivity growth" (2002: 2, n. 2).[3]

It is notable that the industries with large increases in the contribution of ICT capital saw the greatest acceleration in labor productivity, includ-ing wholesale and retail trade, telephone communications, non-depository financial institutions, and business services, among others. At the same time, most of the service industries which have not had com-parable productivity gains and or even experienced negative multifactor productivity (MFP) rates during the 1990s made relatively smaller ICT investments (Jorgenson, *et al*. 2002).[4]

ICT-attributed productivity gains also vary within industry sectors. A US Department of Labor, Bureau of Labor Statistics (BLS) study (Sieling *et al*. 2001) reveals that total retail trade labor productivity grew steadily between 1987 and 1999, especially after 1990, at an average rate of 2.0 percent per year. It accelerated rapidly between 1995 and 1999 at an average annual rate of 3.1 percent, or about twice the rate between 1990 and 1995 (1.6 percent). Productivity growth for certain retail sectors – building materials stores, general merchandise stores, apparel stores, home furni-ture, furnishings, equipment stores, and miscellaneous retail stores – greatly exceeded average growth for all retail trade throughout the 1990s. Food stores and eating and drinking places, in contrast, had negative pro-ductivity growth between from 1990 to 1995, and less than 1 percent per year growth, over the 1995–1999 period (Sieling *et al*. 2001: 3–5).

The BLS study links the productivity increase, as well as the variation among retail sectors, to growth in ICT investments by retail firms over this period, and especially during the 1995–1999 period. Retailers' widespread use of Universal Product Codes (UPCs), machine-readable labels on product packaging (bar codes) and numbers – providing information on the manufacturer, item description, and the price – allows them to gather data at the point of sale (POS) with laser-based bar codes, helping them to target markets and better manage inventories. First used by food retailers, UPCs quickly spread to general merchandise and then to all parts of the retail sector. Increased use of POS, electronically linking cash registers, laser scanning devices, and credit card processing machines with sophisticated software packages has been one factor feeding the speed-up in labor pro-ductivity in retail trade during the last half of the 1990s, as it enables retail-ers to expand service and sales without increasing sales personnel.

The retail trade study also illustrates how factors other than techno-logical change – particularly, shifting consumer purchasing patterns and preferences (i.e., demand changes) and disparate changes in industry structures – affect productivity growth. These non-technical factors may in fact determine whether or not potential gains from introducing new technologies are actually achieved. Increasing concentration in retailing since even before 1987 and the resulting dominance of retail chains have been accompanied by growth in ICT investments, largely from the spread of UPCs. For example, as lumber and building materials retail became increasingly characterized by large-sized chain stores, ICT investment (in POS terminals and associated software) increased to improve the management of inventories and make ordering from manufacturers easier. In contrast, the food retail industry, similarly dominated by superstores and hypermarkets over time, also invested more heavily in ICT. But its labor productivity gains were dampened by an increase in specialized, more labor-intensive services offered by these stores, such as delicatessens, full-service bakeries, and specialized meat and fish departments (Sieling *et al.* 2001: 4–5, 7).

Returning to Gordon's critique of the New Economy, we see that the ICT/Internet-driven economic boom of the 1990s was neither a radical departure from earlier periods of rapid technological change, nor historically insignificant. In many respects it was just the latest stage in a longer-term transformation tied to the diffusion of technologies stemming back to the first modern computer over fifty years ago, and even earlier. Moreover, the forces shaping – as well as limiting – the role of ICT in fostering economic growth are not just technical, but consist of a complex interweaving of social, institutional, organizational and economic processes with the technical. As Triplett and Bosworth (2002) point out:

> much of what happened in the U.S. after 1995 was a continuation of processes that were as old as the Industrial Revolution itself – managerial innovations that disturbed the competitive balance in an industry, investment in new kinds of machinery and equipment that improved labor productivity by increasing capital per worker, and the relative absence or reduction of economic regulation and monopoly power that stifles innovation.

Rather than debating whether the Internet era measures up to earlier Industrial Revolutions, therefore, a more fruitful analytical approach would be to examine the Internet and associated ICT innovations within a larger historical framework. Like Gordon, economic historian Paul A. David (1999) compares the economic consequences flowing from the spread of electricity, specifically, the invention and diffusion of the electric dynamo in the late nineteenth century, with the impacts of ICT. David, however, draws the historical analogy between the "computer and the dynamo" primarily to shed light on the spread of "computerization" and the economic growth it generated. Concerned with explaining the "productivity paradox," he notes the long time lag from the

25

introduction and early spread of electric motors and its widespread penetration in manufacturing in the decade of the 1920s, suggesting the possibility of a similar lag before the economic impacts of ICT are fully felt.

David also recognizes the influence of non-technical forces in both
facilitating and limiting the diffusion of the electric dynamo and its
impacts on productivity, which also holds true for ICT:

> An understanding of the way in which the transmission of
> power in the form of electricity came to revolutionize industrial
> production processes tells us that far more was involved than
> the simple substitution of one new, form of productive input
> from an older alternative. The pace of transformation must be
> seen to be governed, in both the past and the current regime
> transitions, by the ease or difficulty of altering many other, tech-
> nologically and organizationally related features of the produc-
> tion systems that are involved.
>
> (David 1999: 25)

But he urges skepticism in drawing the analogy too far. It is not foreor-
dained that ICT will live up to its potential to transform the organization
of production. He identifies several potential obstacles to ICT generating
high productivity gains, for example, deriving from the difficulties and
costs modern organizations confront when they adopt new ICT innovations. Such difficulties were obvious in the failure of numerous dot.coms,
as well as many bricks-and-mortar businesses, in successfully adopting
electronic commerce applications. History can provide guidance based
on past experiences for identifying and addressing these obstacles, but
offers little help in determining whether or not these efforts will succeed.
As David states:

> One cannot simply infer the detailed future shape of the dif-
> fusion path in the case of the ICT revolution from the experience
> of previous analogous episodes, because the very nature of the
> underlying process renders that path contingent upon events
> flowing from private actions and public policy decisions, as well
> as upon the expectations that are thereby engendered – all of
> which still lie before us.
>
> (David 1999: 24)

The first industrial revolutions

Economic historians agree that there have been one or more "industrial
revolutions" since the original Industrial Revolution at the turn of the
nineteenth century. The defining features of the Industrial Revolution

26

included the replacement of multi-skilled artisanal craft workers by mechanically (water and steam) powered machines and the proliferation of factories which brought large numbers of machines and workers into hierarchically structured organizations under a single roof. Work organization in the new factory system was characterized by a detailed division of labor and the routinization of tasks. Factories (or "manufactories"), large-scale production sites, highly developed divisions of labor, mechanically-powered equipment, and precocious forms of mechanization, predated the Industrial Revolution. But even in the largest enterprises, almost all work was carried out by hand, under the control of master craftsmen. The crucial innovations that sparked the Industrial Revolution, the spinning jenny and the power-loom that transformed textile manufacturing, were mechanical devices that replaced human muscle power and skill.

The initial motive force in the new textile factories was water. The invention of the steam engine and major improvements in metallurgical and chemical processing, however, spurred the rapid spread of mechanization throughout British industry, followed by similar developments in Continental Europe and the United States by the mid-1800s. The introduction of spinning machines in Britain led to both the demise of the rural cottage spinning industry and the spread of cotton spinning factories – the "Satanic mills" lamented by nineteenth-century Romantic writers – employing large numbers of men, women, and children as operatives. The introduction of power-looms, accelerated by the glut of yarn produced by the mechanized spinning mills, caused a precipitous decline in hand-loom weavers, and their eventual elimination as a class of workers by the 1860s and 1870s.

The "Second Industrial Revolution" of the last half of the nineteenth century was characterized by continued widespread technological innovation and productivity growth, as well as remarkable scientific progress (Mowery and Rosenberg 1989: 23). Of particular import was the revolution in transportation driven by the application of the steam engine to new modes of transport – first the steamboat and then the railroad. These technologies dramatically shrank the times and distances involved in economic transactions, making it cheaper and easier to transport large quantities of materials and goods across larger distances in shorter times. The railroad opened up the continental United States west of the Appalachians to settlement and economic development in the last half of the nineteenth century (Rosenberg 1976: 177). Reduced transportation costs led to a dramatic increase in agricultural productivity, as bulky agricultural products could be exchanged across geographical areas larger than ever before. The railroad, and later, the iron steamship – along with the innovation of refrigeration – contributed to the steady expansion of transcontinental and transoceanic shipping and trade.[5]

The revolution of transport, the new machines of the Industrial Revolution, and the great feats of construction and civil engineering of that period would not have been possible without the availability of large quantities of cheap iron and later, steel, which in turn was made possible by the improvements in metallurgy, especially after the 1850s (Rosenberg 1976: 182). These innovations not only cut the cost of steel, they enabled the production of steel which could sustain higher temperatures and pressures, with a higher degree of uniformity and reliability.[6] The metallurgical advances, and other systematic improvements in materials (e.g., superior abrasives), also spurred improved capabilities in machine tools such as the introduction of high-speed steel in machine-cutting tools. These improvements, along with a stream of machine tool innovations – turret lathes, universal milling machines, precision grinders, and numerous highly specialized tools – subsequently drove advances in a wide range of metal-using industries, enabling the United States to take the leadership in making such products as reapers, threshers, cultivators, rifles, hardware, watches, sewing machines, typewriters, and bicycles. As David Mowery and Nathan Rosenberg (1989: 27) note, a distinctive characteristic of US manufacturing was its production of large quantities of highly precise and standardized metal components by use of a sequence of specialized machines that "could be easily assembled rather than laboriously fitted." By contrast, the fitting process in craft-dominated industries was time-consuming, labor-intensive, and costly.

End of the craft paradigm

Industrialization ended craft production as the dominant paradigm of industrial organization in Western economies. Age-old craft skills and occupations were eroded and broken down, though some traditional craft occupations persisted in several industries well into the first decades of the twentieth century. The rate of mechanization in the United States was uneven across and within industry sectors, as not all forms of skilled work were easily divided into routinized tasks or substituted by machines. Hence, pockets of craft workers, whose skills were still necessary for the successful functioning of the production process, survived within industries as diverse as steel forging, shoe fabrication (Mulligan 1981), and even textiles (Freifeld 1984), until more advanced technologies and new forms of work organization eliminated the need for them. Even early automobile production was carried out by skilled craftsworkers in craft workshops. Nevertheless, by 1900, the unskilled factory operative had replaced the skilled craft worker as the predominant type of worker engaged in industrial production.

The primary unit of industrial organization shifted from the small-scale, independent, artisanal workshop to large-scale, multi-level, highly subdivided, and eventually bureaucratically administered factory. In the latter part of the nineteenth century, reductions in the cost of goods transport, made possible by a dense network of railroads, spurred further growth in the size of industrial enterprises and the range of functions they performed (Mowery and Rosenberg 1989). The new modes of transport allowed a more intensive exploitation of economies of scale by expanding the markets available to firms in any given location. That is, greater volumes of goods were needed to serve growing, distant markets made economically possible because of new modes of transportation and communication (Rosenberg 1982: 58). By the end of the century, the first great integrated corporations began to appear, with highly subdivided functional departments devoted to engineering, production, and marketing (Braverman 1974: 261).

The decline of small craft workshops and the rise of mechanized factories and large-scale industrial organizations were accompanied by dramatic sectoral reallocations of the labor force. Aside from the disappearance of numerous traditional craft occupations, rural cottage and agricultural workers and their families moved in large numbers to the new industrial towns to take factory jobs. By the beginning of the twentieth century, agricultural workers ceased to be the largest occupational category. In Britain and the United States the agricultural and related workers' share of the total working population shrank to less than 10 percent by 1901, while workers in manufacturing, mining and related industries accounted for the largest share of industrial occupations. The share of trade and transport workers of the total working population also jumped between 1801 and 1901, rising from about one-tenth to over one-fifth of the British labor force, reflecting the growing importance of transportation and trade in the new industrial order (Rosenberg 1982: 250).[7]

The industrial revolutions of the nineteenth century also transformed the nature and organization of work and skills. The defining characteristics of craft work include the integration of design, production, and even marketing functions; embodiment in the crafts worker of a high level of skill and mastery of the media, means, and methods involved in material goods production; a limited division of labor – skills were divided by product and process area not by task; an emphasis on non-standardized, customized products; and a work process, pace, and rhythm set by the craft worker. Most of these qualities were eroded or eliminated by the new machine-based factory system, though some vestiges of craft persisted because of the uneven adoption of mechanization. Indeed, some highly skilled jobs with craft elements, albeit in truncated, industrialized forms, remain occupational categories in the modern economy (in construction trades and skilled repairmen, and mechanics in manufacturing). But the traditional, artisanal craftsworker had all but disappeared by the early twentieth century (Yudken 1987).

Taylorism and organizational change

The new form of industrial organization that replaced the craft workshop emphasized greater subdivision of work tasks, structured around and driven by machines. The order and pace of work tasks were now set by machines not by workers. Steady improvements in machine production – and the tools that made the machines – and the increasing scale of production, called for and enabled increasing standardized, interchangeable components and greater precision in their manufacture to allow parts to more easily fit together. They also called for a more systematized transformation in the structure and organization of the labor process.

In the latter part of the nineteenth century and the early twentieth century, Frederick Winslow Taylor succeeded in introducing a highly rationalized system of work organization that matched the needs of bureaucratized and mechanized, large-scale industrial organizations of that period. As a manager and engineer in the steel industry, Taylor wanted to develop a better system of shop management and organization to increase the productivity of the emerging machine-based industries. The findings of the extensive time-and-motion studies of factory work he conducted were published in his *Principles of Scientific Management* in 1911, though they began to be put into practice much earlier. Harry Braverman (1974) argues that scientific management was designed specifically to wrest control of labor power from the shop floor. First, Taylor sought to subordinate the skills and abilities of workers entirely to the control of management practices. Once skilled jobs were subdivided into very small components and the actions of the workforce strictly regulated. Second, the processes of design and planning were separated from the execution of tasks. As Braverman notes, "mental labor is first separated from manual labor and ... is then itself subdivided rigorously according to the same rule." Third, as both skill and knowledge are removed from the labor process, it is brought under the control of management which now oversees and guides all its aspects (1974: 42).

Taylor's main accomplishment was to articulate, systematize, and diffuse a movement toward rationalization of the labor process already underway in the emerging industrializing, capitalist economies. But it is indisputable that these principles have dominated management approaches to workplace organization for most of the twentieth century, and remain a powerful influence on organizational strategies even today. Moreover, observes Charley Richardson, Taylorism or scientific management "is, and has been for almost a century, the primary culture and method driving the development and implementation of workplace technologies." But he cautions that the "built-in imperatives of Taylorism" are so deeply ingrained in the system, that "it is important to keep this method and culture in mind as we examine the current approaches to workplace technological change" (Richardson 1992: 154).

Airplanes, autos and Fordism

The early twentieth century saw new technological and organizational innovations building on the advances of the previous decades. The invention of the internal combustion engine in the 1870s made possible the automobile and airplane, both invented at the turn of the century. These inventions not only revolutionized transportation but helped shape the modern industrial economies of the twentieth century.

The aircraft industry – airframe and engine producers, and parts suppliers – is one of the largest, most technologically advanced and economically important manufacturing industries. The story of the civilian aircraft and airline industries properly begins in the late 1920s when a series of mergers created several vertically integrated firms combining air transport, airframe manufacture, and engine production. These concentrated firms dissolved in the 1930s due to the Depression, airmail scandals and federal anti-trust legislation. Demand for aircraft sharply declined after World War I, but rose slowly through the 1920s spurred by government airmail service and growth in commercial air travel. But military demand dominated by the late 1930s, ultimately giving a dramatic boost to aircraft production during World War II. The military still plays a major role as a customer and supporter of R&D for the aerospace industry. The introduction of the jet engine played a decisive role in making civilian aircraft manufacturing and the airlines major industrial sectors from the 1950s on (Mowery and Rosenberg 1982).

The manufacture of airframes and engines includes many craft-like elements, more akin to shipbuilding and large-scale construction projects, than mass manufacturing. Aircraft (and engine) firms produce relatively small numbers of large, somewhat customized, highly complex products, requiring the coordination of numerous precision-made parts in both the design and fabrication processes; industry managers and engineer half-jokingly refer to their product as "a million spare parts flying in formation." The bulk of the workforce in aerospace plants includes skilled assembly workers, highly skilled machinists and technicians, and a large complement of engineering and managerial workers, often accounting for a third to a half of total employment at large facilities. Both the civilian and military sides of the aircraft industry have been major sponsors of automation innovations and their application – including, more recently, the use of advanced computer-based networking and Internet commerce technologies – during the 1980s and 1990s. Nevertheless, despite the stream of technological innovations that have "spun off" from this sector over the past 50 years – and despite the growing importance of air travel in the global economy – the advent of the airplane has not had as great an impact on the organization of production and work, or on the structure of labor markets, as the automotive industry during the twentieth century.

Like aircraft manufacturing, automobile manufacturing in the late 1800s and early 1900s was carried out in craft-production workshops. Unlike aircraft production, the auto industry pioneered mass production modes of organization, merging with and perfecting Tayloristic methods, eventually adopted throughout most of the manufacturing sector. Automobiles initially were produced in small volume by an extremely decentralized collection of small machine, assembly, and supplier shops. These shops employed a workforce highly skilled in design, machine operations, and fitting, using general-purpose machine tools to perform drilling, grinding, and other operations on metal and wood. By 1905, there were hundreds of companies in Western Europe and North America producing autos using craft techniques (Womack et al. 1991: 24–25).

Henry Ford changed all this with his system of mass production. In 1908 Ford introduced the Model T, designed to achieve two objectives: greater ease of manufacture based on the complete and consistent interchangeability of parts and the simplicity of attaching them to each other; and user-friendliness, in which anyone could drive and repair the car. Some analysts argue that it was Ford's success in achieving a very high level of interchangeability, based on using the same gauging system for every part, that enabled him to introduce the moving assembly line in 1915, the innovation for which he is best known. With part interchangeability, Ford could have his assemblers perform only one task, first moving from vehicle to vehicle around the assembly hall, reducing the task cycle for the average assembly worker from 514 to 2.3 minutes. The next step was to have the car move past the stationary worker on a moving or assembly line, who repeatedly performed the same task; the task cycle time shrank further, from 2.3 minutes to 1.19 minutes (Womack et al. 1991: 26–29).

Ford's innovative mass production process required comparable, radical changes in the workforce, in technology, and in business organizations. As James Womack, Daniel Jones and Daniel Roos, from the MIT International Motor Vehicle Program, note, "Ford not only perfected the interchangeable part, he perfected the interchangeable worker" (Womack et al. 1991: 30). He took the division of labor to its ultimate extreme. The assembler on the assembly line had only one task – to put two nuts on two bolts or perhaps to attach one wheel to each car. He didn't order parts, procure his tools, repair his equipment, inspect for quality, or even understand what the workers on either side of him were doing.

Only a few minutes were needed to train the assembler in these tasks. The pace of the line determined and disciplined the worker's pace. Gone were the skilled fitters common in craft production auto plants who

> gathered all the necessary parts, obtained tools from the tool room, repaired them if necessary, performed the complex fitting and assembly job for the entire vehicle, then checked over his work before sending the completed vehicle to the shipping department.
>
> (ibid.: 31)

At the same time, Ford achieved Taylor's goal of separating the design and engineering functions from the shop floor, and placing these functions – as well as the assembly process – more firmly under management control. Engineering shops included various specializations and subdivisions: industrial engineers who designed assembly line operations – how the parts came together and the assemblers' tasks; production engineers who did the parts and inventory scheduling and designed assembly line equipment; manufacturing engineers who designed production machinery, including assembly hardware and special-purpose machines for each part, and product engineers, who designed and engineered the car. Womack *et al.* noted that these early "'knowledge workers' ... replaced the skilled machine-shop owners and the old-fashioned factory foremen of the earlier craft era," although, unlike their predecessors, they rarely touched an actual car or even entered the factory. Over time, as cars and trucks became more complicated, these engineering jobs branched out into many subspecialties, resulting in an increasingly minute division of labor in the engineering workshop (ibid.: 32).

The new auto assembly plant needed new kinds of machines, illustrating how technologies can be shaped by institutional and organizational requirements. Inexpensive, standardized, interchangeable parts required new tools that not only could cut hardened metal and stamp steel with very high precision, but could do this job at a high volume with low or no set-up costs between pieces. Ford achieved this by making special purpose machines dedicated to doing one task at a time. Like the assembly line, these machines could be operated by unskilled workers with only a few minutes' training. The skills once required to carry out these tasks, such as milling, were now embodied in the machine. Ford then placed his machine in a sequence so that each manufacturing step led directly to the next, prompting the observation by visitors to his High-land Park, MI, plant that Ford's factory "was really one vast machine" (ibid.: 36).

To better implement his mass production system, Ford created a completely vertically-integrated company, which made everything connected with producing his cars, from the raw materials on up. Driven by the need for parts with closer tolerances and on tighter delivery schedules than ever required before, Ford took all the functions of engine, chassis and parts production and assembly in-house, culminating in the giant Rouge complex, opened in 1927.

The dramatic productivity gains from his system gave Ford an obvious competitive advantage over other auto assemblers. Ford was able to significantly reduce cycle times, capital requirements and the amount of human labor required to assemble an automobile. By the early 1920s, Ford reportedly cut real costs by two-thirds of the 1908 price for the Model T. To stay competitive, other automakers soon followed suit, adopting Ford's mass production methods into their own operations. Only a handful of small firms continued to produce autos using craft methods, some of which, such as Aston Martin, Bentley, and Rolls-Royce, still make customized, luxury, and specialty autos today.[8]

In adopting Ford's mass production model to General Motors in the 1920s, GM president Alfred Sloan introduced new management and organizational strategies, to address the bureaucratic rigidities and operational problems Ford experienced in running his company that also plagued his firm. Sloan created decentralized divisions for each of the five model cars and major components (generators, steering gears, carburetors) produced by GM-owned companies, run "by the numbers" from a small corporate headquarters. Womack *et al.* argue that Sloan made the "system Ford had pioneered complete, and it is this complete system to which the term *mass production* applies today." He devised the organization and management system required to effectively manage the total system of factories, engineering operations, and marketing that mass production calls for. "It isn't giving Sloan too much credit to say that his basic management ideas solved the last pressing problems inhibiting the spread of mass production" (ibid.: 41).

The features of the Ford–Sloan mass production system – standardized products produced in high volume, the interchangeability of parts, the use of dedicated, special-purpose machinery, the assembly line, the management "by the numbers" – made the situation for auto workers worse than before, creating the conditions for successful unionization during the Depression. Womack *et al.* note that Sloan's innovations "did nothing to change the idea, institutionalized by Henry Ford, that the workers on the floor were simply interchangeable parts of the production system" (ibid.: 42). It was this mass production system, developed by Ford and elaborated and enhanced by Sloan, which transformed manufacturing, setting the stage for the first waves of computer-based automation in the 1950s, 1960s and 1970s.

Electricity and automation

Few would dispute Robert Gordon's assessment of electricity as one of the "great inventions" of the first industrial revolutions. Electricity is the primary energy source for powering industrial processes and equipment, to light our streets, workplaces, and residences, and to heat and cool buildings. We depend on electric power for most home appliances (refrigerators, washing machines, microwave ovens), most major forms of entertainment (radio, TV, movies, CDs, videos, DVDs, video games), and the computing and telecommunications systems that make up the New Economy, including the Internet.

The scientific discoveries (Michael Faraday's and James Clerk Maxwell's work on electromagnetism) and major innovations (incandescent light, electric dynamo, central power stations, transformers, and transmission systems) that made the practical application of electricity possible, largely originated during the last half of the nineteenth century. Thomas A. Edison's invention of the incandescent light bulb in 1882 provided one of the initial impulses to the spread of electric power. It offered a safer, cleaner, and cheaper alternative way to provide lighting for streets, buildings, factories, and private residences. Edison also opened the first central electricity generation station in New York City in 1882, to generate and distribute the electricity needed to power his invention on a large scale.

Electrification spread rapidly at the end of the nineteenth century and the early decades of the twentieth century, fostered by its increasing application to industry, communications, and an ever growing list of household and consumer devices. From 1901 to 1932, electric utility capacity and generation grew at annual average rates of about 12 percent per year (US Dept. of Energy 1996: 106). By the 1930s, the generation and transmission of electric power had become such a large and important industrial sector that Congress passed the Public Utility Holding Company Act of 1935 (PUHCA) to establish a new regulatory regime over the rapidly expanding electric utility industry.

Electricity's great advantage was not just that it reduced the cost of a lumen of light or provided a cheap substitute for other energy sources. It was, as Nathan Rosenberg writes, "a form of energy possessing certain characteristics that are economically desirable," used for a wide range of technologies for which there is no alternative energy form (1982: 94). Its great versatility is reflected in its use in lighting (the electric light), as a source of process heat (the electric furnace) and motive power (the electric motor), and most importantly for our purposes, as *a carrier of information* (automation equipment, computers).

Metallurgical industries became increasingly reliant on electric power over the twentieth century. Electricity is a primary source of process heat in the chemical transformation of materials, particularly, in the production of steel and aluminum. The electric furnace, developed in the nineteenth century and mainly used to produce specialty steels until after World War II, has since become an attractive way to produce inexpensive additions to primary steel making. The basic oxygen furnace which produce most steel today became commercially feasible with the availability of cheap oxygen, produced by electricity-intensive processes including the liquefaction and rectification of air. Similarly, the processing of aluminum was made commercially possible by electricity. Other important electricity-intensive processes include electrolytic techniques employed in the chemical industry and copper refining (ibid.: 95–97).

The electric motor was probably the main invention that spurred widespread use of electric power. Beginning in the last decade of the nineteenth century, electric-powered machinery transformed the nature of industrial production. As a source of motive power, the electric motor accounted for only a little under 5 percent of mechanical horsepower in US industry in 1899. Ten years later, it had jumped to over one-quarter of the total, by 1919 the figure was 55 percent, by 1929 it was over 82 percent, and by 1939 it was just under 90 percent. The relatively small scale and portability of electric motors freed manufacturing processes from reliance upon very large steam engines and the cumbersome network of belts and shafts that transferred energy from the engines to operations on the floor. Floor space requirements could be radically reduced while offering increased freedom in the organization and layout of the workplace. By decentralizing the power source, electric motors made possible flexible portable tools and machines. Because of these qualities, which helped make work flows on the factory floor simple, easy, and automatic, the electric motor is credited with helping to drive the productivity improvements of the assembly-line and mass-production systems (Rosenberg 1982: 100; Cohen *et al.* 2000). At the same time, by the mid-twentieth century, electric motors were embodied in a wide range of consumer appliances that dramatically improved the quality of life in the home. Washing machines and dryers eliminated the drudgery associated with manual laundry, refrigerators eliminated food spoilage, and air conditioners made summers enjoyable and opened the southern United States for economic development (Gordon 2000: 21).

The application of electric power to automated equipment and systems was another important stage in the evolution of industrial production and work organization – yet another "industrial revolution" (Dubin 1970) – setting the stage for the current digital information "revolution." In automated production, electricity not only provides the motive power for machinery, but is a medium for conveying information. As Edward B. Shils observes, "Automation depends more on the handling of information than on any other single factor" (1970: 147). By the mid-twentieth century electricity as an information carrier, involving the transmission of electrical impulses, was well developed. It was employed in all forms of long-distance communication (telegraph, telephone, radio) and major entertainment media (phonographic records, motion pictures, television). Invented in the nineteenth century,[9] these technologies became the basis of major, new industries during the first few decades of the twentieth century – except for the television industry, which took off after World War II (Rosenberg 1982: 94).

Beginning in the 1930s, the spread of automated systems accelerated in the 1950s and 1960s, with office automation following suit shortly after. The impetus for automation is the same that drove mechanization and mass production – to cut costs (especially labor costs) and increase profits. As mass production grew in scale and complexity, industry managers turned to automation as a way to integrate their production processes and expand their ability to control, regulate, and coordinate these operations. Made more feasible by improvements in electronic machinery and new electronic devices, automation depends on the ability to transmit and process electrical impulses within and between machines, which benefited from technical advances in communications and media (electronic tubes and other electronic components, switching devices, magnetic tape). This convergence is reaching its highest levels in the current era, with the marriage of broadband, multi-media, digital electronic networks to modern industrial processes and business practices. Hence the story of the Internet and its impacts on industrial organization and jobs properly begins with the automation of industrial processes, well before digital communications and computers.

An extensive literature on automation was produced in the first three decades after World War II (Friedmann 1955; Dubin 1958; Bright 1958; Shils 1963; Faunce 1965; Buckingham 1961; Blauner 1964; Marcson 1970; Braverman 1974; Shaiken 1984; Noble 1984; Greenbaum 1995). It is generally agreed that automation brought in new features and had impacts that were qualitatively different from earlier forms of mechanization. The first industrial revolutions substituted inanimate power for human and animal power in the use of tools, and machinery for human skills in carrying out processing tasks. Skilled craftworkers were replaced by semi-skilled and unskilled factory workers performing a small number of operations by hand and with machines in an extensive division of labor. At best, the new production worker was a machine operator or "tender," their range of motion and use of skill constrained by special-purpose machines dedicated to one or a small number of operations. The assembly-line, mass-production system subdivided work tasks into ever more minute operations. It tied workers' motion to the pace of machines which brought the work past them, the repetitious tasks they performed dictated by their place on the line.

Automation seeks wherever feasible to take the human element out of production processes altogether. In automated production, the human worker disappears from a host of operations, such as checking the quality of output, adjusting machine errors, handling materials between processing tasks, and even simple repetitive tasks performed on the assembly line. Machine operators are replaced by machine "monitors" who oversee a group of linked special purpose machines, and in some instances, integrated production systems (Faunce 1970: 86), with little or no ability to influence the internal operations of these systems. Managers and engineers set the parameters guiding the production process to desired performance and output levels. Machines perform dedicated tasks to achieve these objectives, and machines with automatic controls make adjustments as needed within these parameters without human intervention. Aside from managers and engineers, the only skilled workers are machinists and maintenance workers responsible for maintaining, repairing, and adjusting the automated equipment as needed.

Automated machines have two key properties. First, they are *self-acting*, in that their operations can be preset or "programmed" in advance, to be carried out without human involvement and control while the equipment is running. Second, and unique to automation, they have the facility of *self-regulation* through the application of "feedback" control. An automatic feedback control system – otherwise called a "servomechanism" – sends back information ("feedback") about the machine's output collected using a sensing device, compares that information with a predetermined objective, and then regulates the input and operations of the machine to correct for any deviation from the objective. A simple example of feedback control is the thermostatically controlled heating system found in homes and buildings. Machines employing feedback controls can automatically start, stop, accelerate, and decelerate their operations. They can count, inspect, test, remember, compare, and measure the dimension of space, time, sound, temperature, and other physical qualities, and apply this information to automatically regulate the quality and quantity of their output (Buckingham 1970: 127–134).

Automated devices based on mechanical, hydraulic and pneumatic principles can be found throughout history.[10] Elements of automation could be found in the spinning machines of the Industrial Revolution (Friedmann 1970: 121), "self-acting" metalworking machinery using mechanical stops, cams and hydraulic (and later electrical) actuators, and machine tools after the Civil War (Noble 1984: 66). It is arguable, in fact, that most mechanization of industrial processes entailed a degree of automaticity, as the purpose of machinery was to embody skills and knowledge once the sole province of craftsworkers.

Fully automated production occurs, however, when self-acting and self-regulating machines are linked and integrated into a continuous flow process. Not surprisingly, continuous process industries (petroleum refining, chemicals, papermaking, ore refining) were the first to embrace automation, even before the word was coined. Automatic industrial control mechanisms had long been used for measuring and adjusting variables such as temperature, pressure, and flow rates in batch processes of the tobacco, canning, dyestuff, rubber, and paper industries, based upon the fluid-tube diaphragm motor valve and pneumatic, hydraulic, and later electro-mechanical devices (Noble 1984: 59). In petroleum refining, where automatic controls are highly developed, crude petroleum is fed in at one end of the plant, flows continuously through a series of automatically controlled chambers and pipes, finally pouring out in a variety of finished products at the other end (Shils 1970: 139, 143). David Noble notes that automatic industrial controls were first applied in these sectors, where "careful and constant control over complex, high-speed operations became a necessity and a high volume of production could offset the considerable capital outlay for fixed automated facilities" (1984: 66).

The reduced role of human workers in automated production is acutely apparent in this sector. In modern process control plants, human operators monitor dials, make minor corrections in automatic control equipment settings, and change product properties as indicated by laboratory analysis. Automatic feedback devices handle the turning of valves, the starting and stopping of pumps, and other operations. Recording instruments display the quality of the process at key points for operator observation. The operator is in control of the process only during start-up, shutdown, or emergencies. Edward Shils estimated in 1963, that if a petroleum refinery plant employing eight hundred people were fully automated, the operating staff (except for maintenance staff) could be cut down to a mere dozen employees (1970: 151–152).

Achieving the same level of automation in the metalworking and similar manufacturing industries was more difficult. It was harder to replace the skilled machine operators in a metalworking facility, which historically had retained control over critical parts of production. Automation in these industries began with the linking up of self-acting, special-purpose machines by conveyors and work-handling devices forming assemblages called "transfer machines," enabling long sequences of metalworking operations without operator involvement. This kind of integrated, automatic factory production was pioneered in the metalworking industry as early as the 1920s by A. O. Smith's Milwaukee automobile plant (Noble 1984: 67).

Because of its widespread application in automobile plants during the 1930s and later, the linking of machine tools with automatic materials transfer and handling equipment was dubbed the "Detroit" model. The use of automatic and semi-automatic transfer devices to supplement conventional assembly-line operations greatly sped up mass production in other industries after World War II (Buckingham 1970: 132). Shils describes an example of continuous automatic production in 1952, when Ford started operations in a plant

> to machine automobile engine blocks with a battery of seventy-one machines linked together into an automatic line about 1600 feet long. Automatic machine tools perform more than five hundred boring, broaching, drilling, honing, milling, and tapping operations with little human assistance. The timing of each operation is synchronized so that the line moves forward uniformly.
>
> (1970: 150)

"Detroit" automation, while excellent for implementing a fixed sequence of dedicated operations to produce long runs of identical products, lacked the flexibility found in automated continuous process production. Some preferred to call it advanced mechanization rather than automation. When auto industry manufacturing executive Del Harder first coined the term automation in 1947, he defined it as "the automatic handling of parts between progressive production processes" (ibid.: 138–139). Detroit-style automation also lacked the capacity to adjust production operations to changing product requirements, make special set-ups, carry out product runs, and adapt the machine's function to a specific job order. These were common requirements in metalworking, especially in smaller companies using general-purpose equipment. Human operators were needed to carry out all these operations (Noble 1984: 67).

Advances in electronics, electronic communications and servo systems, and in computers, before, during and in the first decades after World War II, however, provided capabilities that could help overcome these limitations. Automatic equipment did not need electric motors and electronic devices to exist – it had long used controls employing mechanical, hydraulic, and pneumatic principles. But by the 1930s, electronics had come of age, and analog electronic computers and other devices were applied in early generations of automatic control. Before the war, basic electronic components had become reliable and cheap, and hence suitable for a wide number of applications. Many new devices also emerged, including phototube amplifiers for photoelectric actuators (to open doors and control motors), testing equipment such as voltmeters and oscilloscopes, and pulse transmitters, among others.

David Noble (1984) details how World War II spawned major improvements in electronics in the effort to develop radar, sonar, and related capabilities (e.g., radar-directed ordinance control systems). Government-supported work at the MIT Radiation Laboratory and elsewhere generated advances in pulse technology (essential to digital technologies) and microwave detection, as well as fundamental research into the properties of semiconductors. MIT's Servomechanism Laboratory produced a range of remote control devices for position measurement and precision control of motion. In short, the war generated a large number of components and devices, greater theoretical and empirical understanding of electronic technology, and a large number of trained experts in these areas. By the war's end, Noble observes, a universally applicable and easy to manipulate theory of servomechanisms had emerged, along with a "mature technology of automatic control," including precision servomotors, pulse generators, transducers, and a wide range of actuating, control, and sensing devices (ibid.: 48).

Nevertheless, electronic automated control systems diffused at a modest rate into the major manufacturing sectors. Electronics, feedback control and computer applications were rarely in use in the metalworking industries in the late 1940s and 1950s (ibid.: 67). Small analog computers applied to control technology in the process industries were installed in a number of plants in the early 1950s, and the first application of large-scale analog computers to a process problem was carried out under Air Force auspices in 1955 (ibid.: 60–61). However, the emergence of digital computer applications to automated systems eventually enabled widespread diffusion of truly automatic control devices throughout the economy in the decades that followed.

The digital revolution

The story of the digital computer over the past half-century, tracing in particular its military roots and the federal government and industrial roles in its development have been the subject of numerous studies and books (e.g., Flamm 1987, 1988; NRC/CSTB 1999; Castells 1996; Freeman and Perez 1988). The first large-scale, general purpose, electronic computing machine in the United States, the ENIAC (Electronic Numerical Integrator and Computer) – perhaps Vonnegut's inspiration for the EPICAC supercomputer in his book *Player Piano* – was built to calculate ballistic trajectories for airplane bombing raids at the end of World War II. ENIAC's successors in the 1950 were primarily employed to handle the enormous accumulation of paperwork and information accompanying the emergence of large bureaucratic organizations. In the 1950s and 1960s, large corporations, financial institutions, and government agencies were the first major users of mainframe computers, which become faster and more compact when "second generation" computers were introduced in 1959, using transistors instead of vacuum tubes and easier-to-use programming languages.[11]

As with most major innovations in history, such as machine tools, the internal combustion machine and electricity, the development and widespread diffusion of digital computing required a slew of complementary technical and organizational innovations. Flamm tracks the huge number of advancements in components, computer hardware, and software technology (1988: Tables A-1–A-4) that drove the evolution of the computer from the late 1940s through the 1970s and later. For example, magnetic core memory, the transistor and semiconductor integrated circuits were key components that began use in computers during the 1950s and 1960s.

The invention of the transistor was crucial for the growth of modern computing. It enabled the creation of faster and more power electronic devices in smaller, more compact packages. The transistor supplanted the vacuum tube in most electronic applications, and was widely used in analog and digital devices well into the 1970s.

The next important advance was the integrated circuit (IC), invented in 1957 by Jack Kilby and Robert Noyce, who co-founded Fairchild Semiconductor, and then Intel (in 1968), the spawning ground for most of the chip-making, computer and software businesses that proliferated during the late 1960s and 1970s, putting Northern California's Silicon Valley on the map. The IC packed multiple transistor circuits, ranging from digital logic gates to memory devices, on a single silicon wafer chip. From the 1960s on, as the technology of design and manufacturing semiconductor devices steadily advanced, IC chips packed in electronic circuits in increasing numbers (Castells 1996: 42). In 1971, Intel engineer Ted Hoff invented the microprocessor – the computer on a chip – which some consider the opening shot of the information technology revolution. Castells (1996: 42) calls the microprocessor the "great leap forward in the diffusion of microelectronics" as it allowed information processing power to be installed everywhere. The subsequent advances in chip design and manufacturing technology prompted Intel co-founder Gordon Moore in the 1960s to predict that the density of transistors on a silicon chip – and hence its processing power – would double every 18 months (later updated to 18–24 months), which has since been dubbed Moore's law. Chips produced in 2000 have 256 times the density of those manufactured in 1987, and 66,000 times the density of those of 1975.

The dramatic advances in microchip technology enabled the creation of computing devices with faster and more powerful microelectronic components at decreasing costs, accelerating their diffusion into a wide range of consumer and industrial applications. The economic impacts of the microelectronic "revolution" are especially apparent in three applications of computing technology – computers, embedded computing devices, and high-speed digital networks.

Computers

As microchips increased in speed and power, the processing power of computers also expanded, at the same or lower cost. A $1,000 personal computer today has the processing power of a $20,000 scientific workstation of only five years ago. It is estimated that the installed base of computer power has increased a billion-fold over the past forty years (Cohen *et al.* 2000: 8–9). The speed and data storage capacity of today's desktop personal computer (PC) far exceed that of ENIAC's, whose vacuum tubes and wiring filled a huge room. ENIAC operated at a speed of 5,000 operations per second, while the typical desktop PC in 1995 operated at nearly 100 million instructions per second, and the fastest supercomputers operated at over 1 trillion instructions per second (NRC/CSTB 1999: 26). By 2002, PCs were an order of magnitude more powerful still.

Spurred by the "revolution" in components, computer technology advanced rapidly. Throughout the 1950s and 1960s large mainframe computers were virtually the only commercially available computers. By the mid-1970s, smaller, minicomputers had made inroads into the business computer market once dominated by mainframes, accounting for 9 percent of computer sales in 1974, and twice that of ten years later. The first mass market personal computer (PC), the Apple II, was introduced in 1977. IBM introduced its Personal Computer in 1981, and by the mid-1980s the new PCs and minicomputers combined accounted for more than half the computer market in sales (Flamm 1988: 237–239). By the 1990s, desktop PCs were ubiquitous artifacts in offices, schools, and homes, their sales far outstripping those of minicomputers and mainframes.

Large mainframe computers were first applied to industrial problems in the aircraft industry during the late 1950s. In March 1959, the first computer built specifically for plant process control, by TRW, was installed at the Texaco Port Arthur refinery. By 1964, there were approximately one hundred digital computers either in operation or on order in the petroleum-refining industry for use in a large number of industrial processes (Noble 1984: 61). Computers, large and small, have found a wide range of applications in service-related industries, including finance, airlines, entertainment, education, transportation, and government. Finally, computers have been transforming offices since the first

43

mainframes were introduced to manage large corporate databases. But over time, PCs have played an ever more critical role in bringing automation into the office.

Embedded microelectronics

Often ignored in discussions about the IT revolution are the innumerable microelectronic devices embedded in consumer and industrial products. Today, microchips can be found in myriad consumer devices, such as toys, games, televisions, radios, VCRs, DVDs, video and photographic cameras, automobiles, home security systems, and telephone systems, to name only a few. In this sense, we have truly become a digital society – and the penetration of digital devices into our lives continues unabated.

But, microelectronics' greatest economic impact may come from its application to automatic control systems in manufacturing. Microelectronic components have enabled the diffusion of programmable automation technologies into industrial processes to a degree that was not economically, and perhaps not technically, feasible when automation was first introduced. As Harley Shaiken (1984: 1) observes:

> The flexibility of microelectronics extends computer technology to every corner of manufacturing. On one automobile assembly line, for example, 98 percent of over 3,000 welds on the car body are performed by swiftly moving robots, computer-controlled mechanical arms. In an aerospace machine shop, the complex contours of a jet-engine support are carved out by the whirring cutter of a numerically-controlled machine tool, itself directed by a computer that is simultaneously supervising over a hundred other machines.

In process industries, microchip devices can be found in a slew of devices used in process control equipment, such as programmable logic controllers, intelligent sensors, actuators, batch process control systems, and intelligent pumps. Similarly, microchips are embedded in automated equipment employed in goods production, such as in the machine tool and other metalworking industries (auto, aircraft). After the war, the military supported research on programmable machine tools that could overcome the difficulties of efficiently automating manufacturing operations geared to short-run production involving special set-ups, frequent retooling, and the like. Out of these efforts came numerical control (N/C). In N/C machines, mathematically coded information stored on magnetic or punched paper tape guides the motion of a machine tool in cutting out a part (Noble 1984: 84). N/C machines became ubiquitous in metalworking plants, ultimately superseded by computer-numerically

44

controlled (CNC) machine tools with embedded microelectronic control devices that allowed far more flexibility at lower costs.

Microelectronics also enabled other important classes of programmable tools, such as Flexible Manufacturing Systems (FMS) and robots. FMS, which came into vogue in the 1980s, is a complex of CNC machine tools and automatic shuttles to move parts between them, tied to a centralized computer (Shaiken 1984: 140). By the 1980s robots were widely employed in the auto and other industries performing such tasks as welding, painting, assembly, loading and unloading, and inspection. Machine vision technologies (smart cameras, vision sensors), actuators, motion controllers, and other devices with embedded microprocessors are also employed in programmable equipment.

Digital networks

Microelectronics have been a primary enabler, along with other innovations, such as optical fiber, in fostering the development and diffusion of digital networking and high-speed data communications technologies. The history of the Defense Department's Advanced Research Projects Agency's (ARPA) early support for efforts to link up geographically separated stand-alone computers that can interactively exchange information ("talk" to each other) which led to the creation of ARPANET and ultimately to the Internet, is well known. As industries transformed their operations with computers and digital automation equipment, there emerged a new impetus to link and coordinate the diverse machines and processes employed throughout factories – to create the "highly integrated manufacturing system, the computerized factory" (Shaiken 1984: 2). The goal was to "integrate the various parts of the factory, speed the transfer of information, and remove the limits of time and space from the direction of a corporation." In addition, computers would not only control machine tool operations, "but track raw materials coming into the shop, inventory completed parts, monitor robots on the assembly line, and schedule production" (ibid.: 7–8). Toward this end, an alphabet soup of computer-based applications involving internal networking (local area networks or LANs) has proliferated over the past two decades: CAD (computer-aided design); CAM (computer-aided manufacturing); CIM (computer-integrated manufacturing); MIS (management information system); MES (manufacturing execution system); SCADA (supervisory control and data acquisition); MRP (manufacturing resource planning); and ERP (enterprise resource planning), among others.

In some industries, such as auto and apparel, there also emerged efforts to link up their factories' operations with those of their suppliers and customers. Called electronic data interchange (EDI), this entailed the establishment of dedicated "wide-area networks" using existing telephone lines to make this connection. For example, in the apparel industry, EDI ties together sewing shops with company warehouses and retailers. Each of the Big Three auto firms established EDI links with their major parts suppliers. This was expensive and cumbersome for suppliers, who were required to maintain separate dedicated EDI systems for each of their customers. The use of EDI and dedicated data communications links between manufacturers, customers and suppliers, and between corporate headquarters and globally dispersed branch plants, with ever more emphasis on increased integration, flexibility, productivity, and control, continues today. The great gains in microelectronics and in data communications – a steady increase in bandwidth at lower and lower costs – have facilitated these trends.

The Internet offers even greater potential to reduce the transaction costs involved in achieving higher levels of integration on the factory floor. Microelectronics has been called "a revolution within a revolution." The larger, earlier revolution refers to automation, which was a departure from the mass-production system of the first half of the twentieth century. Unlike mass production, which subordinates workers to a mechanized system under managerial control, automation seeks to eliminate the worker. As the first computers were linked to industrial plants where earlier forms of automation already existed, fears of a workerless economy, as expressed in Kurt Vonnegut's *Player Piano*, were heard in the early 1950s. At the same time, others extolled the emergence of another industrial revolution culminating in the fully-automated factory (Dubin 1970) – with its counterpart, the automated "office of the future" (Greenbaum 1995). As it turns out, these claims were premature, as neither the technical means nor the economic incentives yet existed to realize this vision. Nonetheless, as automation technologies penetrated into the economy, a process accelerated by a steady stream of advances in computers, microelectronics, and communications, fundamental transformations in the structure of production organizations and businesses, and in workplace organization, jobs, and labor markets have occurred.

It is important to note that these changes were not simply the product of technological change. Rather they came about as a result of a complex interaction between the processes of technical change, major innovations in managerial organization, and larger economic, social, and political forces (e.g., globalization) since the 1980s. The *lean production* model of industrial organization, in particular, swept through manufacturing, and then into other sectors, such as services and construction, over the 1980s, 1990s and up to the present, introducing new innovative management practices such as "just-in-time" delivery, total quality management, and supply chain management. As we describe in the next chapter, US industry's embracing of the lean model was a response to the growing threat of foreign competitors – especially the Japanese and Europeans – who in 1970s began to challenge the once dominant American manufacturers in market after market (consumer electronics, auto, steel, semiconductors), both at home and abroad.

ICT-based automation also was widely adopted during this period, largely as an element of companies' efforts to restructure their operations along the lean model. A central insight from our historical review of "industrial revolutions" over the past two hundred years is that technological advance is never the actual driver of change in itself. There is a tendency to associate "industrial revolutions" with particular technologies, which can obscure the organizational, institutional, economic, and social factors actually underlying the adoption and diffusion of these technologies into the economy. Part of the reason for this perspective lies with the faulty assumption of neo-classical economic theory that treats technology as an independent variable. In contrast, alternative schools of economic thought, for example, the so-called "evolutionary" economists (Nelson and Winter 1982; Dosi et al. 1988), treat technology as a mediating variable, one that works in a codetermining way with other institutional, economic, and social forces to produce economic change. New technologies present opportunities for change as well as defining the upper boundaries of what is possible at any given time. Technological innovations are selected for introduction to productive processes according to whether or not they contribute to the bottom-line goals of industry owners and managers. We have seen that, in the end, the driving forces of increasing efficiency and productivity, usually associated with lowering labor costs, are the decisive factors in whether or how a new technology is adopted and diffused throughout an economy.

A second insight is that a technology innovation never occurs in isolation, but is the product both of cumulative technical advances over time and the existence of complementary technologies that enable its full potential to be realized. The Internet might be thought of as a "revolution within a revolution, within a revolution," recognizing that its transformative potential must be tempered by its roots in the automation and microelectronic revolutions that preceded it. Keeping in mind these contextual concerns, whether the Internet will ultimately produce qualitative and quantitative changes on a par with the "industrial revolutions" that spawned it is a subject to which we now turn our attention.

References

Berman, D. K. (2002) "Innovation Outpaced the Marketplace," *The Wall Street Journal*, 26 September, B1, B8.

Blauner, R. (1964) *Alienation and Freedom,* Chicago: University of Chicago Press.

Braverman, H. (1974) *Labor and Monopoly Capital,* New York: Monthly Review Press.

Bright, J. R. (1958) Automation and Management, Boston: Division of Research, Graduate School of Business Administration, Harvard University.

The Brookings Institution (2002) *Summary of the Workshop,* Brookings Workshop on Economic Measurement, Service Industry Productivity: New Estimates and New Problems, Washington, DC, May 17.

Buckingham, W. (1961) *Automation: Its Impact on Business and People,* New York: Harper & Row.

Buckingham, W. (1970) "Principles of Automation," in Marcson, S. (ed.) *Automation, Alienation, and Anomie,* New York: Harper & Row, 126–136.

Castells, M. (1996) *The Information Age, Economy, Society and Culture,* vol. I, *The Rise of the Network Society,* Cambridge, MA: Blackwell Publishers.

Cohen, S. S., DeLong, J. B. and Zysman, J. (2000) *Tools for Thought: What is New and Important About the "E-conomy"?,* BRIE Working Paper #138, Berkeley, CA: Berkeley Roundtable on the International Economy, February 22.

David, P. A. (1999) "Digital Technology and the Productivity Paradox: After Ten Years, What Has Been Learned?", paper prepared for presentation to the conference "Understanding the Digital Economy: Data, Tools and Research," US Department of Commerce, Washington, DC, May 25–26.

Dosi, G., Freeman, C., Nelson, R., Silverberg, G. and Soete, L. (eds) (1988) *Technical Change and Economic Theory,* London: Pinter Publishers.

Dreazen, Y. J. (2002) "Behind the Fiber Glut, Telecom Carriers Were Driven by Wildly Optimistic Data on Internet's Growth Rate," *The Wall Street Journal,* 26 September, B1, B8.

Dubin, R, (1958) *The World of Work: Industrial Society and Human Relations,* Englewood Cliffs, New Jersey: Prentice-Hall Inc.

Dubin, R, (1970) "Automation: The Second Industrial Revolution," in Marcson, S. (ed.) *Automation, Alienation, and Anomie,* New York: Harper & Row, 152–161.

EIA, US Department of Energy, Energy Information Administration (EIA) (1996) "History of the U.S. Electric Power Industry, 1882–1991," *Changing Structure of the Electric Power Industry: An Update,* DOE/EIA-0562(96) (Washington, DC, December), Appendix A, 103–112.

Faunce, W. A. (1965) "Automation and the Division of Labor," *Social Problems,* vol. 13, no. 2, Fall.

Faunce, W. A. (1970) "Automation and the Division of Labor," in Marcson, S. (ed.) *Automation, Alienation, and Anomie,* New York: Harper & Row, 79–96.

Flamm, K. (1987) *Targeting the Computer: Government Support and International Competition,* Washington, DC: The Brookings Institution.

Flamm, K. (1988) *Creating the Technology: Government, Industry, and High Technology,* Washington, DC: The Brookings Institution.

Freeman, C. and Perez, C. (1988) "Structural Crisis of Adjustment, Business Cycles and Investment Behaviour," in G. Dosi, C. Freeman, R. Nelson, G. Silverberg and L. Soete (eds) *Technical Change and Economics Theory,* London: Pinter, pp. 38–66.

Freifeld, M. (1984) "The Impact of Technological Change on the Sexual Division of Labor in the Cotton Textiles Industry: The Reconstitution of Craft Skill on the Self Acting Mule, 1925–1920," paper presented at the Berkshire Conference of Women Historians, Smiths College, June 1–2.

Friedmann, G. (1955) *Industrial Society*, New York: Macmillan Company/Free Press.

Friedmann, G. (1970) "Three Stages of Automation," in Marcson, S. (ed.) *Automation, Alienation, and Anomie*, New York: Harper & Row, 113–125, 177–188.

Gordon, R. J. (2000) *Does the "New Economy" Measure Up to the Great Inventions of the Past?* Working Paper 7833 (http://www.nber.org/papers/w7833), Cambridge, MA: National Bureau of Economic Research, August.

Gordon, R. J. (2002) *Technology and Economic Performance in the American Economy*, Working Paper 8771 (http://www.nber.org/papers/w8771), Cambridge, MA: National Bureau of Economic Research, February.

Greenbaum, J. (1995) *Windows on the Workplace: Computers, Jobs and the Organization of Office Work in the Late Twentieth Century*, New York: Monthly Review Press.

Jorgenson, D. W., Ho, M. S. and Stiroh, K. J. (2002) "Information Technology, Education, and the Sources of Economic Growth across U.S. Industries," paper prepared for Brookings Workshop on Economic Measurement, Service Industry Productivity: New Estimates and New Problems, The Brookings Institution, Washington, DC, May 17.

Marcson, S. (ed.) (1970) *Automation, Alienation, and Anomie*, New York: Harper & Row.

Miller, S. and Lundegaard, K. (2002) "The $85,000 VW: Its Seats Can Be Adjusted 18 Ways," *Wall Street Journal*, 7 March, B4.

Mowery, D. C. and Rosenberg, N. (1982) "Technical Change in the Commercial Aircraft Industry, 1925–1975," in N. Rosenberg, *Inside the Black Box*, Cambridge: Cambridge University Press, pp. 163–177.

Mowery, D. C. and Rosenberg, N. (1989) *Technology and the Pursuit of Economic Growth*, Cambridge: Cambridge University Press.

Mulligan, W. H. Jr. (1981) "Mechanizing the Gentle Craft: The Introduction of Machinery into the Lynn, Massachusetts Shoe Industry, 1852–1882," in Robert W. *et al.* (eds) *Essays from the Lowell Conference on Industrial History 1980 and 1981*, Lowell, MA: Lowell Conference on Industrial History, pp. 33–45.

National Research Council, Computer Science and Telecommunications Board (NRC/CSTB) (1999) *Funding A Revolution: Government Support for Computing Research*, Washington, DC: National Academy Press.

Nelson, R. R. and Winter, S. G. (1982) *An Evolutionary Theory of Economic Change*, Cambridge, MA: Harvard University Press,.

Noble, D. F. (1984) *Forces of Production: A Social History of Industrial Automation*, New York: Alfred A. Knopf.

Richardson, C. (1992) "Progress for Whom? New Technology, Unions, and Collective Bargaining," in Labor Policy Institute, *Software and Hardhats: Technology and Workers in the Twenty-First Century: A Report of Two Conferences*, Washington, DC: Labor Policy Institute, pp. 151–174.

Rosenberg, N. (1976) *Perspectives on Technology*, Cambridge: Cambridge University Press.

Rosenberg, N. (1982) *Inside the Black Box: Technology and Economics*, Cambridge: Cambridge University Press.

Shaiken, H. (1984) *Work Transformed: Automation and Labor in the Computer Age,* New York: Holt, Rinehart and Winston.

Shils, E. B. (1963) *Automation and Industrial Relations,* New York: Holt, Rinehart and Winston, Inc.

Shils, E. B. (1970) "Automation: Technology or Concept," in Marcson, S. (ed.) *Automation, Alienation, and Anomie,* New York: Harper & Row, 137–152.

Sieling, M., Friedman, B. and Dumas, M. (2001) "Labor Productivity in the Retail Trade Industry, 1987–99," *Monthly Labor Review,* December, 3–14.

Thomas, R. (1994) *What Machines Can't Do: Politics and Technology in the Industrial Enterprise,* Berkeley, CA: University of California Press.

Triplett, J. E. and Bosworth, B. P. (2002) "'Baumol's Disease' Has Been Cured: IT and Multifactor Productivity in U.S. Services Industries," paper prepared for Brookings Workshop on Services Industry Productivity, The Brookings Institution, Washington, DC, May 17.

US Department of Energy, Energy Information Administration (EIA) (1996) *The Changing Structure of the Electric Power Industry: An Update,* DOE/EIA-0562(96), Washington, DC: US Dept. of Energy, December.

van Ark, B., Inklaar, R. and McGuckin, R. H. (2002) "'Changing Gear,' Productivity, ICT and Service Industries: Europe and the United States," paper presented at ZEW Conference 2002 on Economics of Information and Communication Technologies, Mannheim, June 19.

Womack, J. P., Jones, D. T. and Roos, D. (1991) *The Machine That Changed the World,* New York: HarperCollins.

Yudken, J. S. (1987) "The Viability of Craft in Advanced Industrial Society: Case Study of the Contemporary Crafts Movement in the United States," unpublished PhD dissertation for Graduate Special Program, Stanford University, California.

3

THE WIZARD OF OZ AND THE
JOBS DILEMMA

Visiting the Santa Clara, California, corporate headquarters of Intel, maker of the Pentium microprocessor and the world's largest microchip manufacturer, is a little like visiting the Wizard of Oz. Except, unlike in the Judy Garland movie, what happens here is truly a kind of technological wizardry. A tour through Intel's facilities and its small, on-site museum reminds visitors that they are not in Kansas anymore. An exhibit in the museum illustrates how a microprocessor is fabricated, from the wafers cut from cylindrical ingots of pure silicon, made by processing ordinary beach sand (SiO_2), to the photolithography process used to reproduce a chip's circuitry pattern on the wafer surface, to the ion implantation (or "doping") processes that alter in desired ways the electrical properties of silicon elements in the device. To put this in perspective, Intel claims that its current volume production line of microprocessors – each about the size of a dime – features transistors on the scale of 60 nanometers (nm; a nanometer is a *billionth* of a meter) and interconnect lines of 130 nm. It recently unveiled chips produced using a 90 nm process which allows printing of individual lines smaller than a virus.

The production facilities where these incredible devices are fabricated are correspondingly impressive (and expensive). An enormous amount of sophisticated technology is employed, not only in design and fabrication, but in creating an extremely clean environment to ensure that not even the tiniest speck of dust can contaminate the wafers while they are being processed. The "cleanrooms," where chips are made, are said to be 10,000 times cleaner than a hospital operating room. Enormous air filtration systems completely change the air in these rooms about ten times per minute, and every employee in a cleanroom must wear a "bunny suit" made from a unique non-linting, anti-static fabric, to protect the chips from human particles, such as skin flakes or hairs.

Intel was a pioneer in the microelectronics revolution, and it continues to practice its technical wizardry in generating ever more powerful microelectronic devices that drive advances in almost every area of information technology. In 1971, Intel's 4004, the world's first commercial microprocessor, contained only 2,300 transistors and performed about 60,000 operations per second. Its Pentium 4 processor today packs 55 million transistors on a chip operating at a speed of greater than 2.2 gigahertz (GHz; a billion hertz or cycles per second). Moore's law is still in effect, and Intel predicts that by 2007 it will produce a processor with over 1 billion transistors operating at a speed of 20 GHz. Equally important is the increasingly lower cost of this exponential growth in processing power. A transistor once cost $5; today, $5 in effect can purchase 5 million transistors.

Intel views itself as being at the heart of the Internet revolution, a claim that is hard to argue with. Its revenues of $26.5 billion in 2001, while down 21 percent from the previous year, is way above that of its nearest competitors in microchip sales. Its products are building blocks for the PCs, servers, communication products, and digital cellular components and software, that make up the Internet. At the same time, the continued growth of the Internet will continue to drive up demand for its products. Intel's annual report (Intel 2001) predicts that over the next two decades it will be one of the main suppliers of microchip devices for the growth over the next two decades of "ubiquitous networks worldwide, with tens of millions of servers connecting billions of PCs and other clients." It adds that it is "well positioned to be at the heart of this long-term build-out, with innovative architectures targeted at key Internet areas."

A ride around the industrial parks surrounding the Intel campus, however, is not quite such an upbeat experience for the visitor. A number of sleek, high-tech-looking industrial buildings are closed, their parking lots empty, and parking lots attached to many other high-tech companies – most obviously owned by microelectronics and information technology firms – are at best half-full. With nearly 80,000 unemployed workers, the unemployment rate in Silicon Valley rose to 7.9 percent in October 2002, the highest level since 1983, and way above the statewide average of 6.4 percent and the national average of 5.7 percent. It was less than 2 percent during the dot.com boom. Even Intel, with over 80,000 employees in forty-five nations, has cut jobs, shedding 6,000 jobs in 2001, and it reported that it would cut 4,000 more in the second half of 2002. When the Internet bubble burst, ICT spending dropped dramatically and chipmakers, computer and telecom equipment manufacturers, and software developers saw their markets suddenly dry up, sending a ripple effect through these firms' supplier chains which also suffered huge losses. As a local resident only half-jokingly observed, a side benefit from the economic slump is a much faster commute between Berkeley and Silicon Valley because of the ease in traffic congestion (Bolton 2002; Steen 2002).

Nevertheless, Intel remains optimistic that there will be a rebound. It is investing a total of $10 billion building new fabrication facilities by 2004 for its newest, state-of-the-art processor chips, each containing a quarter-billion transistors, starting with its $2.5 billion D1D semiconductor factory in Hillsboro, Oregon. The chipmaker is gambling that its efforts to speed up the introduction of extremely powerful chips will take the Internet to the next level, enabling hundreds of millions of computers, phones, and other devices to be tied to wireless networks. It is not alone in this optimism, as other industry leaders and analysts are also expecting a comeback as the nation emerges out of the recession of 2000, in part grounded in a faith in the future of digital wireless communications. For example, *Fortune* quotes Intel chairman of the board and former CEO Andy Grove:

> You know that saying, "The Internet changes everything"? People are backing away from it but I say, just wait five years. Hundreds of billions of dollars we now spend on voice telecommunications will become a freebie – just like [Cisco CEO] John Chambers has said. That's Moore's Law at work. The entire entertainment industry will be digitally distributed over broadband networks. [Media companies are] going to tip over, because one of them, with its back to the wall, will make the transition, and the others will have to follow. That's Moore's Law at work. Houses will be wireless, broadband will be delivered wirelessly, and home and portable computers and consumer electronics are going to be built to facilitate all of the above. Okay, it hasn't happened in the first five years; it's going to take ten. And there will be a lot of pain for some. But it will happen, and we'll all benefit.
>
> (Schlender 2002)

Similarly, Microsoft is dedicating large numbers of its programmers to developing all-wireless PCs. Its "dotNet" strategy reportedly encourages programmers to develop software capable of running on any device, including cars, watches, refrigerators, stereos, clocks, and the like. The wireless PC would be at the center, coordinating the flow of information between these devices. As Microsoft chief technical officer and strategist Craig Mundie says, "The computer not only gets revamped, it becomes part of an ecosystem of intelligent devices, services, and novel applications that live on the network" (Kirkpatrick 2002a). This in turn, Intel and other chipmakers hope, would require new generations of faster, more powerful microprocessors.

Whether this optimism is warranted or turns out to be wishful thinking depends upon a number of mostly non-technical or indirectly technical factors, many outside industry leaders' control. The telecom sector is still on life-support, and there are no signs yet of a resuscitation. An Intel executive whose division supplies network processors notes that his telecom customers have laid off 270,000 people in the past two years. But there is some doubt that even a telecom industry back on its feet would use enough chips to keep companies like Intel growing (Schlender 2002).

Much of the ICT industry's hope for the future hinges on the deployment of broadband and wireless communication. Broadband communications (high-bandwidth, high-speed) technology enables much faster, more powerful multi-media digital processing applications than can be employed using standard Internet telecommunications connections. Industry leaders lament the relatively slow growth of broadband Internet services in the United States and their higher costs compared to other countries, especially Korea, Japan and China. They believe that it is the platform on which powerful applications of the future will be developed, and its adoption will stimulate huge amounts of spending on hardware and software (Kirkpatrick 2002b). Microsoft boss Bill Gates has called the lack of widespread broadband access a significant obstacle in the way of broader residential use of the Internet (Waters 2001).

Broadband deployment, however, has been hindered by a combination of complex regulatory issues and an apparent lack of consumer demand. Consumer and media public interest advocates are especially concerned that the unregulated cable industry's dominance in providing high-speed broadband services in the United States – the slower Digital Subscriber Loop (DSL) technologies provided by telephone companies over existing copper wires is cable's only competitor – could allow cable providers to limit access to their facilities and discriminate in Internet services it provides, exercising control over the content and applications that operate on their networks (Lessig 2001: 62–63; NRC/CSTB 2000: 1–13, 14). At the same time, most consumers, especially residential users, have yet to see what extra value they would receive from broadband at the costs being offered. Although 85 percent of US households potentially have access to broadband in one form or another, only a little more than one in ten households actually use it (Waters 2001).

The spread of high-speed Internet wireless technology suffers from similar problems concerning regulation over public use of the technology and spectrum availability, and other technical and financial difficulties confronting the wireless industry (NRC/CSTB 2000; Dombey and Guerrera 2002: 1–15). As with broadband, there is still undeveloped consumer demand for the kind of services offered by wireless, though some believe the popularity of the i-mode phone service provided in Japan by DoCoMo indicates a potential for rapid adoption of wireless data services elsewhere (NRC/CSTB 2000: 1–15). Consumers also need to see applications of the technology, such as the wirelessly networked home, up close and working before they will buy into it. Whether efforts, like Sony's push into wireless – it plans to introduce next year a little wireless device called RoomLink, that attaches to a TV, allowing users to use their PC's media on the TV (Kirkpatrick 2002a) – or Intel's plan to introduce radio-enhanced processors – radio transceivers incorporated into processors in PCs that automatically detect and connect to wireless and even cellphone networks (Intel 2002; Schlender 2002) – will help generate sufficient consumer demand for a new generation of Internet products to get the ICT industries going again, remains to be seen.

ICT and economic trends

The resurrection of the ICT sectors is also inextricably linked to national economic recovery. The ICT industries' technology-driven growth fueled the economic expansion of the 1990s, and could be important to future economic growth. At the same time, healthy ICT-using industries (manufacturing and services) which are major customers for ICT products, are essential to the successful re-emergence of the ICT sector as the leading edge of the economy. Several other factors, such as the war on terrorism, the war with Iraq, the status of global financial markets, the strength of the US dollar and trade policies, also will strongly influence the extent and speed of the nation's economic revival – and hence the rate and extent of continued penetration of ICT and Internet technologies into the economy.

In any case, ICT and the Internet probably will remain important drivers of productivity and economic growth for many years. Most significantly, they will continue to influence workplace organization and labor markets as they have for the past five decades. The rise of ICT created industry sectors and occupations that did not exist prior to World War II. These sectors and jobs, moreover, were among the fastest growing in the US economy in the decades after the war, and are expected to be major areas of growth in the future, current uncertain political and economic conditions notwithstanding. Our concern, however, transcends the rollercoaster ride that ICT workforces have been on over the half decade, or what they might experience in the coming decades. We are equally concerned with the consequences of ICT and the Internet on the remaining 95 percent of the nation's workforce.

Advances in ICT helped fuel manufacturers' efforts to automate their operations in the post-World War II decades, which contributed to the productivity gains enjoyed by the manufacturing sector over most of that period. Yet up through 1980, despite automation steadily spreading throughout the major industrial sectors, total manufacturing employment grew (with notable fluctuations), reaching its highest level of a little over 21 million in 1979 (see Figure 3.1). However, the size of the total workforce grew much faster than the manufacturing workforce over these years, and as a result, manufacturing's share of the total steadily declined (see Figure 3.2). According to Bureau of Labor Statistics (BLS) data, in 1950, manufacturing jobs accounted for 34.4 percent of total non-farm employment, while private services accounted for 45 percent and government jobs for 13.2 percent. By 1980, manufacturing's share had dropped to 22.3 percent, while services increased their share to 54 percent and government to 17.9 percent. This trend has continued to the present day: manufacturing's share fell to 13 percent in 2001, services' proportion increased to 65.3 percent, and government employment dropped a little to 16.1 percent.

The steadily diminishing share of manufacturing jobs, even as they grew in absolute numbers, reflected the rapid growth of service industries after the war. Employment in category of services steadily grew, especially after 1960. The largest, fastest-growing sectors included retail and wholesale trade, finance, insurance and real estate (FIRE), communications, transportation, health, educational, social, legal, and personal services. Employment growth in what some have called "producer" services – engineering and management services, business services (inclusive of computer and data processing services) – also began to take off in the 1960s, though its most dramatic increases occurred during the 1980s and 1990s.

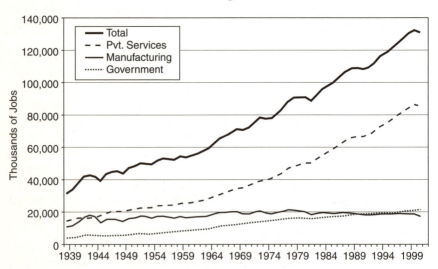

Figure 3.1 US non-farm employment, total and selected sectors, 1939–2001 (seasonally adjusted)

Source: US Department of Labor, Bureau of Labor Statistics

Note
For data used to compile this figure, see Appendix 1.

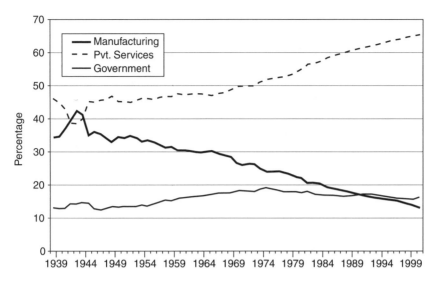

Figure 3.2 Percentage of total US non-farm employment, selected sectors,
1939–2001

Source: US Department of Labor, Bureau of Labor Statistics

Note
For data used to compile this figure, see Appendix 2.

Multiple, interrelated forces produced these trends. The end of the war, especially following the deprivations of the Depression, unleashed enormous pent-up demand for material goods. Mass production was matched by mass consumption in a new era of prosperity, and an army of sales people emerged to distribute the goods produced by the revved-up engines of civilian manufacturing industries. Returning soldiers went back to school with the help of the G.I. Bill, new families moved in droves into newly built suburban developments, and a new generation of children flooded – and put a strain on – the nation's educational system (the Baby Boomers). As suburban communities grew up around the urban, largely manufacturing-based, centers, so did the need for improved and expanded transportation and communication services, public utilities, and many other personal services. Internationally, the United States emerged from the war as the pre-eminent industrial power and the dominant exporter of manufactured goods. Its only potential trade competitors, Europe, especially Germany, and Japan, needed to rebuild their industrial systems shattered by the war, an endeavor undertaken with the help of US aid programs (e.g., the Marshall Plan). Until the 1970s, Japanese imports were synonymous with cheap, poor quality goods.

The huge industrial mobilization for the war effort presided over by the Federal Government played a crucial role in giving US manufacturing industries their competitive edge. The automobile and aircraft industries rapidly converted from their wartime production, emerging stronger and more technologically sophisticated than they were before the war. American manufacturers were well positioned to exploit for commercial use the many technological advances in materials, electronics, aircraft design, communications, and manufacturing methods, among others, that had been developed for the war effort. For example, the Boeing 707 began as a military transport (Dertouzos *et al.* 1989: 11). Some inventions like the computer saw limited application during the war, but became critically important commercial and industrial technologies in the civilian economy during the decades that followed.

The defense aerospace and electronics industries emerged as important economic sectors in their own right, with strong links to their commercial sides; Boeing and McDonnell Douglas (now owned by Boeing) and Lockheed (now Lockheed Martin) produced both military and commercial aircraft. The military–industrial–academic complex that emerged out of the war, and consolidated and grew to meet the challenges of the Cold War, continued to be a major source of subsidy and stimulus for technological advances that often (though not as much as some proponents have argued) led to commercially important "spin-offs." The integrated circuit was invented in commercial laboratories, but its development benefited from prior military-supported R&D in semiconductors and materials technology, as well as from large military markets for its use. The Internet itself began as a major initiative of the Defense Advanced Projects Research Agency. Indeed, the Pentagon was a major early sponsor of automation technologies (see Noble 1984), leading to the development of N/C machine tools; it continues to be a major government sponsor of advanced manufacturing technology R&D.

Computers, N/C and then CNC machine tools, automatic control devices and other new technologies were diffused throughout the nation's production facilities and offices over those first post-war decades, raising the specter of massive job displacement. As the employment data shows (Figure 3.1), however, the feared job losses were not realized, at least on the aggregate level. In manufacturing, at least up until the late 1970s, whatever displacement of jobs that took place at the factory and industry sector levels when automated equipment was introduced – and displacements assuredly did occur at these levels – was offset by economic growth. The argument is that automation results in greater efficiencies, higher productivity and lower costs, which in turn leads to increased demand for manufactured goods. Manufacturers increase their investment in new production capacity to meet this demand, creating new jobs that offset the job losses resulting from the new technologies. In addition, new jobs are created in the computer and software, machine tools, machinery and parts sectors, and other emerging technologies – both production and services – which supply the new automation equipment purchased by upgrading manufacturers. This argument appeared to hold true up through the late 1970s, as long as the US economy was growing at a reasonably healthy rate, and US manufacturers distributed their goods mostly at a national level, with relative immunity from foreign competition.

On the other hand, the low rate of job growth in manufacturing relative to other sectors undoubtedly is due, at least in part, to increasing automation. By definition, automation reduces labor requirements, and the resulting productivity gains equates with increased output by fewer workers. This relationship is affirmed by manufacturing's remarkably constant share of total private non-farm output over the period 1945–1985 – in 1948 it was 27.9 percent, and in 1985 it was 28 percent – while its share of employment steadily fell, to 19.4 percent in 1985. In contrast, within the non-manufacturing sector (in particular, FIRE, retail trade, wholesale trade, services) rapid output growth, in absolute terms and as a share of GDP, and low productivity growth resulted in a strong demand for labor (COSEPUP 1987: 74–75, Table 3–7). This is consistent with the relatively lower service sector investment in new technology compared to manufacturing at least until the 1980s.[1]

Joan Greenbaum (1995) notes that although there was much talk of introducing computers into offices during the 1950s and 1960s, there was very little computerization of office work until the 1970s. The earlier decades, she observes, were "a period for preparing for it." The post-war period saw the rise of large corporate and government bureaucracies on a far greater scale than ever before. Insurance companies, banks, airlines, securities firms, and government agencies, in particular, had huge and growing volumes of data they needed to process and a large amount of repetitive work, making them ripe for the introduction of computers. Large mainframe computers had been employed in these sectors as early as the 1950s. As the volume of work and labor costs skyrocketed and computer technology advanced, managers introduced computers into their organizations on a much larger scale. Thus, writes Greenbaum:

> During the 1970s, mainframe computers became a fact of organizational life. Most of the "bugs" or programming quirks, in the mainframe operating systems had been ironed out and companies were beginning to develop applications that could handle large volumes of transactions.
>
> (1995: 53)[2]

Office automation did not cause massive displacement of office workers, any more than automated machinery produced large-scale job losses in manufacturing. On the other hand, computer-based automation has fostered the restructuring of work organizations and produced changes in skill requirements and occupational composition in offices.

By 1980, the US economy was undergoing its most significant transformation since World War II. The United States entered a major recession in 1980, resulting in the economy losing a net of about 2 million jobs between 1979 and 1982. The manufacturing workforce was hardest hit, shedding about 3 million jobs in this period (private services job growth decelerated, but still registered positive job growth), dropping to 18 million workers in 1982. But manufacturing's malaise ran deeper than a mere recession – the changes were structural. For the first time since before World War II US firms were confronted with major foreign competitors, who rapidly cut into their markets, both overseas and in the United States, the largest and most lucrative market of all. Japan's and Europe's (especially Germany's) industrial sectors emerged from their post-war economic reconstruction – ironically with US assistance – stronger and more competitive than ever before. Equally important, these nations' industries adopted innovative management and organizational practices, that enabled their companies to produce higher quality products, at lower costs and with better service, than many US firms. Moreover, their governments embraced industrial policies to support technological advances, foster new product development and sales (e.g., Airbus), and promote more favorable trade conditions.

The signs that US industry was losing ground to foreign competition were already evident in the early 1970s. One of the earliest indicators was the decline in the US consumer electronics industry. The MIT Commission on Industrial Productivity (Dertouzos *et al.* 1989: 12) reported that the "history of consumer electronics is a history of successive retreats by American firms, with the result that foreign manufacturers have won an entire market without ever having to fight a pitched battle." For example, in 1955, 96 percent of all radios sold in the United States were made in the United States. By 1965 this share was down to 30 percent, and by 1975 it was near zero. Similarly the US steadily lost ground in the television market, over the 1970s and 1980s; it was down to one sole US producer, Zenith, with 15 percent market share, by 1987.

The US trade balance also turned a corner in the 1970s. Up until 1970 the United States had maintained a positive merchandise balance. Over the first half of the 1970s, however, the trade balance began to show small deficits, indicating growing penetration of foreign imports into US markets relative to exports. After 1975, the trickle of imports had become a stream, as the merchandise trade deficit increased to between $25–$40 billion up until 1982. But from 1983 on, the stream turned into a flood, as the goods trade deficits sharply increased to well over $100 billion for the rest of the decade, reaching a high of $159.6 billion in 1987.[3]

In one major industrial sector after another, from the late 1970s through the 1980s, US manufacturers saw their markets at home and abroad severely cut into by foreign competitors. In automobiles, foreign imports rose from a mere 1 percent in 1955 to 31 percent in 1987. The United States went from being a net exporter of automobiles in 1967 to an auto import deficit of $60 billion in 1987, the largest element in that year's overall trade deficit. Steel, from 1975 to 1985, saw declining demand for its products, loss of domestic markets, shrinking production and employment, and low or negative earnings. Textile imports went from 2 percent in 1963 to 50 percent in the late 1980s. Leading US firms in high-tech industries such as semiconductors, semiconductor manufacturing equipment, computers, telecommunications, advanced machine tools, and pharmaceuticals, saw large bites taken out of their market shares. In machine tools, with Japan pushing at the low end of the market and Germany down from the high end, the United States fell from being a net exporter in 1964, to importing 50 percent of its machine tools in 1986. In one of the most troubling trends, US firms saw their share of semiconductor production drop from 60 percent to 40 percent between 1975 and 1985. In 1978, the United States was dominant in every major category of semiconductors. By 1986, Japan had established overwhelming leadership in several major categories and achieved parity in others (Borrus 1988; Yudken and Black 1990). For example, in the dynamic random-access memory chip (DRAMs) market, Japan became the dominant player, holding 75 percent of the market by the end of the 1980s (Dertouzos *et al.* 1989: 9–21).

The sudden decline in US industrial competitiveness, defined as the ability of US products to preserve or increase their share of international markets, led to a vociferous policy debate, generating a slew of government, industry and academic-sponsored studies and books (Borrus 1988; Council on Competitiveness 1988; Dertouzos *et al.* 1989; Congress of the United States 1988, 1990). President Reagan appointed the President's Commission on Industrial Competitiveness, chaired by Hewlett-Packard CEO, John Young, to study the problem. The Commission's report, however, was ignored, as it recommended a much more active role of the Federal government in addressing the problem, by an administration (and that of the successor Bush administration) that loathed the very concept of "industrial policy."

Meanwhile, a parallel debate was taking place about how declining US competitiveness was affecting the defense industrial base. Defense policymakers grew concerned that the defense production reliance on strategic products, from steel fasteners to specialized high-tech materials and components increasingly produced overseas, would be vulnerable to disruption, hence threatening military preparedness.[4] Much emphasis was placed on expanding the role of the Defense Advanced Research Projects Agency (DARPA), to promote advances in "dual-use" technologies –

technologies with both significant commercial and military potential (for discussion, see Yudken and Black 1990).

Many reasons have been given to explain the drop in US economic performance: the over-strong American dollar; the trade and industrial policies of competitor nations' governments; the high cost of capital for US firms; US corporations' failure to invest in modernizing their capacity and commercial innovation; the advanced management and organizational innovations employed by foreign businesses, while American businesses held onto short-sighted and outdated practices. Each of these factors undoubtedly played some role in diminishing the competitiveness of US industry. For example, the appreciation of the US dollar during 1980–1985 drove up the price of US goods in international trade, regardless of changes in quality, making imports more attractive to US consumers while exports suffered. Other evidence, however, shows that US industry's declining competitiveness predated the exchange rate increases. Import penetration increased in 28 of 40 major US manufacturing industries between 1972 and 1982, a period during which the dollar was both overvalued and undervalued (COSEPUP 1987).

Failure of US industrial firms to invest in new technologies and modernization was thought to be another factor. Some blamed this problem on the high price of capital in the United States. Others noted the industrial policies of foreign governments that provided financial support and trade protections for its industries – Japan's Ministry of International Trade and Industry (MITI) and the European government-funded Airbus consortium – to make them internationally competitive. In any case, some analysts claimed that the large integrated steel makers did not make needed investments in new technology to upgrade their capacity, such as the basic oxygen furnace, continuous casting, and computer controls, which were being employed by competitors in other parts of the world (Dertouzos *et al.* 1989: 12–14). Similarly, US automakers were criticized for not investing in product changes and innovations that had made Japanese and German imports so popular, such as smaller, fuel-efficient vehicles that undercut the sales of US automakers making large, gas guzzlers during the OPEC-created oil shortage (Halberstam 1986).

Another advantage said to be enjoyed by foreign competitors over US manufacturers was lower-wage workers (which is no longer the case). But COSEPUP (1987: 80) observes that by the 1980s much low-wage foreign competition in manufacturing was no longer low productivity competition. "In part because of more rapid rates of technology transfer, as well as increased technological sophistication in many foreign economies, production, product and product technologies" now approached or exceeded those of the United States in quality and product sophistication. In fact, US dominance in world markets was bound to erode once Europe and Japan had completed their economic recovery and began to flex their new industrial muscles. But the US system of mass production suddenly found itself confronting industrial powers that not only invested heavily in the most advanced, state-of-the-art production technologies, but had introduced effective new management and organizational practices.

Lean production

What captured the attention of many industry leaders, academic and government policy-makers was the innovative production strategy employed by Japanese manufacturers, most notably Toyota and other Japanese automakers, known as *lean production* or, alternatively, *flexible production*. Many believed that it was this system that enabled Japan to become the world's premier industrial competitor (Congress of the United States 1990; Dertouzos *et al.* 1989; Womack *et al.* 1991). "Alone in the 1980s," an Office of Technology Assessment report wrote, "Japan managed to combine great productivity growth in manufacturing with rising manufacturing employment, rising wages and benefits, and greatly rising output" (Congress of the United States 1990: 2).

Lean production refers to a combination of management techniques, workplace practices, and technological processes designed to continuously cut costs, slim inventories, improve product quality, and meet customers' needs. According to Womack *et al.* (1991: 13) lean producers "employ teams of multi-skilled workers at all levels of the organization and use highly flexible, increasingly automated machines to produce volumes of products in enormous variety." MIT's John F. Krafcik (1989: 29) contrasts the traditional "buffered" mass production system with lean production systems. The former are characterized by large stocks of inventory, large repair areas, and narrowly specialized workers. The latter have small inventory stocks, small repair areas, multi-skilled workers, and a team approach to work organization. The goal of lean production is to create highly flexible systems that can quickly respond to changes in demand (ibid.: 30). Japanese lean production entails several strategies, which include:

- Total quality control, an approach which enables and trains workers to detect defects and then correct them while the product is still on the line, and to trace problems to their ultimate causes. Hence, there is less need for large repair areas for faulty products coming off the line.
- *Kaizen* or "continuous improvement," in which workers are expected to improve the production system by proposing new ideas. Hence, workers are involved in making incremental improvements in the production process, such as introducing new tooling or redesign of a

part. As Kosuke Ikebuchi, head of manufacturing at NUMMI (a joint Toyota–GM-operated auto plant in Fremont, CA), in the early to mid-1980s, explained, "To be effective, a plant must use its production workers' ideas. To do otherwise is to waste a tremendous resource" (cited in Krafcik 1989: 33).

- "Just-in-time" (JIT) inventory system – called *kanban* by the Japanese – in which the manufacturer reduces or eliminates the need for an inventory "buffer" by ordering parts or components from suppliers only as needed. In contrast to the traditional automakers' traditional vertically integrated organization, which excelled in producing high volumes of standardized products, the Japanese automakers use networks of small suppliers. To make JIT work, automakers must establish very close working relationships and excellent communications at one end with their customers and at the other end with their suppliers, who in turn strive to guarantee high quality parts to the auto assemblers (ibid. 1989: 31).

- An emphasis on work teams, in which each worker is cross-trained so he or she can do any other job in the work group and tasks can be rotated with each worker able to fill in for the others. They also need to acquire other skills, such as simple machine repair, quality-checking, housekeeping, and materials ordering. In the Japanese model of lean production, teams are not just employed on the shop-floor to address problems and engage in *kaizen*, but in production development and in working with component suppliers. A comprehensive information display system is employed which allows each team member the ability to respond quickly to problems and understand a plant's overall situation (Womack 1987: 99).

- Employment of flexible automated equipment on a large scale. Recognizing that to build a variety of parts on each stamping line required a change of dies several times during a shift, the Japanese by the 1970s had developed automated machines capable of fast change-overs. Their stamping presses could change dies in five minutes compared with eight to 24 hours for American machines (Dertouzos *et al.* 1989: 180). Japanese investment in automation equipment, particularly assembly-line robots, by the early 1980s, was far greater than that in the United States or Europe (Womack 1991: 236).

The American response to the Japanese and European competitiveness challenge in the 1980s and into the early 1990s took several forms.[5] In efforts to make their operations more "flexible," many firms attempted to restructure their operations, by closing plants, drastically cutting workforces, "re-engineering" their organizations, investing in automation, or adopting many of the management practices – or variants of them –

employed in lean production. Some initiatives were more successful than others. The MIT Commission on Industrial Productivity contrasts the ability of the steel minimills to thrive at a time when the integrated steel makers were suffering huge cuts in their capacities and workforces. While the integrated steel mills "lacked an international perspective, characterized by mature, relatively inflexible organizational structures," the Commission reported, the minimills were "technological leaders":

> They built new mills using electric furnaces and continuous casting; they pioneered new management techniques and built cooperative labor–management relations; they scoured the world for new technologies; and they sought close cooperation with their customers. Close cooperation with customers was particularly important to the success of the minimills.
>
> (Dertouzos 1990: 14)

Lean production has become a major paradigm guiding the restructuring of work organization in almost every industry sector. Later we will contrast and compare the "lean" concept to that of the "virtual" organization, arguing that the latter is an extension of the former, coupled with the earlier corporate visions of "factory (or office) of the future," (e.g., the "lights-out" factory and the "paperless" office), built around the advantages of advanced networking technology (e.g., the Internet). In any event, the principles of lean production, or variations of them, have been applied by manufacturing firms throughout the United States and Europe since the 1980s. Boeing Aircraft and Dell Computers are examples where lean production methods have been used with great success. But it also has been employed with varying degrees of success by government agencies and by services providers, from transportation to health care to financial organizations. It is even being applied to software development.

A 1993 *Business Week* article (Byrne 1993) touted the coming of the "horizontal organization," essentially, a version of lean production, which it argued was a trend toward "flatter organizations in which managing across has become more critical than managing up and down in top-heavy hierarchy." Aside from a flattened hierarchy, the elements of "horizontal organization" include organizational structures built around "core processes," self-managed teams, customer-driven performance, maximized supplier and customer contact, multi-skilled, empowered employees, and a team-based performance reward system. The article cited such firms as Eastman Chemical, General Electric, Lexmark International, Motorola and Xerox, and AT&T's Network Systems Division, as moving toward the horizontal model. Noting that the changes associated with the lean or horizontal organizational model had been going on for several years under the guise of total quality management (TQM), re-engineering, or business-process redesign, *Business Week* observed that many corporations were "moving to this new form of corporate organization after failing to achieve needed productivity gains by simple streamlining and consolidation" (ibid. 1993).

Many firms did try in the late 1980s and 1990s, to implement at least a few of the principles of the lean or horizontal model, such as teamwork, worker empowerment, and quality control, some even forming partnerships with unions to implement these strategies. Many others, probably in larger numbers, interpreted lean production as streamlining or downsizing their operations through draconian cuts in their workforces, both in management ranks and on the shop-floor, and by outsourcing of various functions to external suppliers. The "deindustrialization" of the 1980s, in which thousands of plants shut down and hundreds of thousands of workers were laid off, was a consequence of US industry's failure to compete against international competitors for the reasons enumerated above. The wave of corporate downsizings that reached its peak during the early to mid-1990s was a product of corporate America's attempt to restructure itself, largely in response to the competitiveness crisis of the previous decade, but also to Wall Street demands on corporate managers for higher short-term earnings.

To be sure, the concept of horizontal organization requires trimming some management layers and encourages some outsourcing. But its emphasis on teamwork, worker empowerment and training, customer responsiveness, and closer supplier relationships, have at best been given lip service by the corporate downsizers, and merger icons such as "chainsaw" Al Dunlap who specialized in eviscerating the firms they acquired. The *Business Week* article reflected a growing awareness by at least some part of the corporate world, that the "softer," human dimensions of the lean model, whether it entails a focus on the role of workers or on the supplier–customer relationship, were needed for restructuring to produce positive results (Byrne 1993).

The introduction of advanced automation also did not necessarily lead to the flexibility and productivity gains sought by company managers. Fueled by steady advances in microprocessors, computers, software and networking technologies, many companies in the 1980s and 1990s invested heavily in computer-based automation equipment (CNCs, robots, Flexible Manufacturing Systems), as a key part of their restructuring initiatives. A number of industrial experts have argued, however, that in order to be effective, new technology needs to be accompanied by organizational changes, such as those called for by the lean production model. For example, Womack *et al.* noted that the Japanese had managed to gain major benefits from their huge investments in automation, while Western firms seemed to spend more than they saved from similar investments (1987: 236). Krafcik cited the example of the General Motors Corp., which since 1981 invested more than $40 billion in a comprehensive effort to modernize its production. But this infusion of technology did little to improve the company's performance. GM's share of the US car market dropped from 45 percent to 37 percent, and its profitability also fell, "under the double impact of weak sales and the soaring fixed costs caused by all that new technology" (1989: 29).

Similarly, Harvard Business School professor David M. Upton noted that, based on a study of automation in sixty-one fine paper factories in North America, the "flexibility of the plants depended much more on people than on any technical factor" (1995: 75). Many firms had collectively invested tens of billions of dollars in hardware and software in the hope that computer-integrated manufacturing CIM would transform their factories into highly flexible operations, without success. He found that computer integration alone was not sufficient to improve changeover times or increase product range in a plant. That is, computer integration does not necessarily guarantee greater flexibility. Instead, he concluded:

> Although high levels of computer integration can provide critically needed advantages in quality and cost competitiveness, all the data in my study point to one conclusion: Operational flexibility is determined primarily by a plant's operators and the extent to which managers cultivate, measure, and communicate with them. Equipment and computer integration are secondary.
>
> (ibid.: 75)

To achieve the promise of CIM that companies sought, attention must be placed on involving and training workers in the process of introducing and implementing the new technologies. For example, he described the efforts of one company to transform itself to achieve greater flexibility and improve its responsiveness to customers. The company replaced its old mill-wide computer systems with a new system custom designed to support operators at each operation. It allowed them to control the manufacturing process, giving them freedom to make changes based on what they saw was needed on the production line. In short, he observed, "the system was designed from the outset to help workers make better decisions rather than to cut them out of the decision-making process" (ibid.: 80).

Lean and mean

As Upton himself recognized, this approach runs counter to the conventional wisdom that the purpose of automation is to place machines over (or replace) the human operators – to control and circumscribe, if not eliminate, the human element in productive processes. Unfortunately, from the 1980s on, managers have introduced computer-aided automation into workplaces more often governed by the conventional view than by Upton's insight that building on and enhancing workers' capabilities result in greater flexibility and productivity. While a number of lean production elements, such as just-in-time delivery, total quality management, work teams, and manufacturing cells, have become common corporate practices, most restructuring companies have attempted to introduce lean production methods within organizational frameworks that preserved much of their original, traditional Tayloristic and hierarchical characteristics.

As a consequence, a number of critics have argued that there is a "dark side" to lean production that deserves greater attention. Speaking from a militant union activist perspective, Charlie Post and Jane Slaughter (2000) note that although by the late 1990s corporations were doing better than any time in the past thirty years, most ordinary working people were doing worse. After the sharp recession of 1990–1991, US corporations appeared to have made a remarkable recovery from the 1980s' crisis. During the halcyon Clinton years, corporate America regained much of its competitive edge over foreign competitors. The restructuring efforts of the previous decade – aided by government budget policies (i.e., elimination of the budget deficit) and technology-driven economic growth – seemed to have paid off. The United States enjoyed one the longest periods of sustained economic growth in the post-war period. Even manufacturing experienced general employment growth between 1993 and 2000 (Figure 3.1). Nevertheless, Post and Slaughter point to evidence that most American workers were doing less well and were less secure in their jobs. Except for slight gains at the end of the 1990s, average real (inflation adjusted) earnings for workers were below what they were in the early 1970s. Economic disparity has also increased. The minimum wage remained 15 percent below its average purchasing power in the 1970s. Corporate CEOs in 1995 were getting paid 173 times the average worker's income, compared to 60 times in 1978.

According to Post and Slaughter, lean production lies at the heart of the problem. In their view, lean production is an extension of other "schemes" – Taylorism, automation, and computerization – designed to get more work out of fewer people, i.e., increased productivity (output per worker). In their view, lean production "stresses workers to the limits of their capacities." They equate it with speeding up the pace of work, increased contracting out, outsourcing or privatization of work previously done by unionized workers, greater use of temporaries, part-timers and contract workers, and greater management control over setting workers' hours and tasks. Tasks forces and teams are just another type of management-applied pressure to engage workers in actively speeding up their own jobs. What management calls "empowerment" they call "cutting your own throat." The introduction of new, expensive computer technology does not necessarily mean workers gain more skills, but often means deskilling. They lament the spread of lean methods in "all walks of life, from phone companies to health care to coal mines. Hospitals have turned nurses' work over to unlicensed aides; universities replace tenured professors with part-timers and use e-mail and the Web to increase workloads" (Post and Slaughter 2000).

Some noted economists have echoed these concerns. In a 1994 *Technology Review* article, Carnegie Mellon University Professor of Political Economy Bennett Harrison connected the corporate search for "flexibility" with lean production, downsizing, outsourcing, and dispersed production. Thus he wrote:

> as fast as the big firms are going flexible, the number of safe, stable, secure occupations seem to be shrinking. In fact, when we characterize the prototypical business organization of the new era as lean, mean, and flexible, we are implicitly recognizing that the workforce in the new economy, is systemically being divided into insiders and outsiders. Some people are employed on full-time, year-round schedules, receive health insurance and paid vacations, and benefit from formal and informal job training. But a growing fraction of Americans have become so-called contingent workers, facing involuntary part-time or part-year work, low wages, and few benefits. This is the dark side of flexible production.
>
> (1994: 39–40)

He cites Nike as typifying the central tenet of flexible production in which managers divide permanent ("core") from contingent ("peripheral") jobs. The core is cut to the bone, which he associates with lean production. In order to reduce labor costs, peripheral activities are largely handled by part-time or temporary workers with low wages and few benefits. Many of these activities are outsourced to whatever suppliers can work expediently and cheaply – often in far-flung geographic regions. He also notes how major corporations, "from IBM and Prudential to Xerox and Boeing, are slashing their home-office and core-production operations, farming out a growing share of the work to external partners and suppliers around the globe" (ibid.: 42). He particularly laments the shift in work away from bigger, more established, sometimes unionized firms where workers receive relatively high wages and benefits, and where the gap between the highest and lowest paid earners is relatively narrow. Hence, the growing use of outside subcontractors reinforces the long-term trend toward polarization of earnings in the United States (ibid.: 45).

In his 1996 book *Fat and Mean,* the late New School for Social Research economist David M. Gordon examines the downsizing movement of the 1990s, associated with corporate efforts to make themselves "lean and mean." Instead of becoming lean by shedding management jobs, he argues, they have actually remained "fat" and top-heavy, while cutting large numbers of permanent front-line jobs. At the same time, despite many experiments to increase worker involvement (Quality of Work Life programs, high-performance workplaces), more and more corporations appear committed to taking a "low" road to improving their economic performance and profitability by cutting labor costs, outsourcing and increasing their reliance on contingent workers. In the end, managers are reluctant to provide strong worker rewards or accept reductions in their managerial power or prerogatives (Gordon 1996: 93) and strive to maintain their hierarchical structures. Gordon connects the corporate "low" road movement to the decline in US workers' real earnings since the 1970s, especially compared to other major industrial nations. BLS data shows that in terms of average real hourly compensation, US manufacturing employees in 1994 were lower paid than their counterparts in Germany, Japan, Norway, Sweden, Denmark and Belgium. Gordon also links the drive for "flexibility" to growth in the number of contingent, or what he calls "disposable" workers. As US corporations travel the "low road," he writes, "growing numbers of workers have faced their employers without any protection against dismissal, without benefits, without rights, without even a modicum of job security" (ibid.: 223).

The jobs dilemma

Unlike Post and Slaughter and their colleagues, for whom only a democratic socialist revolution can provide a corrective, both Harrison and Gordon seemed to hold out some hope that appropriate policies could help push the economy toward the "high road." They also seemed to accept that under the right conditions there could be "flexible" work organizations favorable to the interests of workers.[6] Both agreed that strengthening unions and labor laws were among the most important of these conditions. Similarly, as cited in an American Psychological Association (APA) article on the mental health impacts of lean production (Clay 1999), Michelle Kaminski of the Institute of Labor and Industrial Relations at the University of Illinois has argued that the new, flexible-types of work organizations do not have to sacrifice workers' health and well-being for the sake of profits, if they are properly implemented. The APA article reports on evidence that suggests that lean production can increase workers' mental stress levels and physical injuries. Kaminski, however, presents an example where strong unions and cooperative managers successfully implemented a lean production approach based on profit-enhancing benefits and strong worker involvement and control over their work, without harming workers' mental health or fostering injury. Indeed, mental health measures improved while injury rates declined.

Unfortunately, as Kaminski points out, this is "a very unusual plant in the American landscape." Admitting that success stories are atypical, she notes that, "[m]ost plants trying to implement changes like this don't allow worker input." Therein lies what we call the *jobs dilemma* associated not only with lean production, but with more recent, evolving variations of work organization and production linked to the emergence of advanced digital networks – that is, *virtual organizations* – that have their roots in flexible/lean production models. In defining the jobs dilemma, we refer back to the long-standing debate over the impacts of technological change on work. Does new technology destroy or create jobs? Does it deskill workers or expand their skills? Does it demean or enhance the quality of work? Does it weaken or strengthen workers' right to collective representation through unions?

In assessing the innovations of lean production, including the introduction of "flexible" automation technologies (e.g., robots, CNCs), we see arguments on both sides of these questions. Lean production proponents have touted how it empowers workers and enhances skills. Moreover, lean production, by increasing business competitiveness and productivity, in time generates many more new, good jobs. On the other hand, as we saw above, lean production critics stress just the opposite. Lean production increases the level of mental stress and injury on the job. Permanent jobs are outsourced and eliminated, at best replaced by insecure, poorly compensated contingent jobs. While some workers may upgrade their skills, many more will see their job skills diminished.

A similar polarity arises if we examine more closely the emerging digital economy. The Internet/ICT-driven economic growth of the last half of the 1990s fostered a belief that the New Economy is about creating numerous new, high-skilled jobs. Although usually admitting some job dislocation in certain sectors is probable, studies on the economic impacts of the Internet generally have projected a net increase in jobs. For example, an Organization for Economic Co-operation and Development (OECD) study concludes that "in the longer term, the combination of new products, extended product reach, and income gains and lower prices derived from productivity increases will lead to net employment gains" (1999: 17). Of course, the bursting of the dot.com bubble has dampened much of this optimism, as least for the time being. As noted above, the job loss impacts have been as deeply felt in Silicon Valley and other high-tech havens as they have been in other sectors, most notably in manufacturing. In fact, manufacturing employment has dropped precipitously, with over two million lost jobs between 1998 and 2002; it is now at its lowest level since the early 1960s. This represents 90 percent of all job losses in the economy since the current recession began. While it is likely that there will be some reversal of this trend with an economic recovery, it is not unreasonable to speculate that employment in many manufacturing industry sectors, if not in manufacturing as a whole, could remain permanently depressed under certain conditions.

A multiplicity of factors can affect this outcome, including, most notably trade policies. However, we also need to consider the potential loss of jobs from continued corporate efforts to implement "flexible" production strategies on a global basis enabled by powerful, new high-speed, broadband digital networks. Bennett Harrison, writing in 1994, foresaw such an outcome of the New Economy, noting that

> All the major automobile assemblers, from General Motors to Mercedes Benz, buy components from all over the world, many of which (such as seat belts and wiring harnesses) they formerly manufactured using full-time, in-house core employees. And in Silicon Valley, actual production once handled by core workers has dispersed to such an extent that journalist John Dvorak has called the valley a "virtual reality."
>
> (1994: 44)

We return to a closer examination of these potential impacts, especially at the sectoral level, in the next chapter. As suggested in the earlier discussion, whether we see a positive or negative impact on jobs and the quality of work largely depends on institutional and organizational factors, which are co-determinant of how technological change is actually implemented within an economy. That is, technological change does not by itself determine the direction of economic change. There is always a strong element of social choice involved in determining how a technology is implemented, and consequently, its social and economic consequences.

This perspective is inherent in that most of the serious critiques of computer and information technology' impacts on jobs predate the Internet revolution. Shosana Zuboff's *In the Age of the Smart Machine* (1988) examines the evolution of computer-based machines in the 1980s, and what they might mean for organizations and workplaces. Zuboff acknowledges that centralized, rationalized policies common to most management practices would result in computer systems that "automate" the workplace, displacing the human body and its know-how and skills (a process known as "deskilling"). She alternatively argues that the new technology has properties which, if introduced with decentralized, enhancement-oriented management practices, could lead to systems that "informate" work, resulting in the *reskilling* of jobs. This suggests the element of choice: human agents choose how technologies are introduced, and in particular, whether new computer and information-based techonology – including the Internet – will displace and deskill work, or whether it will be used to informate and reskill work.

For example, computer numerical controlled machine-tools (CNCs) can be programmed locally, allowing a skilled machinist to continue to run the machine, and even override the computer, if necessary. Or they can be programmed in a way that restricts operators' actions to simply following directions prompted by the internal computer and displayed on the machine's video screen, similar to the way people operate their microwave ovens and VCRs. Managers have the choice to follow one or the other of these options designed into the machines by equipment manufacturers, with very different implications for the skills of workers operating these machines.

Harry Braverman's *Labor and Monopoly Capital* is probably the classic scholarly work on deskilling and alienation of the modern workplace in the 1950s through the 1970s. Braverman, however, was not a technological determinist. On the contrary, he argued that it was management's continued, systematic adoption of scientific management principles, to assert greater and greater control over the labor process, that causes the deskilling and demeaning of contemporary work. The new computer-based automation technology emerging at the time he wrote his book, complemented and enabled, but did not drive the diffusion of Taylorist managerial practices.

In more recent studies, Harley Shaiken (1984) and Joan Greenbaum (1995) have written important, critical analyses of how computer-based automation has been transforming manufacturing work in the 1980s and the office workplace of the 1990s, respectively. But like Braverman, Shaiken and Greenbaum, without downplaying the important role of new technology, place the primary onus for the transformation of jobs on managerial strategies and organizational practices; technology serves as a mediator and enabler, rather than as an active agent of change. Indeed, both emphasize that the properties of technologies introduced into workplaces are themselves largely determined by choices made by people. For example, Shaiken argues that "the design of new forms of automation reflects not only technical requirements but social decisions as well." Changes in the workplace and in the nature of jobs, therefore, "are not a mandate or even simply a by-product of the technology but a result of conscious choices" (ibid.: xi). Similarly, Greenbaum describes how the design of new computer programs first employed in office systems were based on principles provided by "[t]he standardization and division of labor that were the mainstays of corporate organization" (1995: 47).

Charley Richardson, director of the Technology and Work Program, University of Massachusetts in Lowell, also examines how new technology is restructuring workplaces:

> robots doing welding, spray painting, or machine loading and computerized numerically controlled (CNC) machine tools operating "by themselves" are among the common images of new workplace technology. Computers, imaging software, artificial intelligence, ceramics, fiber optics, bar code scanners, manufacturing cells, and computer vision systems are other examples.
>
> (1992: 151)

Like Shaiken and Greenbaum, he stresses that:

> Technology must be seen as a social process. It is in their application in the workplace that machinery and equipment become socially significant. Hardware and, more recently, software are enabling factors for changes in the organization of work which ... have many significant impacts on workers, on production and on society as a whole.
>
> (ibid.: 152).

Their emphasis on the importance of social factors shaping workplace technologies – and therefore workplaces and jobs – notwithstanding, these authors are on the whole pessimistic about the consequences of new technology for jobs and work, within the modern industrial organizations and markets. They argue that computer-based automation, coupled with Tayloristic management and organizational practices, results in increasing routinization, standardization, deskilling, restructuring, and in many instances, displacement of jobs. Other negative outcomes are increased stress and health and safety problems.

The focus of these studies largely has been on the introduction of computer-based hardware and software into workplaces in the decade and a half before the Internet revolution took off. Nevertheless, they presage the potential job implications of the new wave of advanced digital networks first introduced into workplaces in the 1990s. For example, Shaiken examines the emergence of what he calls "super-automation," whose "more potent capabilities are based on the ability to tie separate computerized machines and systems into larger networks." He further notes how combining telecommunications with computers removes the geographic limits from management, enabling transnational companies to "maintain the advantages of centralized control over managerial decisions in far-flung subsidiaries without sacrificing the benefits of decentralized operations" (1984: 9). Greenbaum observes that networks were as central to the 1990s' office workplace as personal computers were in the 1980s. She reports that by 1994, 87 percent of large firms and 32 percent of smaller companies had some sort of Local Area Network (LAN), which links computers within offices and between offices within a building. She also notes that at the time of her writing there was an increasing number of Wide Area Networks (WANs) installed by organizations, linking computers in different departments, buildings, and cities, and more and more individuals and organizations "hooked into worldwide networks, like the Internet, joining what the media likes to call the 'information superhighway'" (1995: 109).

Given the relative newness of these networking technologies, these writers could only speculate about the likely job implications. As long as the primary managerial principle driving investments in these technologies is to increase control over labor processes and reduce labor costs, their findings strongly argue for further job displacement, deskilling, and restructuring. Greenbaum also predicts increased job restructuring and polarization of workforces into high and low-wage tiers, and growth in outsourcing, home-work (now called "telework"), and contingent work.

Empirical studies of automation impacts on jobs in the 1970s and 1980s have tended to be more ambiguous (for a review of this literature, see COSEPUP 1987: 86–111). They usually recognize that dislocation and deskilling do occur in some instances, but they also present evidence of job creation and skill upgrading in other situations. There also is evidence that while early forms of computerization can cause fragmentation in office work, more advanced computer technologies introduced later into offices have enabled an electronic reintegration of work tasks, increasing skill requirements. Assessment of impacts on skills is especially difficult, particularly at the aggregate level. One reason is the difficulty in obtaining agreement on a definition of job-related skills. Another is the significant weaknesses in the methodologies and data used in measuring skills and technology change. COSEPUP (ibid.: 100) also concludes that the

> skill effects of technological change are sensitive to the ways in which new technologies are implemented in the workplace. Managers have considerable discretion in such implementation, which may affect skill requirements ... Thus, identical innovations introduced in different firms can alter skill requirements in different ways.

In the same vein, Shaiken (1984: 4) observes that "[c]omputers and microelectronics present a dazzling array of alternatives in the workplace: more worker autonomy or greater managerial authority, more skills or fewer skills, increased hierarchy or more democratic decision-making." But, he adds "in a market economy, the selection and assemblage of these electronic building blocks into a production system is largely the prerogative of management."

Any attempt to evaluate the employment and workplace impacts of ICT and the Internet therefore requires understanding the organizational and institutional context within which these technologies are implemented. Lean production represents a particular set of business organizational strategies and practices. But how they are implemented affects whether workers' jobs are created or eliminated or their skills diminished or enhanced. Organizational restructuring coupled with technological change also affects jobs on an aggregate level, with consequences for occupational composition, compensation patterns, and union representation. We briefly review these patterns later in the next chapter. But, first, we turn our attention to understanding how organizational structures in productive enterprises (both private and public) are interacting with the rapidly evolving advanced digital networking technologies, to generate new organizational models.

References

Bolton, A. (2002) "Drop in Employment in Silicon Valley Eases Traffic Congestion," online (http://beta.kpix.com/news) (accessed: 15 September).

Borrus, M. G. (1988) *Competing for Control: America's Stake in Microelectronics*, Cambridge, MA: Ballinger Publishing Co.

Braverman, H. (1974) *Labor and Monopoly Capital*, New York: Monthly Review Press.

Byrne, J. A. (1993) "The Horizontal Corporation," *Business Week*, 20 December, 76–81.

Clay, R. A. (1999) "'Lean Production' May also Be a Lean Toward Injuries," *APA Monitor Online* (www.apa.org/monitor/may99/lean.html) 30, 5, May.

Committee on Science, Engineering, and Public Policy (COSEPUP), National Academy of Sciences, National Academy of Engineering and Institute of Medicine, Panel on Technology and Employment (1987) *Technology and Employment, Innovation in the U.S. Economy*, Washington, DC: National Academy Press.

Congress of the United States (1988) *Paying the Bill: Manufacturing and America's Trade Deficit*, OTA-ITE-390 Washington, DC: US Government Printing Office, June.

Congress of the United States, Office of Technology Assessment (1989) *Hold the Edge: Maintaining the Defense Technology Base*, OTA-ISC-420, Washington, DC: US Government Printing Office, April.

Congress of the United States, Office of Technology Assessment (OTA) (1990) *Making Things Better: Competing in Manufacturing*, OTA-ITE-444, Washington, DC: US Government Printing Office, February.

Congress of the United States, Office of Technology Assessment (1998) *The Defense Technology Base: Introduction and Overview – A Special Report*, OTA-ISC-374, Washington, DC: US Government Printing Office, March.

Council on Competitiveness (1988) *Picking Up the Pace: The Commercial Challenge of American Innovation*, Washington, DC: Council on Competitiveness.

The Cuomo Commission on Trade and Competitiveness (1988) *The Cuomo Commission Report: A New American Formula for a Strong Economy*, New York: Simon and Schuster.

Dertouzos, M. L., Lester, R. K., Solow, R. M. and the MIT Commission on Industrial Productivity (1989) *Made in America: Regaining the Productive Edge*, Cambridge, MA: MIT Press.

Dombey, D. and Guerrera, F. (2002) "Brussels Pushes States over Wireless Technology," online (www.ft.com) (accessed 12 August).

Gordon, D. M. (1996) *Fat and Mean*, New York: Free Press.

Greenbaum, J. (1995) *Windows on the Workplace: Computers, Jobs and the Organization of Office Work in the Late Twentieth Century*, New York: Monthly Review Press.

Halberstam, D. (1986) *The Reckoning*, New York: Avon Books.

Harrison, B. (1994) "The Dark Side of Flexible Production," *Technology Review*, May/June, 40–45.

Intel Corporation (2001) *Intel 2001 Annual Report,* online (http://www.intel.com/intel/annual01/letter), Santa Clara, CA.

Intel Corporation (2002) *Expanding Moore's Law: The Exponential Opportunity, Fall 2002 Update*, online (http://www.intel.com/intel), Santa Clara, CA.

Kirkpatrick, D. (2002a) "The PC's New Tricks," online (http://www.fortune.com), *Fortune*, 28 October.

Kirkpatrick, D. (2002b) "Will the U.S. Fall Behind in Tech?" Online (http://www.fortune.com), *Fortune*, 22 October.

Krafcik, J. F. (1989) "A New Diet for U.S. Manufacturing," *Technology Review*, January: 28–36.

Lessig, L. (2001) "The Internet Under Siege," *Foreign Policy*, November–December, 56–65.

National Research Council, Computer Science and Telecommunications Board (NRC/CSTB) (2000) *The Internet's Coming of Age*, Washington, DC: National Academy Press.

Noble, D. F. (1984) *Forces of Production: A Social History of Industrial Automation*, New York: Alfred A. Knopf.

Organization for Economic Co-operation and Development (OECD) (1999) *The Economic and Social Impact of Electronic Commerce: Preliminary Research Agenda*, Paris: OECD.

Post, C. and Slaughter, J. (2000) "Lean Production: Why Work is Worse Than Ever, and What's the Alternative?" *A Solidarity Working Paper*, online (http://solidarity.igc.org/LeanProduction.html).

Richardson, C. (1992) "Progress for Whom? New Technology, Unions, and Collective Bargaining," in Labor Policy Institute, *Software and Hardhats: Technology and Workers in the Twenty-First Century, A Report of Two Conferences*, Washington, DC, 151–174.

Schlender, B. (2002) "Intel's $10 Billion Gamble," online (http://www.fortune.com), *Fortune*, 11 November.

Shaiken, H. (1984) *Work Transformed: Automation and Labor in the Computer Age*, New York: Holt, Rinehart and Winston.

Steen, M. (2002) "No Upturn Near in Silicon Valley Job Market," *Mercury News* online (http://www.bayarea.com/mld/mercurynews), 20 November.

Under-Secretary of Defense (Acquisition) (1988) *Bolstering Defense Industrial Competitiveness*, Report to the Secretary of Defense, US Department of Defense, Washington, DC: US Government Printing Office, July.

Upton, D. M. (1995) "What Makes Factories Flexible?" *Harvard Business Review*, July–August, 74–84.

Waters, R. (2001) "Broadband's Slow Start Hides its Potential," *Financial Times*, online (www.ft.com), 12 December.

Womack, J. P., Jones, D. T. and Roos, D. (1991) *The Machine That Changed the World*, New York: HarperCollins.

Yudken, J. S. and Black, M. (1990) "Targeting National Needs: A New Direction for Science and Technology Policy," *World Policy Journal*, VII, 2, 251–288.

Zuboff, S. (1988) *In the Age of the Smart Machine: The Future of Work and Power*, New York: Basic Books, Inc.

4

E-BUSINESS AND THE VIRTUAL ORGANIZATION

Dell Computer is the poster-child of the virtual organization. Almost every article and study examining the emergence of virtual organization and the Internet refers to Dell's success in setting up the "fully integrated value chain" (*The Economist* 1999; see also Dedrick and Kraemer 2002; McClenahan 2000; Sheridan 2000). The Austin-based computer manufacturer has mastered the art of "build-to-order" production, electronically mobilizing its internal operations and globalized supplier chain to build and deliver computers in response to Web-originated orders from its customers. Case-Western University Economics Professor Susan Helper and Wharton Management Professor John Paul MacDuffie review the key features of Dell's accomplishment. They note that Dell's direct sales model is based on a reconfiguration of the supply chain, tight integration of B2B and B2C operations, and new approaches to handling customers. In particular, they write:

> Consumers choose a custom configuration at Dell's web-site, arrange purchase and payment details online (often with phone support ...) and then can track the progress of their order through every phase of production, right up until delivery. Orders go directly from the web-site into Dell's production schedule, parts are ordered from suppliers only after the order (and payment) is received, parts are kitted immediately before production and built up in cells, and the final product is tested and loaded with software before shipment.
>
> (Helper and MacDuffie 2000: 6)

Similarly, an industry executive quoted in McClenahen (2000), concludes that: "What [Dell] did is use technology to make their supply chain so darned efficient that it seamlessly melded with their in-house information systems. And they got to a point where they could do one-on-one marketing and one-on-one buildouts." Interestingly, although Dell makes extensive use of outsourcing, it considers its build-to-order model so strategic to the company, that it does not outsource its final assembly; it doesn't want to share the secrets of its model with its subcontractors (Dedrick and Kraemer 2002). This contrasts with other PC makers, communications equipment, and semiconductor producers who farm out assembly work to contract manufacturers.

By any indicator, Dell's model has achieved superior performance, giving it distinct advantages in an industry marked by accelerating product cycles and rapid product depreciation. It is now the world's number one PC seller (Dedrick and Kraemer 2002: 9). By the end of 1999, Dell reportedly was bringing in $40 million a day in online sales. In 2001, Dell's net profit margin was 5.5 percent compared to the industry average of 2.7 percent. Similarly, Dell chalked up a return on equity of 26.1 percent and an inventory turnover per year of 74.7 percent, compared to the industry averages of 4.7 percent and 53.5 percent, respectively (Dedrick and Kraemer 2002: 9).

Many firms in many industries have been trying to emulate Dell's success, applying the elements of its model with varying degrees of success. In the PC industry, although market forces have driven a transformation in the industry's structure, Dedrick and Kraemer assert that these changes have been fostered and enabled to a large extent by the use of internal and interorganizational information technologies by firms across the industry network (ibid.: 10). Dell has taken lean production to a completely new level, and offers a model that, while still embracing most of the objectives of lean production and the related customer-focused concept of "agility" (Goldman *et al.* 1995), its approach represents a quantum leap forward. In part, that is because of the existence today of technologies of power and flexibility far beyond what was available in the 1980s, when the lean model swept through US industry.

In the future, Internet intermediation in industries throughout the economy, at some level, undoubtedly is on the cards. But it remains unclear how far the Internet/ICT revolution will be able to penetrate the operations of US businesses. Helper and MacDuffie raise such concerns *vis-à-vis* the auto industry. They ask if all players in the industry will enjoy the same improvements in efficiency and effectiveness. Will those firms that have achieved greater mastery of lean production systems be influenced by or benefit from Internet-related developments different from those firms still heavily influenced by mass production (Helper and MacDuffie 2000: 5)? These questions are not easily answered. But we now shift our focus from the industrial discourse centered around the lean organization to the emerging Internet-enabled industrial models of electronic commerce and the virtual enterprise.

The Internet advantage

Our emphasis on digital networking is inclusive of the Internet, and most of our discussion will focus on the role of Internet and electronic commerce (e-commerce) applications in enterprise behavior and organization. But first we look at the characteristics that distinguishes the Internet from other earlier types of electronic networks, that also give it its economic advantages.

Martin Kenney and James Curry (2000) conceive of the Internet as an "intelligent communications technology" enabling the creation of a vast "virtual space" involving "the complex interaction of millions of intelligent nodes," each with its own computer power. Their central insight is that the Internet's greatest promise lies not only in its ability to reduce the costs of conducting economic transactions, as important as this may be, but in its capacity to generate new and innovative processes in a broad range of economic and social domains. Because of the "extreme flexibility of digital representations," the Internet enables an almost infinite number of diverse activities, from "booking airline flights, purchasing items, playing games, viewing pictures, and listening to music, to accessing public information." Given such an amazing range and breadth of possible applications, they conclude that "[t]here can be no doubt that the Internet is transforming the substance of economic activity" (2000: 3–5).

There is a long history of companies establishing *intranets* and *extranets* built on digital networking technologies. Intranets provide access over dedicated data communication lines to only to those within an organization, which, unlike LANs, may not be within the same building or geographical location.[1] Extranets link, also over dedicated lines, organizations with a common interest, such as customers, suppliers, and other business partners (Hecker 2001: 4). Electronic Data Interchange (EDI), one of the oldest types of extranets, is a standards-based, computer-to-computer link for transmitting orders and payments between firms.[2] EDI systems, however, are cumbersome to use, costly to implement and are usually inflexible and not open to outsiders because of their high costs and proprietary protocols. For example, suppliers cannot connect to each other, and often are required to set up independent, proprietary EDI links for each of their main customers. It is expensive – it costs tens of thousands of dollars per added EDI link – and time-consuming both to add new members to an EDI network and expand the types of information exchanged on it (Upton and McAfee 1996: 128).

Business intranets and extranets, may or may not be linked to the Internet, or Internet-enabled. In many instances, Internet-based commerce has replaced the older EDI systems, although EDI is still the main form of electronic exchange between businesses. What differentiates the Internet from the other types of networking technology – giving it the flexibility, generality of purpose, and broad scope noted above, among other important qualities – is its unique architecture. As Marjory S. Blumenthal (1999) of the National Research Council's Computer Science and Telecommunications Board shows, the Internet's architecture gives it its fundamentally integrative character and explains how it supports a wide range of communications services and their use. The principal distinguishing features of this architecture are described below:

- *Open standards and protocols*. The essence of the Internet's architecture is a "protocol suite," that is, a layered structure of open (nonproprietary) standardized protocols which enables multiple computing devices with diverse operating platforms to communicate with each other[3] – a capability known as *interoperability*. Because of the design of this essential software, the Internet is technology- and application-independent. Blumenthal explains:

  > The Internet uses a common set of communications and related services to deliver information transmitted from a wide and changing range of underlying communications technologies (devices and networks), via a wide and changing range of service providers, to a wide and changing range of applications. With these characteristics, the Internet is open to change: it can accommodate innovation in the underlying communications technologies without forcing changes in the applications, and vice versa.
  >
  > (1999: 6)

  The Internet's "open network" architecture gives it its general and flexible character, differentiating it from other kinds of electronic communication networks, such as telephone and television networks whose architectures are tightly linked to those applications, which subsequently limits their purposes.
- *Edge orientation*. Blumenthal also explains that the Internet's architecture assumes that "intelligence" is at the "edges" of the network, located in the devices and applications software that make use of its services (e.g., software for electronic mail or Web browsing), and not in the systems that comprise the body of the network (the routers) (1999: 8–9). Kenney and Curry refers to this as "node-based intelligence." The Internet builds on existing communications infrastructures – telephony (copper wire and fiber optics), cable, wireless, satellite, and even electric utility – which serve as common carriers transmitting the content in digital "packets" but does not engage in

any processing of this content. The data transport technology is essentially "dumb," its routers only determine how to move around bits of information between end users until they get to a final "address." The Internet's node-based intelligence resides in the hardware the Internet hooks up (computers, servers, PDAs, Internet "appliances," wireless devices) and the software applications that run on them. One of these applications is the World Wide Web (e-mail is another), which adds another layer of protocol – the HyperText Transfer Protocol (HTTP) – onto the Internet protocol (IP) suite. The Web uses the Internet as a communications system, just as the Internet uses telephony or other communications infrastructure.[4] Node-based intelligence, Kenney and Curry contend, makes the Internet much more than a "mere communications medium," however, as it "extends interaction between individuals augmented by intelligent machines, and to ever more sophisticated machine-to-machine interaction" (2000: 15).

- *Network of networks.* The Internet is an *internetworking technology* – its open architecture enables it to be an integrator of multiple networks in many places (Blumenthal 1999: 8). The Internet, Blumenthal writes, has long connected sites in multiple countries, primarily by interconnecting networks in different countries. It has been "able to grow, net by net, to embody the vision of global networking" (ibid.: 13). In short, the Internet is a vast, complex networks of many interconnected networks which span the globe. Anyone with a computer, modem, telephone and ISP (Internet Service Provider) can get online and access the web-site and linked HTML pages of any individual, business, government agency, university, non-profit organization or whatever, anywhere in the world.

The Internet's architecture endows it with several properties that have enabled it to play a powerful economic role. First, the Internet's *generality* and *flexibility* allow it to be employed for a very large number of different commercial and industrial purposes, from advertising, informing, and providing services (e.g., technical assistance) to consumers, to exchanging information and products between businesses and their customers and clients, to coordinating activities of businesses with geographically dispersed internal units, suppliers, or customers. A second characteristic is the Internet's *ubiquity* (Kenney and Curry 2000: 12). Users can access the Internet on an unlimited and equal basis, and go anywhere on the net around the world with a minimum of effort. A third important feature is the *low cost* of this connection, especially compared to the older EDI systems and extranets set up in the 1980s. A fourth important property of the Internet is its *interactivity* which has enabled new forms of collaborative activity, such as, for example, the open source "movement" exemplified by the Linux operating system and Apache web-server software programs. These programs, freely downloadable, have depended on the Internet for their dissemination and continuing technological evolution (ibid.: 13).

The Internet's open architecture, ubiquity, interactivity, and low cost give it distinct advantages in enabling businesses to establish flexible, low cost value-added networks. In contrast to EDI networks, Internet e-commerce networks allow multiple suppliers, customers, and business partners to link with each other in common networks, without being at the same level of network technology sophistication or having the same kinds or intensity of relationship with the dominant business in the network (Upton and McAfee 1996). That is, the Internet connects every node in business value chains, while still making possible easy addition of entirely new intermediaries at low cost (Kenney and Curry, 2000: 21). Easy access and relatively lower transaction costs for implementing commercial exchanges and other business activities underlie much of the Internet's rapid diffusion throughout much of the industrialized world, and increasingly in the industrializing societies. As Blumenthal writes:

> From a global perspective, what matters most in Internet use is the simple fact of having access. Although more of today's Internet and Web use takes place in urban than rural areas (given the superior local infrastructure in urban areas), the location of sought-after resources does not and will not necessarily correlate with typical production or business centers. Even the most modest level of access provides entrée to remotely located resources that can yield far greater benefit, at least in principle, than a long-distance phone call. For example, searching or retrieving information from diverse sources or contacting a large number of people is more cost-effective via a session on the Internet than a series of phone calls.
>
> (1999: 13)

The Internet's distinctive features combined with its global reach have facilitated the efforts of businesses to expand their operations and activities on a global basis, allowing them to combine a high degree of centralized control with the flexibility of decentralization in coordinating multiple, diverse, and geographically dispersed operations. Thus, the Internet facilitates a number of business practices that firms have increasingly engaged in over the past decade, shifting operations to remote, lower-cost regions of the world, outsourcing so-called "peripheral" or "non-core" functions, and globalizing supply chains.

E-commerce models

But are the Internet's characteristics fostering radically new business models that over time are transforming our economy as some propose? Or is it merely furthering new, more successful, efficient variants and extensions of earlier, established business models – such as, mass production or lean production, or both? As we saw in Chapter 2, the electric dynamo was crucial to the rapid spread of mass production in the early twentieth century, and electronic devices, from vacuum tubes to transistors to microprocessors, were instrumental in the spread of automation technologies in the last half of the twentieth century. The Internet may be the vehicle that enables the rapid spread of business organizational structures and practices based on lean or flexible production principles on a much wider-scale, throughout all sectors of the economy, over the next few decades. That is, virtual enterprises may be an advanced stage in the evolution of lean production organizations.

In examining this hypothesis, we first look at the varieties of electronic business (or e-business). The most commonly known types of economic activities building on the properties of the Internet can be subsumed under the rubric of electronic commerce, or *e-commerce*. E-commerce refers to the commercial exchange of products and services over electronic networks, in particular, over the Internet. The three most important types of e-commerce include business-to-consumer (B2C) e-commerce (also sometimes called "e-tailing"), business-to-business (B2B) e-commerce, and consumer-to-consumer (C2C) e-commerce. A related area, that mostly falls under the B2C e-commerce category in the statistics, is *e-services*. We focus only on the first two, though C2C e-commerce, individuals buying and selling through electronic auctions (e.g., eBay.com) has proven to be a successful means of goods exchange between private individuals.

B2C e-commerce refers to consumer purchasing of goods and services over the Internet. Today, there are few types of items not sold over the Internet, whether through B2C e-commerce or online auctions. Areas with the largest B2C e-commerce sales include travel, computer goods, entertainment, gifts and flowers, books, apparel, groceries, and pharmaceuticals. Two major types of enterprises that support Internet B2C include non-store retailers and "brick and click" firms. Non-store retailers include "pure-plays" such as Amazon.com, retail businesses that sell solely over the Internet, and catalog and mail-order operations (e.g., Lands End, MacMall, CDW), many of which sell through multiple channels, that do not operate any outlet stores. "Brick and clicks" are e-commerce business units of retailers which operate one or more (or a chain of) "brick and mortar" outlet stores, such as Barnes & Noble, Amazon.com's leading competitor in online bookselling. Motor vehicles and equipment outlets, mainly auto dealerships, are a major brick and click group (US Census Bureau 2002b).

Throughout 2000 the trends for B2C e-commerce showed rapid growth, with many business forecasters predicting dramatic growth in electronic retail sales in the next half decade. For example, Forrester Research estimated that online retail sales, which were $8 billion in 1998, would jump to a projected $33 billion in 2000, and $108 billion in 2003. It also estimated that the number of US households shopping online, which was 17 million in 1999, would jump to 49 million by 2004. The dot.com crash dampened, but did not stop, this trend. The US Census Bureau for the first time started to track electronic commerce sales starting the 4th quarter 1999.[5] Its data shows that US B2C e-commerce sales have made significant gains over the past year, growing at a much faster rate than total retail sales in the United States. It reported that US online retail revenues in the 3rd quarter 2002 were 34.5 percent higher than one year earlier, compared to only a 5.8 percent increase in total US retail sales over the same period. Total online retail sales were $35.9 billion in 2001 and may rise to as much as $45 billion or more by the end of 2002. Online retail selling, however, remains a very small part of total US retail sales ($3.168 trillion in 2001), although it did grow from 0.9 percent in the 4th quarter 1999 to 1.3 percent in the 3rd quarter 2002 (US Census 2002c).

E-services, services sold or performed online, generally are incorporated under the category of B2C e-commerce. For example, a huge range of services can be purchased online in banking, insurance, real estate, securities trading, travel, airlines, entertainment, educational institutions, health care and government, among others. Travelocity.com and expedia.com are two of the largest, most successful web-sites offering travel-related services, including reserving and purchasing airline tickets, rental cars, and vacation packages. Disney.com allows you to purchase Disney theme park and cruise packages, among many other things. The Delaware state park system web-site allows you to reserve and pay for campsites at any of its parks. Fandango.com and movies.com allow you to purchase movie tickets at your local theaters, and avoid the lines. The list is almost endless. Most of these online services complement, and do not necessarily replace, services that can be obtained by phone or in person at storefronts or office outlets. But the convenience, at least, of taking the first steps toward obtaining these services online (perhaps completing the transaction by phone or in person) is attracting more and more people to using the Internet for conducting everyday personal business.[6]

B2B e-commerce, the electronic sales of goods and services between businesses, dwarfs B2C e-commerce in scale. Firms use e-commerce for coordinating the transactions between purchasing operations and their suppliers; their logistics planners and the transportation firms that warehouse and move their products; their sales organizations, and the whole-salers and retailers that distribute their products; and their customer service and maintenance operations and their customers. Businesses have engaged in B2B for a several reasons: to lower their purchasing costs, to reduce inventories, to lower cycle times, to provide more efficient and effective customer service, to lower sales and marketing costs and to generate new sales opportunities (DOC 1998). A very large number of industry sectors have been engaging in B2B e-commerce, but a handful of industries lead the pack. According to Forrester Research, the largest sectors by far are computing and electronics, motor vehicles, petrochemicals, and utilities. Other important B2B online industries include paper and office products, shipping and warehousing, food and agriculture, consumer goods, pharmaceutical and medical, defense, construction, heavy industries, and industrial equipment.

As in the case of B2C e-commerce, B2B e-commerce projections tended to be highly inflated until the dot.com bubble burst in 2000, and many B2B dot.coms went under along with their B2C counterparts. Forrester Research, for example, estimated a growth in B2B e-commerce sales from $43 billion in 1998 to $251 billion by 2000 and an astronomical $1.3 trillion by 2003. Similarly, the Gartner Group predicted total worldwide B2B sales would grow to $7.2 trillion by 2004. Projections made since 2000 are a little more modest, but still suggest strong steady growth into the future. For example, CyberAtlas reports projections that worldwide B2B e-commerce will be $823.4 billion in 2002 and more than double, to $2.4 trillion, by 2004 (CyberAtlas 2002).

Meanwhile, the US Census Bureau reports that 94 percent of e-commerce in 2000 was B2B. Manufacturing leads all industry sectors with 78 percent of all B2B e-commerce, with e-commerce shipments in 2000 of $777 billion, accounting for 18.4 percent of the total value of manufacturing shipments. Merchant wholesalers had 22 percent of total B2B e-commerce with e-commerce shipments of $213 billion in 2000, accounting for 7.7 percent of their total sales. E-commerce sales in both sectors grew at significantly faster rates than total B2B sales between 1999 and 2000. The overwhelming bulk of e-commerce sales, however, were conducted over EDI systems in both sectors. EDI sales accounted for 88 percent of B2B e-commerce sales for merchant wholesalers in 2000. Two-thirds of e-commerce shipments of manufacturing plants primarily used EDI networks in mid-2000, compared to only 5 percent of e-commerce shipments of plants primarily using Internet networks (US Census Bureau 2002b). EDI's high showing reflects its long-standing use in these sectors, and the difficulties of replacing such well-entrenched legacy systems by the newer Internet systems, despite their purported advantages.

Although the business sector has not embraced Internet-enabled e-commerce to any great extent, so far, most firms have introduced the

Internet into their operations at some level. In a US Census Bureau survey of 38,000 manufacturing plants in 2000 regarding process use, three-quarters reported that the Internet is present and 20 percent report using EDI networks. Many report more than one type of network present, so there is some overlap of EDI and Internet users (US Census Bureau 2002a). Much, if not most, Internet use in these plants is not directly related to e-commerce, though it is used for other important functions, as we will discuss shortly. Nevertheless, Internet B2B e-commerce is likely to grow. Those companies that do engage in this type of e-commerce have adopted a variety of strategies:

- *Direct sales* – Firm web-sites establish e-commerce linkages with suppliers.
- *E-marketplaces* – Online venues enable multiple buyers and sellers to conduct commerce.
- *Business intermediaries* – Online aggregators pool supplies in a searchable one-stop shopping mall, online auctions, catalogues, trading and spot markets (e.g., ChemDex).
- *Large-scale Internet exchanges* – Large, global Internet exchanges set up by large corporations, or on an industry basis, to manage transactions with suppliers, retail outlets, and dealers. Industries that have set up such exchanges include auto, steel, aerospace, chemicals, and construction.

Some of the largest industrial firms have committed billions of dollars with much fanfare to create the larger exchanges. For example, several of the largest aerospace corporations – Boeing, Lockheed Martin, Raytheon, and BAE Systems – joined with CommerceOne and took out an advertisement in the *Washington Post* (29 March 2000) announcing the formation of a world-wide trading exchange open to all buyers and sellers of aerospace and defense goods and services. The ad touted that in their exchange "[m]anufacturers, suppliers, and airline and government customers will conduct business through an e-commerce solution that lowers their transaction costs and makes frictionless commerce an industry reality."

Similarly, the world's largest auto companies, including Ford, GM, DaimlerChrysler, Renault and Nissan, announced in May 2000 the formation of Covisint, an Internet trading platform to facilitate parts and materials procurement, supply chain management, and collaborative product development on a global scale. Covisint's stated goals include enabling optimization of customers' existing supply chains, facilitating collaborative information exchange and work processes between business partners, creating the technological infrastructure for built-to-order vehicle manufacturing, and creating a frictionless market for goods and services (Weiss

2000). To appreciate the scale of the operation, GM spends approximately $90 billion per year on parts, materials, and services, and works with 36,000 suppliers. Ford spends about $80 billion on purchases from more than 30,000 suppliers. When the corporations joined the exchange, GM expected to trim its purchasing operations by $1 billion per year and Ford expected to save 10 to 20 percent of its procurement costs, or from $8–16 billion (Girard 1999; Reuters 1999; Bloomberg News 1999).

Whether Covisint and the other large industrial Internet exchanges achieve their objectives remains to be seen. Most have encountered difficulties, as have many individual firm B2B initiatives. Expressing disappointment with their experiences with Internet e-commerce, manufacturing organizations in particular have reduced their participation in online auctions and marketplaces (ISM/Forrester 2002a). Skepticism grew after many of the firms involved in Internet commerce applications or services failed. Companies' ICT budgets dropped precipitously after the crash and some reports indicate they are still shrinking (Foremski 2002). But other observers believe that the IT crash in the end may be healthy for the industry. It has eliminated the hype surrounding the Internet, and businesses have become more realistic about their expectations when they invest in new networking technologies. E-commerce is alive and well, but as *The Financial Times* remarks, "it is a very different animal to the cash-hungry monster of the dot.com era. The focus has moved from top-line growth – using the Internet to expand and create new 'scalable' businesses – to bottom-line profits" (London 2001).

The problems, however, are not simply a loss of faith because of the dot.com failures. The Joint Institute for Supply Management (ISM) and Forrester Research reports cite a lack of budget or resources, the impact of the slowing business environment, difficulties integrating with legacy purchasing and internal management software systems (such as Enterprise Resource Planning or ERP) and supplier readiness, as factors slowing business online efforts (ISM/Forrester Research 2002a, b, c). Although three-quarters of small firms with PCs are now on the Internet and are moving quickly to establish their own web-sites, e-commerce has not lived up to their expectations (Pastore 2001). They generally have been more reluctant than larger firms in adopting Internet commerce in part because they have fewer resources and lack adequate technical expertise.

Lean and virtual

Despite the setbacks, there still are many who remain optimistic about the future of e-commerce. Pointing to successful applications of online commerce, *Business Week* concludes that the "Web is business' killer app" (Salkever and Kharif 2002). Wharton Professor of International

Management, Bruce Kogut argues that "The Internet has yet to reach its full potential" (Knowledge@Wharton 2002a). B2C and B2B exchanges are just the tip of the iceberg. They are only different parts of what could in the end be a fundamental transformation in the structure of business organizations. Some commentators argue that the Internet era is ushering in completely new organizational models which, even as they may incorporate elements of lean or even mass production, transcend the older forms. For example, University of California, Berkeley sociologist Manuel Castells contends that a "new organizational form" has emerged through the "interaction between organizational crisis and change and new technologies ... as characteristic of the informational/global economy," which he calls the "network enterprise" (1996: 171). Castells cites the work Dieter Ernst, a well-known analyst of high-tech industrial change, who showed that the convergence between organizational requirements and technological change has established networking as the fundamental form of competition in the new, global economy. Ernst identifies five different types of networks around which, he argues, most economic activity is organized: (1) supplier networks; (2) producer networks; (3) customer networks; (4) standard coalitions; and (5) technology cooperation networks.[7] If we envision that these various types of networks are enabled, expanded, and interconnected through advancing Internet-based networking technology, the "network enterprise" is conceivably, as Castells claims, "the organizational form of the informational/global economy" (1996: 171).

In only a slightly different vein, John Zysman (2002) of the Berkeley Roundtable on the International Economy (BRIE) alleges that a major element of the digital era is what he calls the "Cross-National Production Network" (CNPN).[8] CNPNs constitute a division of labor

in which different value-chain functions are carried on across national boundaries by different firms under the coordination either of a lead MNC [multinational corporation] for its own production or a Production Service Company (PSC) who manages the production value chain for clients.

(2002: 28)

In other words, citing Michael Borrus, Zysman defines the CNPN as:

The organization, across national borders, of the relationship (intra and increasingly inter-firm) through which the firm conducts research and development, product definition and design, procurement, manufacturing, distribution, and support services ... In contrast to the traditional forms of corporate organization, such networks boost a proliferation of non-equity, non-arms-length cross-border, inter-firm relationships in which significant value is added outside the lead firm and entire business functions may be outsourced.

(ibid.: 29)[9]

In this formulation, outsourcing takes on a new significance in the digital economy. Beginning as a tactical response mainly aimed at cutting costs – a product of the flexible production and re-engineering initiatives of the 1990s – it has evolved into a "strategic instrument of supply chain management," a change driven by the shifting character of competition, and facilitated by CNPNs (ibid.: 23).

This model also explains the rapid rise of manufacturing network service companies. Like supply chain management, contract manufacturing has become a significant competitive weapon (ibid.: 31). Contract firms have grown over the last decade from a marginal to a major industry sector accounting for over $40 billion sales in 1995. The top firms, such as SCI Systems and Solectron, grew in 2001 by over 56 percent to almost $10 billion. The largest now approach the scale of MNCs themselves and are growing very quickly. According to some estimates, these firms now represent 10–20 percent of total product-level electronics manufacturing (up from under 2 percent in 1982) and 40 percent of volatile electronics industry segments such as PCs and modems (Zysman ibid.: 30).

Whether we call this emerging form of business organization, a "network enterprise," "cross-national production network," "network organization" (Dedrick and Kraemer 2002: 3), or "virtual organization," the Internet serves as more than just a medium for buying and selling goods and services. In a virtual organization, the Internet is an enabler and integrator of the enterprise's internal operations and its external supplier and customer relationships. The enterprise's core productive functions are electronically integrated with its marketing and sales operations on one end, and its supplier chain on the other. In addition, the internal functional divisions – design, engineering, logistics, scheduling, business offices, and production operations – are also electronically integrated. Moreover, the linkages are not confined to a single plant or office, but can span multiple facilities – including those of suppliers and customers – widely dispersed around the globe.

Figure 4.1 schematically portrays these linkages in a manufacturing context. The electronically integrated enterprise employs many different kinds of information technologies besides the Internet – PCs, servers, routers, communication devices, software applications, intelligent machines, intranets, extranets – to carry out different functions. But the Internet's properties – its accessibility, openness, ubiquity, flexibility, and low cost – have made it much more suitable than other forms of

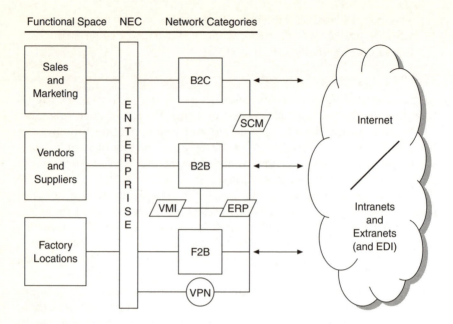

Functional Space   NEC   Network Categories

Legend: VMI = Virtual Management Inventory; VPN = Virtual Private Network; SCM = Supply Chain Management; ERP = Enterprise Resource Planning; NEC = Networked Enterprise Core; B2C = Business-to-Consumer; B2B = Business-to-Business; F2B = Factory-to-Business

Figure 4.1 The virtual organization: a 3-tier E-enterprise core model

Source: Adopted from Lance Gordon, "Factory-to-Business (F2B): Accelerated Change on the Factory Floor," Martcel Insights Frost and Sullivan (http://www2.frost.com/prod/portal.nsf/LuVerticalPortals/F2B) 2 May, 2001, Chart 1.1.

networking technology, such as EDI, to play this integrative role (see Upton and McAfee 1996; Gordon 2001). As Gordon (2001), notes, the long "enterprise" core in the schematic could refer to headquarters' offices in, say, the Sears Tower in Chicago, and its factory locations may be as far-flung as Malaysia, Canada, and Texas. What it suggests, but does not show, is the tendency of virtual organizations to outsource as many functions as possible, including business functions (human resources, personnel compensation systems, accounting, bill processing), and production operations (assembly) – and even research and development – to outside contractors on a worldwide basis.

Outsourcing, of course, is not new. It was a natural outgrowth of the spread of lean and agile business practices in the 1980s, as companies restructured their operations to cut costs and increase their competitiveness. Firms started to slim down their operations, by shedding their so-called non-essential functions to outside contractors and suppliers, so they can focus their resource on core "competencies," such as product innovation and development. Outsourcing has played a major role in restructuring the auto industry's supply base. As reported in a *CNET News* article,

> [a] new core of "Tier 0" suppliers such as Robert Bosch and Johnson Controls – coupled with the spinoffs of Dephi Automative Systems and Visteon (from General Motors and Ford, respectively) – represents a fundamental change. Now, only 10 companies account for 50 percent of the U.S. automotive supply market, compared with 31 companies as recently in 1995.
>
> (CNET 2002)

Companies have been outsourcing a large number of activities, such as call centers, business processes (such as credit card processing, back-office accounting), IT services (such as software development, computer programming, and engineering), and manufacturing, increasingly to overseas service providers and suppliers. IT services has become a particularly large area of outsourcing. Many IT service providers are moving their operations, using technical professionals in low-wage overseas locations such as India, China, and Mexico. For example, HP plans to relocate a major portion of IT services, work to India (Iritani and Dickerson 2002). Similarly, companies such as American Express have been moving more and more of their information extraction and reporting tasks overseas (Aron and Singh 2002). More than 300 of the Fortune 500 reportedly do business with Indian IT services, reports Gartner. By 2004, it predicts that more than 80 percent of US companies will have considered using offshore IT services, and more than 40 percent will have completed an IT pilot program or will be using IT services with an offshore component (Iritani and Dickerson 2002). Auguste *et al.* (2001) meanwhile estimate that what they call the "infra-service" provider market doubled in size from 1997 to 2000 with total revenues at $1 trillion globally, and predict it will grow by 25 percent in 2001 and 2002.

"Strategic operations outsourcing" which encompasses core activities such as manufacturing or logistics is another very fast-growing area. It is estimated that such outsourcing in the United States has been growing at a compound rate in excess of 30 percent over the past five years. Computer, semiconductor, and telecommunications equipment makers are leading outsourcers of manufacturing activities, as are most major advanced manufacturing sectors, such as auto. But even manufacturers of consumer goods such as cosmetics, household, personal care, and healthcare products have been outsourcing their manufacturing operations to contract manufacturers. Similarly, third-party logistics providers (TNT Logistics, Excel, United Parcel Service) are providing services such as optimization planning, spare-parts stocking, and real-time inventory tracking (CNET 2002).

Outsourcing is largely being driven by market forces, in response to the onslaught of lower-cost global competitors in sector after sector. ICT and Internet technology, however, have played an important mediating role in facilitating the spread of outsourcing, especially in areas which can be easily digitized, such as IT services. According to Forrester Research, offshore outsourcing has been aided by the emergence of low-cost high-bandwidth telecommunications linkages, standardized business applications and Internet-based collaborative tools (Frauenheim 2002). Similarly, Wharton professors Ravi Aron and Jitendra Singh argue that the two factors that made the outsourcing of IT business processes possible were "the convergence in corporate computing platforms and the rapid advances made in communications technology" (2002).

In any case, companies like Dell have made outsourcing and supply chain management a central strategic component of their Web-enabled built-to-order, direct sales model. Computer and semiconductor firms have been rapidly trying to adopt Dell's model, though few as yet have matched its success. Many other industries, from auto to banking, have begun to look at this model as they proceed in their own efforts to weave the Internet into their operations to achieve greater integration of their own value chains.

As we saw above, the auto industry has invested heavily in Internet-enabled B2C and B2B e-commerce systems. In their study of the Internet and auto manufacturing, Helper and MacDuffie (2000) note that the auto industry has accelerated its efforts to bring information technologies, such as the GPS-based OnStar system, into their vehicles. Hence, whether or not the auto companies succeed in taking the next step toward fully integrating their value chains, the Internet will likely have a major impact on the industry's structure (Helper and MacDuffie 2000: 33; see also Schulz 2001). Helper and MacDuffie assert that the "built-to-order" model "is the energizing vision of where the Internet takes the auto industry." It is, they add, "where the incumbent automakers potentially gain a competitive edge, by tying their Internet-facilitated relationships with consumers together with their Internet-facilitated relationships with suppliers into one integrated 'end-to-end' package" (2000: 5). Electronic, Internet-mediated procurement they believe, would provide the underpinning for "built-to-order" by facilitating the rapid and low-cost dissemination of order information, production scheduling, engineering changes, and other crucial information.

Schulz (2001) emphasizes that establishing the auto industry along the Dell model would require adopting a modular manufacturing system which would promote greater compatibility among a variety of sub-system alternatives that could be substituted for one another on the assembly line. This would enable rapid assembly of a variety of vehicles in response to specific customer orders. At present, the complexity of the average vehicle precludes the automakers achieving this goal. To explore the possibilities of shifting to this new model, each of the Big Three automakers have initiated pilot projects, mostly in foreign countries, it should be noted, to experiment with modular techniques (ibid.: 39–46).

Several other manufacturing industries, such as aerospace, chemicals, and pharmaceuticals, have long histories and vast experience in automating their production processes, including the widespread use of earlier forms of electronic networking, such a EDI, intranets, and extranets. In recent years they have invested as well in major Internet-enabled applications, especially on the B2C and B2B ends (see above). Aerospace in particular is showing strong interest – prodded as well by the Pentagon – in introducing more Web-enabled technology to foster broader integration across its industry structure. Boeing's "paperless air-craft production" of its 777 passenger plane in the early 1990s represents an early effort to integrate information technology and design and manufacturing processes. The plane was created by some 250 cross-functional teams, including members from supplier companies and airline customers, distributed over many locations. They all were linked electronically and through the use of CAD software (Goldman *et al.* 1995: 138).[10] IBM executive, Pat Toole, argues that aerospace companies will not be able to make their next-generation products unless they employ "an extended digital enterprise [and] collaborating seamlessly around the world with all their systems and business process" (cited in McClenahen 2000).

To give a sense of how Web-enabled systems are helping to transform companies across the industry spectrum within manufacturing, we summarize examples of companies employing the Internet to integrate their operations. Some move toward an approximation of the electronically integrated customer–production–supplier linkages of the Dell model. A few emphasize Internet-enabled integration of internal operations with their suppliers. Others have established remote control of geographically dispersed operations via electronic networks, a partial move toward electronic integration. It is notable that not all these examples are in advanced manufacturing sectors, and some are smaller producers of relatively mundane products, such as corrugated paper.

AeroTech Service Group, St. Louis, MI (Upton and McAfee 1996: 124–125).

In the early 1990s, AeroTech built a highly effective virtual factory with McDonnell Douglas Aerospace (now part of Boeing). Employing standard Internet protocols over a dedicated high-speed link, AeroTech developed a computer-linked manufacturing community of several thousand internal and external users (including suppliers and business partners). The virtual factory employs an electronic bidding system that allows McDonnell buyers to e-mail qualified suppliers throughout the world to notify them a job is available for bidding. The suppliers return bids through the system to St. Louis, which are automatically ranked on the basis of cost. The system also helps members of the community to better coordinate their schedules, and provides the ability to operate large, complex software programs securely from remote locations. In one example, McDonnell Douglas and UCAR Composites, a manufacturer of tooling for high-performance composite components, used the network to jointly build rapid prototypes of complex new parts. CAD files and metal cutting programs developed at McDonnell Douglas were then electronically transferred to UCAR's machines to begin manufacturing. Because of the openness and flexibility that came from using Internet protocols, the AeroTech system permits members with a wide range of technical sophistication. For example, hundreds of small machine shops, with much less IT expertise than UCAR, have been able to transfer cutting programs over the network.

Cutler-Hammer, Moon Township, PA (Bylinsky 2001)

Cutler-Hammer, a $1.4 billion component of Eaton Corp., located outside Pittsburgh, has become a leader in "e-manufacturing" – the "marriage of the digital factory with the Internet." Through its "e-factory" system, it produces complex assemblies ranging from electrical panel boards for industry to large motor control centers, selling for hundreds of thousands of dollars, which run motors in factories, heating and air-conditioning systems in hospitals, schools and office buildings, pumps and vales in pipelines, and turbines and generators at electric utilities. Its Bid Manager software allows a customer, distributor, or a company sales engineer in the field to easily configure the sometimes extremely complex internal works of Cutler-Hammer equipment. The software checks to make sure the engineer has done everything correctly, and sends error signals if there is a mistake. The software is fairly easily mastered by non-specialists. Once a custom design is received by a Cutler-Hammer plant, its machines, robots, and assembly workers spring into action to produce the desired product. The company makes its panel boards in Sumpter, SC, which runs eleven satellite assembly operations, and its motor control centers in Fayetville, NC, which runs eight satellite plants. Another fourteen assembly plants in the US and Mexico also employ Bid Manager. Overall, Cutler-Hammer plants processed over 61,000 orders electronically in 2001.

Corrugated Supplies, Chicago, IL (Richards 2000)

Corrugated, a maker of corrugated paper for industrial users, in the late 1990s, built an integrated, Web-based system linking its customers to its internal, mostly automated manufacturing processes. A single, large database was at the center of the manufacturing system. An easy-to-use Web interface to control what customers would see when they went to Corrugated's web-site is tied into the database linked to the plant's automated machines. Its goal is to make the system available to everyone, from the machinists on the plant floor to customers off-site, in real time, with no delay. Cisco Systems installed a state-of-the-art wireless network, which ties together wireless PCs in the plants. Wireless PCs on a forklift direct the operator to take bar-coded packages to the correct trailer. A truck then comes in, logs into the network to see which trailer it is supposed to take, and then makes the delivery, usually by the next morning.

"Lights-Out Factories"

Long a goal of manufacturing managers and industrial engineers, "lights-out factories," automated factories operating with no on-site employees, is becoming a reality, often with the aid of Internet technologies. In the new "lights-out systems," plant equipment is linked to the Internet where supervisors can check operations at any time from any place, and even do repairs from a distance. For example, Air Products & Chemicals, Inc., an industrial gas maker in Allentown, PA, no longer employs full-time operators at its many small plants producing gases fed directly into larger, neighboring factories, such as steel mills. Machines on the factory floor send signals to alert operators located miles away, who also monitor several other plants, about problems, such as an overheated motor or stuck valve. A safety system automatically shuts the plant down in case of an imminent danger. The operator tries to solve the problem remotely, before going to the site to fix the problems. Evans Findings Co, East Providence, RI, a machine shop that makes small parts, runs without operators for one shift each day (Aeppel 2002). *Business Week* notes that most new factory equipment includes built-in Net connections; machines can be monitored and controlled from a remote location just as easily as from a control room overlooking the shop floor. For example, Unifi Inc, producer of textile fibers, runs twenty-two plants from its headquarters in Greensboro, NC. Using the Net, and aided by new software applications, such as CME, collaborative manufacturing environment and XML, extensible mark-up language, a scheme for tagging data on web-sites, "production data can be captured at each machine, analyzed centrally, and plugged into corporate software systems" (Port 2001).

Many service industries also have embraced the Internet and other electronic network-enabled B2C e-commerce applications to serve individual consumers and clients, and B2B e-commerce to serve industrial customers. In some instances, they have introduced the Internet and digital networks to enable and integrate the internal operations of organizations with their B2C and B2B operations. Some examples:

- Banking and financial institutions have long used electronic networks for certain functions such as electronic funds transfers and ATMs. A large number of banking, securities, mortgage and other financial services are now being offered over the Internet, to both individual and industrial customers with varying degrees of success (McKinsey & Company 2002; Mullaney 2002; Wenninger 2000).
- In health care, hospitals are turning the Internet to share information, perform remote diagnoses, give patients faster access to results, and to cut costs (Salkever 2002).
- The trucking industry is employing IT applications, the Internet and other electronic networking technologies (e.g., EDI) for order tracking (for customers), route optimization, tracking truck movements

(with the help of GPS technology), order processing and sales and marketing (Knowledge@Wharton 2001; Nagarajan *et al.* 2000).

- In education and training, universities and training providers are offering courses and degrees over the Internet. The University of Phoenix Online (http://online.uophx.edu), the nation's largest-for-profit virtual university offers the same educational and technical courses as the University of Phoenix. The University of Maryland University College (www.umuc.edu), the largest state university to offer online courses, allows its 60,000 students to earn about seventy different degrees and certificates online. Corporations and unions have also embraced online training on a large scale to reach adult workers (Symonds 2001).

- Online retail selling on the Internet, while becoming increasingly popular has made only a very small dent on overall retail sales in the United States. In some sectors, such as food retail, there have been notable failures, like Webvan; consumers tend to prefer purchasing some items in person over the supposed convenience offered by Web grocers (Hansell 2001). Established shopping chains, such as Giant, Safeway and Krogers, however, continue to operate online grocery shopping as an adjunct to their bricks-and-mortar stores.

- In the catalogue and mail order industry, the Internet has been a boon, and in a few situations retail applications have even reached back into company operations. For example, taking advantage of the Internet's interactive nature, Lands End allows its customers to input information about their body weight and height and clothing sizes when they order items on the Web. The companies software generates personalized designs based on this data that are digitally transferred to Lands End's Mexican manufacturing plant (Phillips 2002).

- Federal, state, and local government agencies have invested in ICT and the Internet to offer a wider and wider range of services to their constituents. This includes making useful information far more freely accessible, allowing transactions such as auto registration, and applications for services, such as economic adjustment assistance, to be submitted and processed online. One goal of *e-government* is to provide one-stop, non-stop, portals that some believe "will revolutionize not just how public services are delivered, but government itself, as well" (*The Economist* 2000).

The models and examples described above can only suggest what direction industrial organizations may take in the coming decades. The Internet as we know it is less than a decade old, and we are only in the very early stages of industrial applications of the Internet. How much the Internet will penetrate into our economy, producing the organizational and social revolution predicted by some forecasters, depends on a large number of factors, over and beyond market forces. We still are witnessing very rapid technological advance in microelectronics, communications, and software. It is extremely difficult to predict the new computer and networking applications that may emerge if and when Intel's billion-transistor microprocessors become commercially available later in this decade. Broadband and digital wireless technologies are still in their infancy, and have yet to take off commercially, at least in the United States. And who knows what the implications might be when nanotechnology and genetic engineering advances interact with the digital information revolution?

At the same time, a large number of still unresolved policy issues – privacy, taxation, security, access, intellectual property – still need to be addressed, which in fact will probably grow in importance as the Internet grows in power, speed, ubiquity, and flexibility, with new applications that we cannot even imagine, as its underlying technologies advance. How these and other social, economic and political issues are addressed will greatly affect how the Internet and its uses will evolve, and, especially, whether and to what extent the virtual enterprise becomes the dominant business model of the twenty-first century.

References

Aeppel, T. (2002) "In Lights-Out Factories Machines Still Make Things Even When No One Is There," *The Wall Street Journal*, 19 November, B1, B11.

Aron, R. and Singh, J. (2002) "IT Enabled Strategic Outsourcing: Knowledge Intensive Firms, Information Work and the Extended Organizational Form," research paper, the Wharton School, University of Pennsylvania.

Auguste, B. G., Hao, Y., Signer, M. and Wiegand, M. (2001) "The Other Side of Outsourcing," *McKinsey Quarterly*, 1 December: online (http://www.mckinseyquarterly.com).

Bloomberg News (1999) "GM Looks To Cut Costs With Net Purchasing, *CNET News.com* (http://news.cnet.com/category/0-1008-200-1461163.html), 22 November.

Blumenthal, M. S. (1999) "Architecture and Expectations: Networks of the World – Unite!", in *The Promise of Global Networks*, Annual Review of the Institute for Information Studies, Queenstown, MD: Aspen Institute.

Borrus, M. (1997) *Left for Dead: Asian Production Networks and the Revival of US Electronics*, Berkeley, CA: BRIE.

Bylinsky, G. (2001) "The E-Factory Catches On," *Fortune*, online (www.fortune.com), 23 July.

Castells, M. (1996) *The Information Age: Economy, Society and Culture*, vol I, *The Rise of the Network Society*, Cambridge, MA: Blackwell Publishers.

CNET Networks (2002) "Why Outsourcing is Suddenly in," *CNET News.com*, online (http://news.com.com/2009-1001-959785.html), 29 September.

CyberAtlas staff (2002) "B2B-Commerce Headed for Trillions," *CyberAtlas*, online (http://cyberatlas.internet.com/markets/b2b), 6 March.

Dedrick, J. and Kraemer, K. L. (2002), "The Impacts of Information Technology, the Internet, and Electronic Commerce on Firm and Industry Structure: The Personal Computer Industry," unpublished paper, Center for Research on Information Technology and Organizations, University of California, Irvine, July.

The Economist (1999) "When Companies Connect; Business and the Internet Survey," *The Economist*, 26 June, 19–40.

The Economist (2000) "Government and the Internet Survey," *The Economist*, 24 June, 9–15.

Foremski, T. (2002) "Evidence of Falling Technology Budgets," *The Financial Times*, online (http://www.ft.com), 30 May.

Frauenheim, E. (2002) "U.S. Firms Move IT Overseas," *CNET News.com*, online (http://news.com.com/2100-1001-976828.html), 11 December.

Girard, K. (1999) "Oracle, Ford Team on Net Venture," *CNET News.com* (http://news.cnet.com/category/0-1008-200-1427351.html), 2 November.

Goldman, S. L., Nagel, R. N. and Preiss, K. (1995) *Agile Competitors and Virtual Organizations*, New York: Van Nostrand Reinhold.

Gordon, L. (2001) "Factory-to-Business (F2B): Accelerated Change on the Factory Floor," Market Insights, Frost and Sullivan (http://www2.frost.com/prod/portal.nsf/LuVerticalPortals/F2B) 2 May.

Hansell, S. (2001) "Some Hard Lessons for Online Grocer," *The New York Times* online (http://www.nytimes.comk/2001/02/19/technology/19VAN.html), 19 February.

Hecker, D. (2001) "Employment Impact of Electronic Business," *Monthly Labor Review*, May, 3–16.

Helper, S. and MacDuffie, J. P. (2000) "E-volving the Auto Industry: E-Commerce Effects on Consumer and Supplier Relationships," prepared for: *E-Business and the Changing Terms of Competition: A View from Within the Sectors*, sponsored by Berkeley Roundtable on the International Economy, Institute on Global Conflict and Cooperation, The Fischer Center on the Strategic Use of Information Technology, Haas School of Business, University of California, Berkeley, 12 September (Version 2.0).

Institute for Supply Management (ISM)/Forrester Research (2002a) *Report on eBusiness*, online (http://www.ism.ws/ISMReport/Forrester/FROB042002.cfm), April.

Institute for Supply Management (ISM)/Forrester Research (2002b) *Report on eBusiness*, online (http://www.ism.ws/ISMReport/Forrester/FROB072002.cfm), July.

Institute for Supply Management (ISM)/Forrester Research (2002c) *Report on eBusiness*, online (http://www.ism.ws/ISMReport/Forrester/FROB0102002.cfm), October.

Iritani, E. and Dickerson, M. (2002) "Tech Jobs Become States' Unwanted Big Export, Hit Hard in the Global Bust, California May See Some Employment Move Overseas for Good," *Los Angeles Times*, online (http://www.latimes.com), 12 December.

Kenney, M. and Curry, J. (2000) "Beyond Transaction Costs: E-commerce and the Power of the Internet Dataspace," *Working Paper 18*, The E-conomy Project, University of California, Berkeley, 11 July.

Knowledge@Wharton (2002) "The Failure of Customization: Or Why People Don't Buy Jeans Online," *Knowledge@Wharton Newsletter* online (http://knowledge.wharton.upenn/edu), 1 April.

Knowledge@Wharton (2001) "When the Information Revolution Hit the Road: How Computers Changed the Trucking Industry Forever," *Knowledge@Wharton Newsletter* online (http://knowledge.wharton.upenn.edu), for GE Capital, General Electric Corporation.

London, S. (2001) "Grind Replaces Glory for E-commerce Pioneers," *Financial Times*, online (http://www.ft.com), 5 December.

McClenahen, J. S. (2000) "Connecting with the Future," *Industry Week*, online (http://www.industry.week.com), 17 April.

McKinsey & Company (2002) "Banking: The IT Paradox," *McKinsey Quarterly*, online reported in *CNET News.com* (http://news.cnet.com/news/0-1007-202-8491702), 15 January.

Mullaney, T. J. (2002) "Online Finance Hits Its Stride," *BusinessWeek Online* (http://www.businessweek.com), 22 April.

Nagarajan, A., Canessa, E., Mitchell, W. and White, C. C. III (2000) "The Economic Impact of the Internet & E-Commerce On the Trucking Industry," prepared for: *E-Business and the Changing Terms of Competition: A View from Within the Sectors*, sponsored by Berkeley Roundtable on the International Economy, Institute on Global Conflict and Cooperation, The Fischer Center on the Strategic Use of Information Technology, Haas School of Business, University of California, Berkeley, 12 September.

Pastore, M. (2001) "Small Business Embraces Net, Shuns E-Commerce," *CyberAtlas*, online (http://cyberatlas.internet.com/markets/smallbiz), 6 August.

Phillips, S. (2002) "Web's Flexibility Helps Distance Sellers Hit Home, US Mail-Order Companies," *Financial Times*, online (http://www.ft.com).

Port, O. (2001) "Brave New Factory," *BusinessWeek Online* (http://www.businessweek.com), 23 July.

Reuters (1999) "General Motors to Nudge Suppliers Online," *CNET News.com* (http://news.cnet.com/category/0-1008-200-1431136.html), 5 November.

Richards, B. (2000) "Superplant," (http://www.company.com), November, 182–196.

Salkever, A. (2002) "The MD Meets IT," *BusinessWeek Online* (http://www.businessweek.com), 15 April.

Salkever, S. and Kharif, O. (2002) "Business' Killer App: The Web," *BusinessWeek Online* (http://www.businessweek.com), 15 April.

Schulz, E. (2001) *Automobile Retail and Production in the Age of E-Commerce*, Washington, DC: Economic Strategy Institute.

Sheridan, J. H. (2000) "E-Business Case," *Industry Week*, online (www.industryweek.com), 4 December.

Symonds, W. C. (2001) "Giving It the Old Online Try," *Business Week*, 3 December, 76–80.

Upton, D. M. and McAfee, A. (1996) "The Real Virtual Factory," *Harvard Business Review*, July–August, 123–133.

US Census Bureau, Economics and Statistics Administration (2002a) "Detailed Tabulations of Manufacturing E-business Process Use in 2000," *United States Department of Commerce E-Stats*, online (www.census.gov/estats), 1 March.

US Census Bureau, Economics and Statistics Administration (2002b) "E-commerce 2000," *United States Department of Commerce E-Stats*, online (www.census.gov/estats), 18 March.

US Census Bureau, Economics and Statistics Administration (2002c) "Retail E-Commerce Sales in Third Quarter 2002 Were 11.1 Billion, Up 34.3 Percent from 3rd Quarter," *Census Bureau Reports*, online (http://www.census.gov/www/current.html), 22 November.

US Department of Commerce (DOC) (1998) *The Emerging Digital Economy*, Washington, DC, April.

Weiss, P. A. (2000) "COVISINT," PowerPoint presentation to *Auto-Tech 2000*, 12 September.

Wenninger, J. (2000) "The Emerging Role of Banks in E-Commerce," *Current Issues in Economics and Finance*, 6, 3, Federal Reserve Bank of New York.

Zysman, J. (2002) *Production in a Digital Era: Commodity or Strategic Weapon?* Working Paper 147, Berkeley, CA: Berkeley Roundtable on the International Economy, September.

5

JOBS IN THE VIRTUAL ECONOMY

How the Internet's industrial uses evolve also will determine their impact on workers, jobs and unions. Assessing these changes, of course, is greatly hindered by the simple fact that we are only in the early stages of the new Internet business models in our economy. As we saw above, the volume of Internet B2C and B2B e-commerce is still relatively small. There have been empirical studies attempting to assess the job impacts of the growth in these sectors since the mid-to-late 1990s, which we briefly review below. There also is some anecdotal evidence showing the job impacts from these kinds of transactions, as well as from the implementation of the virtual enterprise model in various sectors, which we also discuss.

Historically, periods of rapid technological change have always been associated with a mixture of both positive and negative employment impacts. Even as some trends go up, others may go down. Aggregate job growth, during the 1960 and 1970s, periods when automation began to be applied in manufacturing at accelerated rates, was generally positive, because of relatively strong economic growth over most of this period. But workers in a number of industry sectors, and certainly at the plant level, were displaced. Other economic, social, and political factors may also overshadow technology impacts, although the latter may influence – dampen or deepen – the impacts of the former. The sharp decline in manufacturing employment during the 1980s was mainly driven by non-technical forces, though the new wave of automation applied in this period certainly contributed to jobs losses in several important sectors, such as auto, aerospace, and computers. The composition of the workforce has been shifting over the past century, as the service sector growth outpaced the manufacturing sector. As we saw before, the rate of growth in the manufacturing workforce slowed, in part because of the steady stream of productivity-enhancing technologies. The trends toward greater technological sophistication in all industry sectors also have been associated with the steady growth in certain occupational categories, absolutely and as a share of total employment, such as the managerial, professional, and technical professions. Others, such as skilled craft workers and semi-skilled operators, largely employed in production, have seen their share of jobs decline. Yet, low-end, low-income service-related jobs have grown, and are projected to increase more over the next decade (Parente 2001) suggesting that over the past thirty years we have seen a steady hollowing out of the traditional workforce. Jobs in higher paid, high-skilled and lower paid, low-skilled occupations have been increasing, while middle-income jobs in traditional high-skilled, production-related occupations have been disappearing. Technological change, especially the growth of computer-based automation in factories and offices, has certainly been a contributory factor in these trends, but other institutional, organizational, economic, and even political forces probably played even larger roles.

Whether workers find their skills diminished or enhanced because of technological change has been an area of controversy, as well. A recent econometric study of skill-biased technological change – looking especially at the introduction of advanced manufacturing technology – which reviewed a large body of previous studies on the topic, concludes that "technological change is associated with downsizing and a shift in labor composition in favor of workers with higher levels of education." But it also states that, presumably for the workers that keep their jobs, "new technologies lead to greater empowerment," which is defined "as training of existing personnel, changing job responsibilities, creating new jobs and career opportunities, and increasing extent of employee control" (Siegel 1999). These conclusions have been questioned as well, and actual skills impacts always are subject to localized, sector-specific conditions.

Employment impacts

Focusing now on the employment impacts of the Internet, we can identify six major areas of change:

1   *Displacement of jobs.* First, there is *automation-induced displacement* of jobs as the need for the number of jobs is reduced because of e-commerce or e-business (referring to Web-integrated and enabled business organizations, i.e., virtual organization) applications. When categories of jobs are eliminated, such as intermediary sales, order fulfillment, inventory control, and shipping jobs, because of B2C/retail and B2B e-commerce, this has been referred to as *disintermediation*. For example, as many shipping office functions have been transferred to the Internet, human intermediaries have been replaced by software (Kenney and Curry 2000: 20). *Economic-induced displacement* refers to the elimination of jobs due to loss of economic activity,

directly or indirectly due to e-commerce/e-business activities. For example, state and local governments, labor unions, and consumer and public interest groups have been concerned that the US Congress-imposed moratorium on Internet retail sales would give online sellers a competitive advantage over traditional brick-and-mortar business subject to sales and use taxes. They fear that as Internet retail sales grow in magnitude, "Main Street" retail businesses will lose business and state and local government revenues will fall, undercutting vital public services, both of which could cause job losses.

2   *Outsourcing and contingent jobs.* This is another form of economic displacement, but because it is a central element in the virtual enterprise model, and potentially a major source of job loss, it is worth closer attention. It refers to the elimination of job functions due to the outsourcing of non-core functions, as well as other activities, such as assemblers, to suppliers and contract services (i.e., contract manufacturers). A related job impact is the creation of a large number of new *contingent* jobs that contribute to the loss of permanent jobs performing the same functions, as firms outsource their work to independent contractors. Large-scale outsourcing of jobs and growing reliance on contingent work began during the industrial restructuring of the 1980s, as more and more employers embraced the lean model. Internet-enabled virtual practices will undoubtedly continue to contribute to these trends.

3   *Job creation.* A large number of new jobs have been created by the growth of Internet, e-commerce and related ICT industries (microchips, hardware and software, applications and services, machinery) and in firms that apply e-commerce and e-business applications. There have also been new jobs created as a result of the productivity gains of non-ICT sectors derived from the application of Internet technologies.

4   *Skills impacts.* As businesses restructure and embrace Internet e-commerce/e-business practices, workplaces and jobs are being restructured, resulting in changes in *skill requirements* and *labor force composition*. New computer/Internet-based jobs are requiring new skills, but some jobs may also be deskilled. Helper and MacDuffie (2000) contend that production jobs in auto manufacturing may become more routinized, as they have in consumer electronics, automotive repair work may be deskilled, while diagnosing complex systems may take higher analytical skills and electronics training. In short, both upskilling and downskilling outcomes are likely (ibid.). With new skill requirements, the problem of creating a skilled workforce that can fill these jobs becomes increasingly important. There is an ongoing debate about H-1B visa caps, which sets the limit on the

number of foreign-born workers in high-tech occupations that can be recruited into the United States from overseas (especially from India) to address a so-called skills shortage in IT industries. Industry trade groups have pushed Congress to lift that cap (with some success). Unions, led by the American Federation of Labor and Congress of Industrial Organizations (AFL-CIO), some professional societies (notably the Institute for Electrical and Electronic Engineers (IEEE)) and others have opposed lifting these caps, arguing that the US should be investing more resources in recruiting, training and educating domestic workers to fill these jobs (Smith 1998; Kostek 1999; Yudken 1999; Biggs 2002). A recent National Research Council study (NRC/CSTB 2001) acknowledges that certain types of jobs are in short supply, but does not conclude that a skill shortage, as defined by the IT industry, actually exists.

In any case, workforce training and development will become an increasingly important issue in the digital economy. Special attention will need to be paid to *retraining* and *upgrading* the skills of incumbent workers to help them make the shift to new jobs after being displaced by technology or organizational change tied to the Internet. Finally, we will need to address the *digital divide*, which is widening the nation's economic gap, by training and recruiting more minorities, low-income workers and women so they better qualify for high-end jobs.

5   *Impacts on working conditions.* As jobs and labor markets are restructured, there will be corresponding consequences for workers' earnings and benefits. It is empirically difficult to tie technological changes to changes in workers' wages and benefits, as numerous factors need to be weighed, including the role of unions (which tends to drive up earnings). Impacts on *worker autonomy, empowerment, privacy, job-related stress,* and *health and safety* on the job, are more intangible, but nevertheless need to be assessed as industries restructure to become more virtual. Threats to worker privacy and autonomy especially have grown as employers gain access to increasingly sophisticated software applications that enable them to monitor employees' actions on the job, as well as their e-mail and Web use. Finally, we need to assess the implications of the growth in *telecommuting,* as many workers choose to work at home for at least part of their time enabled by computers and the Internet. In some instances, low-income workers are employed at home engaged in an electronic version of piece-work under questionable working conditions (Ewell and Ha 1999a, 1999b).

6   *Union and collective bargaining impacts.* The Internet economy presents major challenges to unions and their ability to protect their workers in collective bargaining. How will Internet–mediated workplaces

affect job classifications and work rules, union membership and labor–management relations? Union density has declined steadily since the 1950s, with large losses due to the decline of manufacturing jobs since the 1990s. Most of the lost manufacturing jobs have been in traditional heavy industry and metalworking industries with traditionally high union membership. As union jobs have decreased, non-union jobs in US and foreign transplants moving to low-wage, low-union density regions of the nation, and higher-wage, non-union high-tech manufacturing and computer services sectors have increased. Indeed, many firms in these sectors are strongly anti-union. Employer outsourcing and increased reliance on contingent workforces stem from this earlier period, but as noted above, will likely expand with Internet-enabled virtual practices. Helper and MacDuffie assert, for example, that "[t]he role of unions and the structure of industrial relations are also likely to change if there is a linked move to modular design and 'built-to-order'" in the auto industry. They add:

> If power shifts from OEMs and suppliers, "this may further weaken union coverage, particularly locations like the U.S. where the OEMs are unionized and the majority of suppliers are not. Module suppliers are increasingly less likely to fall into traditional industrial segments, like metalworking, given that module design often requires mastery of several production processes and a wide variety of materials; this too could affect union strength.

In addition, they argue that the wage premium for the semi-skilled workers employed in heavily unionized sectors of the industry will probably shrink, while wages differentials between IT-mediated work and manual work are likely to grow, due to increased relative demand for the former (Helper and MacDuffie 2000: 43).

A thorough assessment of these impacts is clearly beyond the scope of this book. However, we think it may provide a useful framework for guiding future research. There is some relevant aggregate data on job growth and some job losses related to e-commerce. The Center for Research in Electronic Commerce, Graduate School of Business, University of Texas at Austin (UT Austin 2001) for a while put out periodical updates of its "Internet Economy Indicators," that was based on a useful analytical division of Internet-related economic activity and jobs. The UT at Austin group divided the Internet Economy into four inter-related layers "based upon the unique elements necessary to facilitate the ultimate revenue producer on the Internet: sales transactions."

107

- The *Internet Infrastructure Layer* consists of the telecommunications companies, Internet Service Providers, Internet backbone carriers, "last mile" access companies and manufacturers of end-user networking equipment, which are necessary for the Internet and the proliferation of Internet-based electronic commerce. Leading companies in this sector include MCI Worldcom, Earthlink, Juniper, Cisco Systems, Dell, HP, and Corning.

- The *Internet Applications Infrastructure Layer* includes the consultants and service companies that design, build and maintain all types of web-sites, from portals to full e-commerce sites. These companies produce the software products and services necessary to facilitate web transactions, as well as transaction intermediaries. Microsoft, Adobe, Oracle, and SAP are leading companies in this sector.

- The *Internet Intermediary Layer* is predominantly comprised of Internet pure-play firms. Many are web content providers, others are market makers or market intermediaries. While not directly generating revenues from sales transactions, their web-based businesses generate revenues through advertising, membership subscription fees, and commissions. Leading companies include Yahoo!, ZDNet, DoubleClick, CommerceOne, CharlesSchwab, COVISINT, Travelocity.com.

- The *Internet Commerce Layer* includes companies that are conducting web-based commerce transactions. These may include companies crossing a variety of vertical industries, "mom and pop" shops generating revenue streams, and e-commerce retailers with significant brick-and-mortar or catalogue presence. Leading companies include Dell.com, Amazon.com, roadrunnersports.com, southwest.com.

The Indicators do not go beyond the 2nd quarter 2000, perhaps reflecting the precipitous drop in probably each sector after the IT crash. The Internet Commerce layer accounted for the largest share, over 1 million jobs, of total Internet-related employment according to the Indicators. The Infrastructure layer was second, with a little over 900,000 jobs and the Applications layer accounted for 741,000 jobs. The Intermediary layer was the smallest, with about 470,000 jobs in the 2nd quarter 2000. Total Internet Economy jobs, after removing overlap, reached a little over 3 million in this period, a 23 percent growth over the 2nd quarter 1999.[1]

In recent studies, the US Labor Department's Bureau of Labor Statistics (BLS) has attempted to specifically address the effects of electronic business (e-business) on jobs. It defines e-business as consisting of marketing and other business processes conducted over computer-mediated networks. It contends that e-business

[is] changing the way organizations in many industries operate. It leads to the automation of some job functions and replaces others with self-service operations, raising output per worker and dampening employment requirements in some occupations, as well as in the industries in which those occupations are concentrated.

At the same time, it observes, "e-business has also spurred employment used by e-businesses and in computer and other occupations associated with websites and networks." They also propose that because of its increasing pervasiveness, e-business may be affecting labor output and employment in virtually every industry (Hecker 2001a: 3). The BLS methodology also distinguishes B2C, B2B, C2C, and management- or production-focused e-business activities. The latter category involves the following functions: procurement, including ordering, automated stock replenishment, payment processing, and other electronic B2B-related activities; personnel-related activities; the use of networks for sharing information and databases; and the expansion of communication and collaboration activities. This preliminary study looks at the likely effect of e-business activities on employment requirements in selected occupations and on output and employment requirements in selected industries. In each case, it indicates whether e-business activities will likely stimulate or dampen outcomes.

For example, it makes the following predictions about e-business impacts:

- It will likely stimulate jobs in the occupational categories of engineering, science and computer and information system managers, management analysts, artists and commercial artists, computer systems analysts, engineers and scientists, and computer programmers.
- It will dampen jobs in the occupations of purchasing managers, purchasing agents, and wholesale and retail buyers, marketing and sales, and administrative support workers, including clerical.
- It will stimulate output and jobs in computer and office equipment, communication equipment, and electric components manufacturing, telephone and cable communications, computers services, and management consulting services (Hecker 2001a: 5).
- It will dampen output and jobs in retail and wholesale trade and dampen jobs in manufacturing.
- While it stimulates output and employment in e-tailing package delivery, it dampens them in other activities in local and long-distance trucking (Hecker 2001a: 7).

These findings of course are highly speculative, as they are not based on hard empirical data. Hopefully the BLS will be able to compile data that allows more accurate conclusions at a future date. The findings on the whole are not surprising. On the one hand, they suggest that computer-related occupations and industries will grow, an obvious conclusion given that these are most closely associated with growth in e-business. On the other hand, the findings recognize that some amount of disinter-mediation will occur as a result of e-business that will slow job growth if not produce net losses in certain occupations (e.g., purchasing agents) and industries. There also needs to be distinctions made within occupa-tions and industries regarding these effects. For example, the BLS sug-gests that, on the whole, jobs and outputs may be negatively impacted in most trucking activities, except in those parts of the industry devoted to delivery of packages of goods purchased online. There is no attempt in the analysis to evaluate skill issues, except in relation to occupational composition, which to some extent is a proxy for skill levels.

Virtual jobs

The BLS makes the useful distinction between web-based activities related to sales transactions and activities tied to internal operations of an organization. While disintermediation from the automation of sales and purchasing activities is an important job impact, the expansion of the virtual organization model throughout the economy, just as the lean concept diffused earlier, could have even greater consequences for jobs and labor markets. The sampling below of situations where virtual prac-tices – from B2C and B2B to web-enabled integration – have affected jobs in various industries suggests the kinds of labor market shifts that might occur in the virtual economy.

- A computer manufacturing company estimates that its move online eliminated seven hundred jobs in order processing, representing $50 million a year savings in labor costs. The remaining employees have changed their job duties: they have become customer relationship managers. They have been retrained and their job responsibilities have been upgraded, with 25 to 30 percent higher pay (Prestowitz and Schulz 2000: 16).
- When GM joined with Ford and other major automakers to form the online purchasing consortium Covisint, it expected to reduce operat-ing costs by $1 billion per year, shedding many of the 3,800 employees in its purchasing organization.
- A package shipping company's introduction of an automated, network-based system for invoicing eliminated the need for a large share of the 1,500 employees previously required to operate the old invoicing system (Prestowitz and Schulz 2000: 17).

- Another company, which puts its recruiting system on the web, reduced the staffing level in its hiring department by 27 percent (ibid.).
- Andersen Consulting estimated that e-commerce applications in the chemical industry could reduce the costs of sales, marketing and order processing by 25 percent to 30 percent, and technical support costs cut by more than 50 percent, creating the possibility that some chemical industry employees will be displaced, or at minimum, their jobs roles will be redefined (Thayer 1999).
- Helper and MacDuffie (2000) suggest that automakers' engineering staffs could be reduced, as suppliers (often non-union and with labor rates one-half those at unionized vertically-integrated plants), enabled by web-based applications, take over module design. They also predict that many transaction-related jobs may be eliminated as coordination efficiencies are achieved through the use of the Internet.
- Corrugated Supplies created an Internet-integrated system linking purchasing, production and purchasing and boasted that after it restructured it managed significantly fewer people than its competitors.
- In a study on Internet impacts on manufacturing, Harvard Business School professor Andrew McAfee observes that "traditional corporate functions from customer support, bill processing, and accounting, to engineering design, architectural design, and manufacturing have been 'virtualized'" – i.e., outsourced, enabled by web-based applications, and the "market for these 'remote services' is projected to expand dramatically in the coming years" (2000: 31).
- Setting up the "lights-out factories" described in Chapter 4 requires consolidation of operator workforces. The original organizations required operators on-site at each plant location. "Lights-out factories" reduce workforce needs by enabling only one or a handful of operator/supervisors who monitor and respond to problems remotely, perhaps in a headquarters in another geographical location.

This small set of examples suggests that as Internet-enabled restructuring based on the virtual-lean model occurs, the disintermediation and job displacement suggested earlier will probably follow. How much displacement has already occurred is difficult to assess. It would depend on how far virtual practices have penetrated into factories and offices. It is likely that those firms that have already adopted lean methods on any appreciable scale will more easily embrace e-business technologies and practices than those still wedded to mass production traditions. Small businesses in particular have found incorporating these technologies into their operations more difficult than larger enterprises with more resources and technical sophistication.

The downsizing of traditional skilled jobs in these circumstances may be partially offset by an increase in new high-skilled positions needed to work with the more advanced ICT systems. There also will be a boost in employment in industry sectors and occupations that provide goods (hardware, software) and services used by "virtualizing" businesses. As the BLS projections suggest (Hecker 2001b), many new relatively high-skilled, high-wage jobs in computer-related services mostly likely will be created as well. All this assumes, however, that we ultimately will have an economic recovery in the near future, that will be accompanied if not spurred by renewed investments in advanced ICT across the economy. But if and when this recovery does occur, things may not go back to the way they were before. As a *Los Angeles Times* article observes, "Experts say what began as a cyclical slump has forced permanent structural changes to the U.S. industry that won't be undone when business revives" (Iritani and Dickerson 2002). The result could be many more losers than winners, and there is a danger that this pattern may become increasingly fixed. That is, the "digital divide" will be harder to bridge, as low-end workers and their families are locked out of the higher-end information and high-tech workforces because of lack of training, education, and opportunity.

As many traditional skilled and semi-skilled production jobs disappear, and high-end jobs increase, we are also seeing larger numbers of low-skilled, low-paid jobs created, primarily in the services sector. In his analysis of BLS employment projections of 1998–2008, AFL-CIO economist Frank Parente writes, "The truth is that low wage employment is not going away in the 21st Century and that many of the ordinary, humdrum, low skill, low paid activities of the past will continue on as before in the years to come." He adds:

> High tech, cutting edge jobs will indeed grow and they are well paid and promise great rewards for those who hold them. But the reality is that low wage employment grows at about the same pace as all employment over the next 10 years. At the same time, some low wage occupations actually grow faster than average ... In a number of instances, the economy produces many more jobs in low wage occupations than are produced in higher paid, cutting edge occupations that receive the most publicity.
>
> (Parente 2001: 5)

According to the more recent BLS occupational projections for 2000–2010, even though eight of the top ten fastest-growing occupations were computer and network related,[2] the occupations of food preparation and serving workers (including fast food), customer service representatives, registered nurses, and retail salespersons, which are relatively low-skilled and paid relatively little, were each projected to experience larger *total* job growth than computer support specialists and computer software applications engineers, which are high-skilled and highly paid occupations. Other low-paid and low-skilled occupations, cashiers, office clerks, security guards and waiters and waitresses filled out the top ten occupations with the largest job growth between 2000–2010 (Hecker 2001b: 80).

One fast-growing area which employs a large number of low-skilled, low-paid workers is the telephone call center, which has grown with the spread of electronically networked enterprises. A University of Pennsylvania Wharton School article calls telephone call centers the "factory floors of the twenty-first century" (Knowledge@Wharton 2002a). It writes that as "millions of 'good' manufacturing jobs have fallen victim to automation and global competition," many low and semi-skilled workers have turned to a "21st century replacement: the telephone call center." The workers range form telemarketers to catalogue order takers to tech support agents for computer and software companies.

Cheap long-distance phone rates and computer systems for taking customers' orders and compiling sophisticated databases make the call centers possible. Center workers sit at phones and computers, electronically linked to faraway corporate databases, making sales calls, taking orders or fielding customers' questions. The centers can be put anywhere, but tend to be located in cheap labor markets of the Midwest and Southwest, and increasingly, offshore. The industry employs 3.5 million workers – some estimate six million – three-quarters of them women, making the centers one of the three or four largest employment categories. These are low paying jobs, with wages running from $7 to $14 an hour. They also are stressful and highly regimented subject to constant electronic monitoring. Employers use computer programs that can record workers' every keystroke, to determine when they have made mistakes (Knowledge@Wharton 2002a).

Call centers also are part of the outsourcing trend in business processing services, called business processing outsourcing or BPO. BPO service providers, which have been attracting the attention of venture capitalists who once funded the dot.com explosion a few years ago, tend to set up their centers overseas, most notably in India and the Philippines. Their primary business selling point is that they provide high-quality service at a low cost, making it attractive to US firms wanting to cut costs by outsourcing some of their back-office services, such as customer-relationship management or document processing. For example, one call center company boasts such clients as Ford, Lexis-Nexis, Dun & Bradstreet, and a major computer firm and major software company (Knowledge@Wharton 2002b).

Call centers and outsourcing are part of the downside of the emerging "virtual economy." Although they may help companies' bottom line and global competitiveness, US jobs are being permanently lost. By definition, outsourcing seeks to find workers with the required technical skills at much lower cost, who can be found in large quantities overseas. A recent Forrester Research report estimated that the number of computer jobs moving offshore due to outsourcing will grow from 27,171 in 2000 to 472,632 five years later. By 2015, it predicts that a total of 3.3 million US jobs and $136 billion in wages will transfer overseas to countries such as India, Russia, China, and the Philippines (Frauenheim 2002). For example, Motorola eliminated 7,000 jobs in its US plants in 2002 as it aggressively shifted its chip manufacturing to contract manufacturers in Asia (Iritani and Dickerson 2002).

Companies are also "outsourcing" permanent jobs to temporary workers and contractors. The number of temporary or contingent jobs, also known as "non-standard work arrangements," has grown since the 1970s. This growth continued over the 1990s, coinciding with the growth of ITC and Internet-producing and Internet-using industries, which have become major users of contingent employees. Such workers often are paid less and receive fewer protections and benefits than full-time employees, even though in many cases, they work side by side with full-time employees, doing the same job. Estimates of the contingent workforce range from 5 percent of all workers, according to the BLS, to nearly 30 percent, according to an Economic Policy Institute report (Birnbaum 2000). Economists Marcello Estevão, and Saul Lach track the growth in the manufacturing sector's use of contingent employees, or what they call temporary help supply (THS) labor. They find that the number of temporary workers in manufacturing grew from about 34,000 in 1972 to about 707,000 in 1997, or roughly equal to about 4 percent of the manufacturing workforce. They also estimate that the number of hours supplied by temporary workers grew from about 53 million in 1982 to about 1.3 million in 1997 (Estevão and Lach 2001).

In their drive to cut labor costs and increase organizational flexibility, firms have turned to temporary workers because they cost less and lack the benefits and worker protections of permanent workers. Although many temps prefer the flexibility of contingent work, many others take the jobs out of necessity. ITC companies in particular have been employing temps on a relatively large scale. Many temps work alongside permanent workers on a year-round basis, for many years, prompting the term "permatemps" to be applied to them.

Attention was drawn to the problem of permatemps a few years ago by the Washington Alliance of Technology Workers (WashTech), now an affiliate of the Communications Workers of America (CWA; Local 37083), located in the Seattle area. Microsoft was employing thousands of permatemps, refusing to hire them permanently and provide them with the benefits offered to their permanent workers. WashTech successfully mounted a campaign, including a court battle (Blain 2002), that ultimately led to Microsoft making many of these workers permanent employees.

They are taking on similar battles on behalf of employees of other ICT and Internet companies, such as Amazon.com. A report for WashTech prepared by the Worker Center, King County Labor Council, AFL-CIO, estimates that in 2000 there were at least 7,935 contingent workers employed in the IT industry, in King, Snohomish, and Pierce counties of Washington State. This is equal to 12 percent of the official tally of IT workers in those counties. The report notes that these workers earn less compensation on average than the directly employed, and have far less job security, often being periodically laid off for one to three months per year. The report, not incidentally, also describes what it calls "a digital divide *within* the digital world." It estimates that about 15 percent of the IT workforce in the three counties, or 7,450 workers, earned less than $16.78 an hour, and 5,000 earned less than $14.44, which is below what would constitute a livable wage in the Seattle area. The median wage was approximately $31.00 an hour. This contrasts with the top 1 percent of the software sector, or approximately 260 people, which averaged over $11,921 an hour (Worker Center 2001).

Unions in a virtual world

The WashTech report highlights the limitations of the "virtual economy." The economic transformation we are witnessing today is the product of the combined forces of what we call *virtualization* and *globalization*. By virtualization, we mean the mix of lean and agile management practices, digitally mediated coordination and integration of enterprises' sales, supplier, and internal operations, and the growing outsourcing and non-traditional workforce trends. Globalization is fostered by international trade agreements, monetary flows, and other macroeconomic factors, as well as by the Internet and advanced information and communications technologies (not to mention advanced modes of transportation). As we witnessed in the 1990s, these forces are capable of generating tremendous economic growth and wealth. We also saw how they can be very volatile, generating economic instability and increasing economic disparity – widening the "digital divide" between the technological "haves and have nots," both within the United States and worldwide.

No institution has been as acutely affected by the contradictions inherent in this combination than labor unions, especially in the United States. Union density in the United States reached its peak during the 1940s and 1950s at about 35 percent of the total workforce, but it has since steadily declined to a little over 13 percent in 2002. Union membership suffered a serious blow during the 1980s, especially in the traditional manufacturing sectors with the highest union density, such as auto and steel, which lost hundreds of thousands of jobs. Union membership share of the total workforce continued to shrink into the 1990s, as unionized manufacturing jobs were shed through outsourcing to non-union US suppliers or overseas. Service unions have made impressive gains over the past two decades in organizing low-end private sector service workers, but this growth has not kept up with the rate of overall growth in services jobs.[3]

Meanwhile, unions historically have had little success organizing any segment of the fast-growing ICT workforce, whether low-end, microchip fabrication workers, high-tech technicians, or computer professionals. Recent efforts by organizations such as WashTech, to organize workers in companies like Microsoft, Amazon, Webvan, and Etown, and the Alliance@IBM, another affiliate of CWA, at IBM have achieved mixed success. The campaigns at Etown and Webvan ended when the dot.coms both folded, and the unionizing effort at Amazon ended when the firm shut down its Seattle service center. On the other hand, Alliance@IBM, open to all IBM's 130,000 employees in the United States, has about 4,000 members and the attention of management. Unions have only achieved a strong presence in high-tech sectors associated with traditional union strongholds, such as telecommunications and aerospace. The United Food and Commercial Workers (UFCW), which already represent retail food market chains such as Safeway, Giant, and Krogers, are having a little success extending coverage to employees of some of these companies' online units (Wolverton 2000, 2001; Gilbert 2002).

Workers and their organizations have been fighting an uphill battle against rapid industrial and technological change since the first Industrial Revolution. The Luddites, in England, are best known for their violent actions against the new industrial factories during the second decade of the nineteenth century, where they destroyed power looms, shearing frames, and other labor-saving machinery. The term "Luddism" has often been applied to people and groups that appear to be in opposition to technological progress. This reflects a general misunderstanding of the Luddites as a historical movement. The Luddite movement was not opposed to technology *per se*. It was mainly comprised of shearmen and croppers, the aristocracy of the woolen workers, who felt threatened by the labor-saving machines that dispensed with the need for their skills. Other artisan working groups participated as well, such as colliers, tailors, shoemakers, and representatives from almost every handicraft. E. P. Thompson (1966) asserts that Luddism was not a "primitive movement." It maintained a high order of organization, discipline, and self-restraint.

One can see Luddism as a manifestation of working class culture of greater independence and complexity than any known to the eighteenth century ... What was at issue was the "freedom" of the capitalist to destroy the customs of the trade, whether by new machinery, by the factory system or by unrestricted competition beating down wages, undercutting his rivals, and undermining standards of craftsmanship.

(Thompson 1966: 601, 559)

The Luddites also were not the only oppositional movement of that period. Cobbetism was a reform movement led by utopian reformer William Cobbett. Its goal was to establish a domestic economy and a way of life in which economic functions would once again be integrated. The Owenites were another utopian movement in the 1820s led by Robert Owen. He proffered a "radical theory of labor" and a vision of an idealistic, cooperative community. His image for an alternative society attracted many different groups of artisan workers, especially after 1825. The Chartist Movement (1836–1854), however, was a strong political and economic movement, the last desperate attempt by artisans and handweavers to stave off the new industrial order and subsequent demise of their own trades (Thompson 1966; Yudken 1987: 107–111).

These movements inevitably failed. They offered no credible alternative for harnessing the technological revolution of their time, to protect and enhance the integrity of their work and the well-being of their communities (Yudken 2000). By the 1850s the thrust of working-class protests, now spurred on by Marx and a variety of other socialists, shifted to a struggle for the needs and rights of the industrial "proletariat," the factory operatives, rather than the plight of a fading artisanal class. The labor movements that emerged in the latter half of the nineteenth century and into the twentieth century were no longer concerned with resisting industrial changes driven by technological change and expanding international markets. They were more concerned with promoting decent hours, pay, and working conditions for the new working class than with confronting the larger forces shaping the structure of their industries.

Until the 1930s, the US labor movement was largely dominated by construction trades and industrial crafts unions, represented first by the Knights of Labor in the mid-1800s and then the American Federation of Labor (AFL). The Congress of Industrial Organizations (CIO) emerged in the 1930s as a more militant industrial union movement fighting for workers' rights in the mass-production industries, such as steel and auto. While the AFL was organized around occupations, the CIO consisted of unions organized around particular industries, regardless of occupation. But neither organization, the AFL or the CIO, nor the merged AFL-CIO (in 1955), directly addressed technological change and the business strategies that were transforming the organization of work and jobs.

Labor historian Nelson Lichtenstein notes the "incapacity of many crafts unions to adapt to technological change." At the same time, he acknowledges:

> This was not endemic to their structure, because skilled workers can often leapfrog from an obsolete technology to one at the forefront of production efficiency. The Teamsters moved from horses to trucks, the locomotive engineers from coal to diesels, and the carpenters from wood to many of its substitutes. But because of their obsession with the control of a certain technological niche, craft unions are vulnerable to employer deployment of a new work process or technique that disrupts, or eliminates outright, their labor monopoly. This happened in long-shoring, where cargo containerization replaced the stevedore gang after 1960; in plumbing construction, where plastic pipe de-skilled the installation job; and it enabled managers in the newspaper business to slash the power and pay of the printing trades, whose legendary control of the press room evaporated with the computerization of the industry.

Industrial unions' members, in contrast, because they were attached to a company and not a trade, had some protection from technological change for workers with high seniority, he claims (Lichtenstein 2002: 71).

The 1960s and later the 1980s saw growing concern over the impacts of automation on jobs. While some craft unions, such as the railroad brotherhoods, the printing trades, and construction fought rearguard actions to restrict specific labor-eliminating technologies, the main issue was who should bear the costs or receive the benefits – labor or management – of technological change. The deals that in the end have been struck between labor and management through collective bargaining provided higher compensation and strong job seniority guarantees for existing workers, while management remained free to introduce technologies that transformed work organizations and unions (ibid.: 133).

In the 1980s and 1990s, a number of unions won technology provisions in their collective bargaining negotiations that guarantee workers advance notification, job seniority, and attrition agreements regarding layoffs, and some assistance for displaced workers, when a new technology is introduced by management. But as Charlie Richardson observes, these "mechanisms operate outside the core technology or production process" (Richardson 1992). Bargaining agreements have rarely allowed unions to have genuine influence over management investment decisions about technology design, development, and deployment; management generally has jealously guarded this decision power as one of its prerogatives.

A recent struggle between the International Longshoremen Workers' Union (ILWU) with West Coast port operators highlights labor's dilemma in the context of the virtual economy. In late September and early October 2002, employers locked out 10,500 longshoremen at twenty-nine West Coast ports that handle more than $300 billion of goods each year. The lock-out occurred after five-month-long contract talks deadlocked over the issue of implementing new technology on the docks. The union argued that this would cost jobs. The Pacific Maritime Association (PMA), representing the port employers, claimed that the new technology was key to remaining competitive.

The new technology would electronically integrate the processes of booking and weighing containers of goods brought in by trucks, and loading them onto ships. The docks' clerical workforce would be the group most affected by the changes. Currently, the clerks have control over the distribution of information in this sequence. With new technology, the processes will be controlled remotely from centrally directed communications centers and many more decisions will be made by machines (Timmerman 2002). The shippers want to give dock trucks computer screens that would enable them to navigate more easily around dock sites, and equip dock cranes with instruments that would create an instant database of where every cargo container is located (Kasler and Schnitt 2002).

The International Longshore and Warehouse Union (ILWU) faced an earlier, similar challenge in 1960, when the port owners sought to introduce standardized shipping containers, which would eliminate longshore jobs. ILWU president Harry Bridges negotiated a "Mechanization and Modernization" agreement that gave ILWU stevedores generous compensation packages and union control over the newly mechanized work. The deal also accelerated the containerization of all West Coast longshore work, which decimated the ILWU's ranks (Lichtenstein 2002: 134), eventually eliminating 90,000 jobs.

In the recent negotiations, the ILWU and PMA reached an agreement on November 23, a few weeks after President George W. Bush invoked Taft-Hartley to end the lock-out, on the basis that it threatened to cause substantial damage to the already sluggish American economy. The six-year contract essentially would give workers a share of the gains resulting from the increased efficiency and cost savings from the technology improvements. This would come in the form of pension protection for ILWU members and their families, sound and secure health care benefits, increased wages, and important safety provisions.[4] Although about 300 jobs, mostly clerks, eventually would be eliminated, the new jobs created to run the new technology would remain union (Kasler and Schnitt 2002).

The ILWU–PMA agreement exemplifies the difficult trade-offs involved in balancing industry's thirst for greater efficiency and profits and labor's need to protect workers' jobs and their working conditions. A common industry perspective is presented by Robert Smiley, dean of the Graduate School of Management at University of California, Davis (cited in Reynolds 2002). "People adjust," he states, "People can find jobs in other sectors or find jobs making the machines that displace them … There will be displacement in the short run, but eventually we will be fine." This view ignores, however, the harsher realities of virtualization and globalization that are limiting opportunities for many even as they create them for few. As we saw above, most of the new jobs being created in the virtual economy are low-end service jobs, if they are not being exported abroad. And displaced American manufacturing workers will be hard pressed to find good new jobs in new industrial sectors, if most new machines (or software) used to automate workplaces are made by foreign competitors, or if most of the jobs to do that work are out-sourced to primarily foreign-based contract manufacturers and low-wage, non-union suppliers.

In this light, ILWU actually did reasonably well in their latest bargaining agreement. Although losing some jobs, they were able to maintain control over any new jobs that were created, while securing decent improvements in compensation and benefits. AFL-CIO Corporate Affairs director, Ron Blackwell, commenting on the ILWU struggle, suggests, however, that ideally unions should be able to go further than sharing in the gains and mitigating losses, in addressing technological change. "We ought to have a say [in the use of technologies]," he states, "We ought to be able to shape whether they are going to be technologies that create jobs and help everyone" (cited in Reynolds 2002). One way to achieve this goal, advocates Charlie Richardson, is to "move from conditions bargaining to technology bargaining, where unions have a role in the process of technology development and implementation" (1992: 171). While guaranteeing basic protections that prevent differential impacts, provide transitional assistance, and improve working conditions, technology bargaining clauses should contain provisions for providing advance notice and triggering appropriate actions when new technologies are introduced. They also should provide unions with access to information needed for effective bargaining and establish a process and organizational form for negotiation and consultation, to effectively carry out technology bargaining (ibid.: 171).

One such organizational form is what has been variously called high-performance work organizations (HPWOs) or high-performance work systems (HPWSs) or "high road partnerships." Key features include the formation of joint labor–management partnership to oversee organizational and technological changes within enterprises to improve their productivity, product (or service) quality, and profits. At the same time, it entails a commitment to training workers, so new skills are available on a timely, high quality basis, an equitable sharing of gains from workplace improvements, and assurances of employment security, so workers do not fear losing jobs as a consequence of workplace changes (Kaminski *et al.* 1996: 2). Above all, HPWOs are based on the principle of building on the skills, expertise, and experience to identify and implement workplace improvements. Researchers Eileen Appelbaum, Thomas Bailey, Peter Berg, and Arne L. Kalleberg (Appelbaum *et al.* 2000: 7) state that the core of an HPWO in manufacturing "is that work is organized to permit front-line workers to participate in decisions that alter organizational routines." Worker participation in these decision processes could occur through using shop-floor production teams or employee participation in problem-solving or quality improvement teams and statistical process control.[5] Many of these elements echo principles of lean production, except that HPWOs require a degree of genuine worker and union participation in enterprise decision-making and strong worker protections not envisioned by lean proponents.

First articulated as a set of principles by University of Texas at Austin management professor and former US Labor Secretary Ray Marshall (Marshall 1991), HPWOs came into vogue, especially among labor unions, in the 1990s. The International Association of Machinists and Aerospace Workers (IAM) initially opposed worker participation schemes in the 1980s because they were then associated with companies' efforts to implement lean production. However, in the 1990s they became a major union champion of HPWOs, as long as they required active union leadership and partnership with management in their implementation. The IAM has since established an HPWO department to support joint labor–management HPWO initiatives at IAM-represented companies (IAM 1994). Several other unions have also experimented with applying HPWO principles with varying degrees of success (see Appelbaum and Batt 1994; Jarboe and Yudken 1996, 1997; Kaminski *et al.* 1996; Appelbaum *et al.* 2000).

In their recent study of high-performance organizations in manufacturing, Appelbaum *et al.* provide evidence that HPWOs can produce positive improvements in manufacturing performance. Productivity and competitiveness gains do not have to come at the expense of lost jobs, lost income or deskilling. To the contrary, companies' commitment to maintaining a high-skilled, well-paid, highly involved workforce may provide an alternative to the "race to the bottom" approach of companies trying to "virtualize" their production through outsourcing, downsizing, and greater use of contingent workers. Moreover, Appelbaum *et al.*

suggest that the use of modern, information-based and advanced digital network technology is not incompatible with HPWOs. For example, they write:

> Several studies provide evidence that information technology used to "informate" [in the sense of Zuboff (1988)] jobs is complementary with high-performance work organization and human resource management (HRM) practices. Because of the complementarities or synergies between workplace practices and information technology, the falling price of information technology increases not only firms' use of such technology, but that they will implement other high-performance practices.
>
> (2000: 10)

Despite their promise, HPWOs have been shown to be difficult to implement and sustain over time. Current US labor law does not provide a supportive environment for initiating and sustaining successful union-led HPWOs. In many instances, the problem also lies with shifting interests and priorities of managers, who in a virtualizing and globalizing world are more concerned with achieving profits by cutting labor costs and increasing organizational flexibility by applying lean and virtual practices. Nevertheless, some unions, such as the IAM, continue to pursue HPWOs as part of their organizational strategy. The AFL-CIO, through its Working for America Institute (WAI), also has been exploring efforts to establish labor-led union-business "high-road partnerships," that also give workers a stronger voice (WAI 2002).

The poster-child for this kind of organization is the Wisconsin Regional Training Partnership (WRTP). Growing out of efforts to address dislocation in durable goods manufacturing in the Milwaukee, WI, area in the 1980s, WRTP has emerged as a model for union-management partnership in promoting worker training, skills standards, and industrial modernization (Neuenfeldt and Parker 1996; Baugh and McDonald-Pines 1997; Friedman 1997; Arendt 1999; WAI 2002: 36). Its modernization work, in particular, involves union-trained labor specialists working as agents of the Wisconsin Manufacturing Extension Partnership, one of the many regional centers established with the help of the federal Manufacturing Extension Partnership (MEP) program. These specialists work with small manufacturers in the region to modernize their production while addressing workforce needs.

A positive union agenda to address the twin challenges of virtualization and globalization therefore should include the elements of technology bargaining, HPWOs, and high-road partnerships. It might also include strategies to promote education and training programs addressing the needs for building a "digital workforce" (NPA 2001), support federal policies and legislation that help address the nation's still glaring "digital divide," and promote federal policies that enhance HPWOs and granting unions and workers a seat at the table in federal "up-stream" technology R&D policies (see Jarboe and Yudken 1996, 1997). At the same time, these strategies need to be tied to labor's broader policy agenda addressing the problems of affordable health care, social security and pensions, minimum wage, and promoting fair labor standards in international trade agreements, among others. On the other hand, labor needs to consider how it should recast these issues in light of the trans-formations occurring in the nation's economic and social structure being driven by the forces of virtualization and globalization.

Last but not least, without a stronger, growing union movement in the United States, it will be very difficult to achieve these objectives. Efforts like WashTech and Alliance@IBM represent embryonic efforts to organize in the ICT sectors where many of the best new jobs have been, and probably will continue to be, created. An equally difficult and important challenge, that needs to be placed centrally in labor's "high road" agenda, is a commitment to organize workers in the numerous low-end services sector jobs also being created in record numbers, to fight for their right to have a greater voice and share more equitably in the bene-fits and economic gains generated by the virtual economy.

References

Appelbaum, E., Bailey, T., Berg, P. and Kalleberg, A. L. (2000) *Manufacturing Advantage,* Ithaca, NY: Cornell University Press.

Appelbaum, E. and Batt, R. (1994) *The New American Workplace,* Ithaca, NY: ILR Press.

Arendt, L. (1999) "Workplace Education, Bringing Classes to the Worksite Saves Time and Money," *Corporate Report Wisconsin,* March.

Baugh, R. and McDonald-Pines, J. (1997) "Taking the Road Less Traveled: Workers, Welfare and Jobs," *Social Policy,* vol. 37, Winter.

Biggs, M. S. (2002) "The H-1B Guest-Worker Program, Prospects for the 108th Congress," prepared for the IFPTE Executive Council, International Federation of Professional and Technical Engineers, AFL-CIO, CLC, Washington, DC, 14 November.

Birnbaum, J. (2000) "The Face of the New Economy" *America@work,* 8–13 August.

Blain, M. (2002) "Court Upholds Microsoft 'Permanent' Settlement," *WashTech News,* online (http://www.washtech.org/wt/news/courts), 12 May.

Bureau of National Affairs, Inc. (2001) *Union Data Book,* Washington, DC: Bureau of National Affairs, pp. 58–67.

Estevão, M. and Lach, S. (2001) "Measuring Temporary Labor Outsourcing in U.S. Manufacturing," Employment Policies Institute, online (http://www.epionline.org/study_lach_12-2001.html).

Ewell, M. and Ha, K. O. (1999a) "High Tech's Hidden Labor," *Silicon Valley.com Special Report* (http://www.mercurycenter.com/svtech/news/special/piecework/d1_piecework.htm), July.

Ewell, M. and Ha, K. O. (1999b) "Long Nights and Low Wages," *Silicon Valley.com Special Report* (http://www.mercurycenter.com/svtech/news/special/piecework/d1_family.htm), July.

Frauenheim, E. (2002) "U.S. Firms Move IT Overseas," *CNET News.com*, 11 December.

Friedman, S. (1997) "We'll Take the High Road: Unions and Economic Development," *Working USA*, November/December, 58–66.

Gilbert, A. (2002) "Unions a casualty of dot.com shakeout," *CNET News.com*, online (http://news.cnet.com/news/0-1007-200-8437119.html), 11 January.

Hecker, D. (2001a) "Employment Impact of Electronic Business," *Monthly Labor Review*, May, 3–16.

Hecker, D. (2001b) "Occupational Employment Projections to 2010," *Monthly Labor Review*, November, 57–84.

Helper, S. and MacDuffie, J. P. (2000) "E-volving the Auto Industry: E-Commerce Effects on Consumer and Supplier Relationships," prepared for: *E-Business and the Changing Terms of Competition: A View from Within the Sectors*, sponsored by Berkeley Roundtable on the International Economy, Institute on Global Conflict and Cooperation, The Fischer Center on the Strategic Use of Information Technology, Haas School of Business, University of California, Berkeley, 12 September (Version 2.0).

International Association of Machinists and Aerospace Workers (IAM) (1994) *High Performance Work Organization Partnership*, Upper Marlboro, MD: IAM.

Iritani, E. and Dickerson, M. (2002) "Tech Jobs Become States' Unwanted Big Export, Hit Hard in the Global Bust, California May See Some Employment Move Overseas For Good," *Los Angeles Times*, online (http://www.latimes.com), 12 December.

Jarboe, K. P. and Yudken, J. (1996) *Smart Workers, Smart Machines: A Technology Policy for the 21st Century*, Washington, DC: Work & Technology Institute.

Jarboe, K. P. and Yudken, J. (1997) "Time to Get Serious About Workplace Change," *Issues in Science and Technology*, 13, 4, Summer, 65–71.

Kaminski, M., Bertelli, D., Moye, M. and Yudken, J. (1996) *Making Change Happen: Six Cases of Unions and Companies Transforming Their Workplaces*, Washington, DC: Worker & Technology Institute.

Kasler, D. and Schnitt, P. (2002) "Age-Old Dispute on Docks Renewed," *Sacramento Bee*, online (http://www.sacbee.com), 2 October.

Kenney, M. and Curry, J. (2000) "Beyond Transaction Costs: E-commerce and the Power of the Internet Dataspace," *Working Paper 18*, The E-conomy Project, University of California, Berkeley, 11 July.

Knowledge@Wharton (2002a) "Telephone Call Centers: The Factory Futures of the 21st Century," *Knowledge@Wharton Newsletter*, online (http://knowledge.wharton.upenn/edu), 10 April.

Knowledge@Wharton (2002b) "How One Venture Capitalist Views Opportunities in BPO Investments," *Knowledge@Wharton Newsletter*, online (http://knowledge.wharton.upenn/edu), 4 December.

Kostek, P. J. (1999) "Testimony on the H1-B Temporary Professional Worker Visa

Program by Paul J. Kostek, President, Institute of Electrical and Electronics Engineers, Inc., United States of America (IEEE-USA)," *At Oversight Hearings Before the Subcommittee on Immigration and Claims of the Committee on the Judiciary, United States House of Representatives*, 5 August.

Lichtenstein, N. (2002) *State of the Union: A Century of American Labor*, Princeton, NJ: Princeton University Press.

McAfee, A. (2000) "Economic Impact of the Internet Revolution: Manufacturing," prepared for: *E-Business and the Changing Terms of Competition: A View from Within the Sectors*, sponsored by Berkeley Roundtable on the International Economy, Institute on Global Conflict and Cooperation, The Fischer Center on the Strategic Use of Information Technology, Haas School of Business, University of California, Berkeley, 12 September (Version 2.0).

Marshall, R. (1991) "Key Elements of High Performance Work Systems," keynote address to AFL-CIO Human Resources Development Institute Conference on "High Performance Work and Learning Systems, Washington," DC, 26–27 September .

National Policy Association (NPA) (2001) *Building a Digital Workforce, Part 1: Raising Technological Skills*, Washington, DC: NPA, November.

National Research Council, Computer Science and Technology Board (NRC/CSTB) Committee on Workforce Needs in Information Technology (2001) *Building a Workforce for the Information Economy*, Washington, DC: National Academy Press.

Neuenfeldt, P. and Parker, E. (1996) "Wisconsin Regional Training Partnership: Building the Infrastructure for Workplace Change and Skill Development," *AFL-CIO HRDI Briefing Paper #96-01*, Washington, DC, January.

Organization for Economic Co-operation and Development (OECD) (1999) *The Economic and Social Impact of Electronic Commerce: Preliminary Research Agenda*, Paris: OECD.

Parente, F. (2001) "The Future of Low Wage Employment," unpublished paper, AFL-CIO Public Policy Department, Washington, DC, January.

Prestowitz, C. V. Jr. and Schulz, E. (2000) *The Networked Economy: Lessons from the Trenches*, Washington, DC: Economic Strategy Institute, May.

Reynolds, D. (2002) "Man vs. Machine, Unions Desperate to Keep Jobs as Technology Replaces Human Labor," ABCNEWS.com online (http://www.abcnews.com), 1 October.

Richardson, C. (1992) "Progress for Whom? New Technology, Unions, and Collective Bargaining," in Labor Policy Institute, *Software and Hardhats: Technology and Workers in the Twenty-First Century, A Report of Two Conferences*, Washington, DC, 151–174.

Schulz, E. (2001) *Automobile Retail and Production in the Age of E-Commerce*, Washington, DC: Economic Strategy Institute.

Siegel, D. S. (1999) *Skill-Biased Technological Change: Evidence from a Firm-Level Survey*, Kalamazoo, MI: W.E. Upjohn Institute for Employment Research.

Smith, D. (1998) "Statement of David A. Smith, Director of Policy of the AFL-CIO, Before the Immigration Subcommittee on Immigration and America's Workforce for the 21st Century," 21 April.

Symonds, W. C. (2001) "Giving It the Old Online Try," *Business Week*, 3 December, 76–80.

Thayer, A. M. (1999) "E-commerce Connects Chemical Businesses," *C&EN*, 12 July, 13–18.

Thompson, E. P. (1966) *The Making of the English Working Class*, New York: Vintage Books.

Timmerman, L. (2002) "Technology Lag is Key to Longshore Dispute," *seattletimes.com, The Seattle Times*, online (http://www.seattletimes.nwsource.com).

University of Texas, Austin (UT Austin) (2001) "The Internet Economy Indicators," online (http://internetindicators.com).

US Department of Commerce (DOC) (1998) *The Emerging Digital Economy*, Washington, DC: DOC, April.

US Department of Commerce (DOC) (1999) *The Emerging Digital Economy II*, Washington, DC: June.

The Worker Center, King County Labor Council, AFL-CIO (2001) *Disparities Within the Digital World: Realities of the New Economy*, a report for the Washington Alliance of Technology Workers (WashTech), Washington, DC: Communications Workers of America, Local 37083.

Wolverton, T. (2000) "Amid Unionization Effort, Electronics Site Etown Cuts Staff," *CNET News.com*, online (http://news.cnet.com/0-1007-200-3957448.html), 1 December.

Wolverton, T. (2001) "Labor Pains," *CNET News.com*, online (http://news.cnet.com/news/0-1007-4385393-0.html), 16 January.

Working for America Institute (WAI) (2002) *High Road Partnerships Report, Innovations in Building Good Jobs and Strong Communities*, Washington, DC.

Yudken, J. S. (1987) "The Viability of Craft in Advanced Industrial Society: Case Study of the Contemporary Crafts Movement in the United States," unpublished PhD dissertation for Graduate Special Program, Stanford University, California.

Yudken, J. S. (1999) "Meeting the Needs of Today's Workforce for Tomorrow: A Labor Perspective on the Information Technology Worker 'Shortage,'" presentation for Panel on "Worker Perspective on Workforce Issues," *Inaugural Meeting, Committee to Study Workforce Needs in Information Technology, Computer Science and Telecommunications Board of the National Research Council*, National Academy of Sciences, Washington, DC, 6–7 July.

Yudken, J. S. (2000) "The Internet and Labor – Riding the Wave!" *Economic Policy Paper, E043*, Public Policy Department, AFL-CIO, Washington, DC, April (reprinted from *iMP*, online (http://www.cisp.org/imp/april_2000/04_00yudken.htm).

Zuboff, S. (1988) *In the Age of the Smart Machine: The Future of Work and Power*, New York: Basic Books.

Part II

THE INTERNET, SOCIAL INTELLIGENCE, AND LABOR

6

LABOR PROBLEMS

In the early part of the twentieth century, many colleges offered courses in "labor problems." These courses reflected the human challenges to the pristine models advanced by economists, as well as the practical issues managers faced on a daily basis. A third theme occasionally emerged in the teaching of labor problems courses: how were labor movements organized and how might they be most effective. (Of necessity, students would address economizing and sociologizing as modes of activity, and might consider praxis.)

Colleges long ago abandoned "labor problems" courses; now professors teach "human resource management." However, labor problems in all three formulations persist, with the new element of virtual enterprise. That is, workers still behave unlike other "factors of production," they still frustrate managers' designs, and labor movements still need to improve the match between strategies and environments.

As should now be clear, the prospects for workers and unions are not accurately described in many popular accounts of the Internet-driven "new economy." Many e-commerce enthusiasts find new fortunes as evidence of the soundness of free market-based Internet development. From this perspective, the fate of the median worker in an organization undergoing change proves nothing; it is the entrepreneur's success, however "unrepresentative," that is significant. Many observers see the Internet as merely another venue for what Schumpeter termed "creative destruction" (Schumpeter 1947), for which reason they expect the net effects for all participants, including workers, to be positive. Microsoft Chair Bill Gates goes further and promises a future without pain: a "frictionless capitalism" (Litan and Niskanen 1998: 12).

Litan and Niskanen predict the workplace of the future:

> Organizations will become flatter. The Internet and organization-specific intranets will reduce the relative number of middle managers and middle staff positions, although the Internet is already

creating new jobs for those who are proficient in navigating through it ...

Organizations will also subcontract tasks, often to other countries, for which the output can be transmitted on-line.

(ibid.: 15)

Like other neoclassically oriented digital optimists, Litan and Niskanen expect the employment outcomes of Internet development to be favorable for all across the globe. Assuming a regulatory climate friendly to new business and product development in the United States, they believe that jobs will be lost but others will be created to sustain employment levels. They assert that developing nations will benefit from their increasing participation in software and other digital industries.

Free market advocates proclaim the emergence of network business which appears to differ from their idealized view of pre-Internet capitalist enterprise in only minor ways. That is, pre-existing capitalist enterprise represented the efficient mechanism for wealth creation. The Internet enterprise is only more so.

Management scholars Crandall and Wallace describe the "virtual workplace" in this way:

a work environment that is bound neither by time nor space, where work gets done by people in harmony with technology to create goods and services on demand. There is a seamless interface among people working together in one place at one time, at different places and at different times, or any other combination that successfully meets customer requirements and demands ...
The *New Capitalism* encompasses a global economy and is driven by information rather than by product and by time rather than space, creating a revolution in the way we do business.

(1998: 1–2)

Crandall and Wallace write from an unambiguously managerial perspective, reinforced by a largely uncritical embrace of technology married to free markets. They write of people in harmony with technology, a seamless interface among people, all successfully meeting customer demands. They stress the information-based character of the emerging economy but fail to note that employees do not live by information alone and need real rather than virtual food and shelter.

The Crandall/Wallace model of Internet enterprise derives impetus from the economies that the virtual workplace offers to managers: the possibility of global reach with much reduced investments in physical infrastructure and labor standards. This combines with the factor of enhanced communication, both within and outside the enterprise, to

130

improve various measures of quality. The authors, however, do advise caution. They warn that people and technology must be "integrated" in ways that allow all stakeholders (companies, employees, shareholders, and customers) to thrive in the next century. In part this appears to mean that employees must take more responsibility to manage their careers (ibid.: 14).

Davidow and Malone (1992) paint the following picture of the "virtual corporation:"

> [The virtual corporation] will appear almost edgeless, with permeable and continuously changing interfaces between company, supplier, and customer. From inside the firm the view will be no less amorphous, with traditional offices, departments, and operating divisions constantly reforming according to need. Job responsibilities will regularly shift, as will lines of authority – even the very definition of *employee* will change, as some customers and suppliers begin to spend more time in the company than will some of the firm's own workers.

The virtual workplace and corporation may not, in fact, be very hospitable to employees. They are driven by the economizing impulse in business, not by any conception of social responsibility illuminated by the needs of workers. While highly skilled computer professionals may benefit from the flexibility a virtual workplace provides, the median worker is likely to find economies that are not in his or her interests, as well as intensified competition over a geographically broader labor market.

Sociologist Manuel Castells is a prominent theorist of the network economy. In the third volume of his opus, *The Rise of the Network Society*, he writes:

> the work process is increasingly individualized, labor is disaggregated in its performance, and reintegrated in its outcome through a multiplicity of interconnected tasks in different sites, ushering in a new division of labor based on the attributes/capacities of each worker rather than on the organization of the task.
>
> (1996: 471)

This implies the attenuation of so-called "internal labor markets," which reward loyal employees with careers and an array of benefits (Doeringer and Piore 1971), and the subjection of employees to intensified competition.

The labor market may grow more like a spot commodity market on the Internet. Contingent employees may compete to be assigned discrete projects for which they receive piece rates. Compensation rates might vary by the individual according to an auction model permitting under-bidding. The work of an online employee might consist of multiple transactions in relative anonymity.

The alleged dynamic pricing experiment of Amazon.com suggests this course. Consumers have charged that the online bookseller had begun to adjust prices based on information in the customer database. That is, two buyers simultaneously inquiring about a product would be quoted different prices (Lewis 2001).

Amazon has already demonstrated the economizing effects of the Internet in its employee relations as well. While Amazon stocks have soared, the company has yet to make a profit. In order to remedy this, customer service has been subcontracted to a low-cost subcontractor in India. (The Internet facilitates instantaneous shifts in supplier relationships.) WashTech, the union-supported workers' rights group described in Chapter 8, has collected a variety of complaints from workers pressed by Amazon's cost-consciousness. Workers are potentially disadvantaged by "instant" sub-contracting or dynamic pricing of labor.

"Telecommuting," like older versions of "homework," is appealing to many because it promises a measure of autonomy. Working at home appears to permit the employee to control his time with a minimum of supervision. Autonomy is a reality for some home-based entrepreneurs and professionals, whose home workplace reflects their affluence, their ownership of homes large enough to accommodate both work and family. They may control much of the production process and command power in the market. However, it is likely that many who work online will find that more powerful employers will dictate less favorable terms of employment. Rather than assume that market forces under new technologies will reach a universally optimal equilibrium, we must be alert to actual developments on the ground (duRivage and Jacobs 1989).

The Internet provides a highly valuable boon to employers in its facilitation of the remote contribution of disparate workplaces. Instructions for production can be distributed to international sites, thereby evading local and national boundaries on profit-maximizing. Intellectual property and capital have enhanced mobility, rendering local groups of workers less powerful.

The Internet can even provide an early warning system for employers seeking to defeat union organizing efforts. Business associations in the Southern United States already alert one another to union initiatives using older technologies. Now names and photographs of union organizers can be easily transmitted instantaneously.

The Internet would serve workers best if it enhanced their power, discretion, and security in craft and profession, while preserving workspace for face-to-face collaboration outside the home. This probably requires more investment in the physical infrastructure of work than employers will provide voluntarily, and depends upon effective models of labor activism.

"Free markets"

The prospects for labor in the Internet economy can better be understood by a broader analysis of labor's plight in the marketplace, independent of any specific technological regime. Classical and neoclassical economists treat labor as a factor of production like land and capital. They argue that only the market can efficiently and justly allocate factors of production. The market wage is the only just wage; wages set by government decree or negotiated through collective bargaining satisfy neither justice nor efficiency. Unionism represents monopoly in the classical/neoclassical model and it necessarily distorts market forces to the disadvantage of all. Accepting this logic, the Internet must remain a forum for market transactions rather than a new plane for organizing against the market (see Boyer and Smith 2001).

The orthodox economic model presented in economic textbooks and championed by conservative business-oriented foundations presupposes perfect competition, an ideal state in which labor demand and supply are equal and unemployment is a temporary aberration. At the equilibrium wage, employers and workers simultaneously maximize profits and individual utility. A union contract or a legal wage floor prevents wages from reaching the level necessary to permit the consumption of all available labor. It will reduce employment unless there is an increase in productivity. In the absence of any such constraints on the market, each worker receives no more and no less than the value of his or her specific contribution to the enterprise (marginal product), which constitutes just compensation.

Not all economists subscribe to this model. So-called institutionalist, evolutionary, and Marxist economists reject portions of the classical/neoclassical edifice. Some critics stress "monopsony" effects, monopoly power among buyers of labor. In the classical/neoclassical model, no employer is in a position to dictate terms to any other employer. However, in reality, some employers may have the power to determine patterns of compensation in their labor markets, depressing wages below marginal product. A higher legal minimum or negotiated improvements in wages might actually attract individuals into the labor market and reduce poverty levels.

Marx argued that employers paid employees only the value of their labor power, that is, the minimum necessary for subsistence and the birth of a new generation. Contemporary facts challenge Marx in two ways. US employers pay a significant proportion of full-time workers an income that exceeds subsistence levels. On the other hand, the declining value of the minimum wage allows employers to pay many workers far less than is required to meet basic living expenses, for which reason these workers are obliged to serve multiple employers.

The efficiency wages argument, pioneered by Fabian Socialist Sidney Webb, holds that higher wages motivate employees to higher levels of performance. Employees work harder and employers are compelled to reduce slack in the system. Employees' physical health may even be enhanced. This argument presupposes that firms are not necessarily fully efficient in the free market and that workers, unlike ordinary commodities, vary in their performance based upon motivation.

Orthodox economists miss a curious fact about human beings: they are conscious and may choose to withhold or intensify effort in work. Their output cannot be fully predicted or deduced from a general model. The Hawthorne studies at Western Electric had a surprising conclusion. Adjustments of the lighting in the plant were associated with improved worker performance regardless of the direction of change. If performance is variable for a given group of employees, and this variance is the result of an interaction of factors, including compensation, consultation, working conditions, and perceptions of justice, within conscious personalities capable of deliberate action, then the orthodox model may have limited relevance to labor markets (Smith 1998).

Orthodox economists also err in their application of the concept of utility, according to which individuals pursue their uniquely ordered preferences in the market. Food and shelter are not mere preferences. They constitute human needs, and as such, neither employers nor society can remain indifferent to their fulfillment.

Most importantly, the orthodox model obscures the role of power in economic relationships. The individual's right of exit or refusal to participate in a transaction does not ensure that he has the power to oppose exploitation. Individuals can surrender under duress to terms of employment that are insufficient to meet their basic needs (and legitimate interests). It is inaccurate to view individuals as autonomous agents exercising rational self-interest while they are at risk of declining market value, dependency, and insecurity.

The classical/neoclassical model relies on a fictitious market in which individuals are the locus of decision, individual choice is decisive, and managers lack power. Imagined market-space obscures particular realms of oppressive labor practices such as domestic and international "sweatshops," where working conditions appear to be inconsistent with workers' health, let alone uncoerced worker preference. While the free market model classifies the worker as a free contractor and thus an end of economic activity, labor's role as factor of production and the reality of power relations confirm the worker as means of profit-making by owners and managers.

John R. Commons' analysis of expanding markets in the 1800s is illuminating. Commons argued that the pressures of managing production for an increasingly competitive and geographically expansive market eroded the conditions and compensation of skilled workers. The breakdown of the master–apprentice relationship and replacement by a manager–employee relationship motivated employees to devise protective associations. In this context the first American unions were born (see Commons *et al.* 1966).

Unionism and free association

Abusive authority in the workplace is an enduring obstacle to justice and human development. Those without authority in a given system have an interest distinct from those who own or manage. Given the persistence of abusive forms of authority in market relationships, trade unionism derives its rationale from workers' need to counter such power. If anything, the consistent growth in size and resources of the corporate enterprise makes the need for counter-organization greater, and nothing about the Internet obviates this need.

The moral case for unionism derives in part from the broadly accepted right to freedom of association (recognized in the US Bill of Rights and the United Nations Declaration of Fundamental Human Rights, among other places). Free association reflects the fundamentally social character of the human species. Individuals reveal their personalities through their individual choices and participation in groups. The need for food, shelter, and belonging motivates the individual to affiliate with an enterprise. However, the employment relationship should not dictate the beliefs or the behavior of the employee, beyond satisfactory performance in the workplace. The enterprise represents one form of association among individuals; it must be limited in its power over members.

It is often union power that preserves a sphere of freedom for employees. Unions negotiate with employers to provide a realm of due process, including protection against unfair discipline and discharge. This countervailing power is best realized when the union secures the right to represent all the employees in a bargaining unit. The individual loses flexibility in the negotiation of individual terms of employment but gains power relative to managers and is less subject to arbitrary control. Despite the arguable loss of freedom implicit in the imposition of union rules, employees retain the right to elect union leadership, form opposition groups, sue the union for failure to provide fair representation, resign from the union (if they continue to pay so-called agency fees in certain states) or vote to decertify the union as their bargaining agent.

Workers cannot be said to possess the right to freely associate if they lack legal protections for organizing and employers are legally empowered to suppress unionism.

Unionism derives legitimacy from the pluralist argument that society is composed of multiple interests. The public interest emerges from a process of articulation, mobilization, and compromise of interests. Within the individual enterprise there are, of course, distinct interests. Owners, managers, and employees share differentially in burdens and rewards. Without unions, employees must depend upon employer recognition of their concerns. The employer is unlikely to make costly concessions in wealth or power to the many employees, although the few who are favored will benefit from special considerations.

Civil society is best understood to be a realm of intermediate associations which check the potential abuse of power by the state and increase society's capacity to resolve vexing problems without violence (see, for example, Levine 2001). In this context, unionism is clearly an important element of civil society. It plays a critical role in problem-solving on economic issues.

Benefits of unionization

Unionism is potentially a desirable remedy for worker exploitation in free markets. Institutional economists have marshalled convincing evidence that collective bargaining potentially improves the treatment of employees while enhancing productivity (Freeman and Medoff 1985). Collective bargaining boosts wages, compelling employers to seek corresponding economies. Management improves its own efficiency, and also strives to improve the quality of labor. One obvious means is training. Lower turnover comes to serve both employees and managers. Senior employees freely share their experience with junior employees. Shopfloor input contributes to product improvement.

Of course, collective bargaining can introduce errors and inefficiencies in management as well as unilateral employer decisions can. Freeman and Medoff (1985) concede both monopoly and voice effects of unionism. They submit that high levels of union density may permit unions to demand excessive wage and benefit increases, thereby overwhelming the voice effects. On the other hand, Rogers (1990) has described a rather different situation obtaining in Scandinavian countries with high union density and centralized union structures. He argues that national labor–management–government accords in these nations have served as effective tools of economic policy-making and have even enhanced national competitiveness. Scandinavian unions have negotiated national wages agreements that maximize wage equality and employment.

Unionism also plays an important role in providing a mechanism for a worker voice in politics. In the absence of unions, employers have the capacity to dominate political debate to the disadvantage of employees. Consider the nature of politics in the southern US. The so-called solid south refers to one party dominance in electoral votes in southern states (now benefiting Republican presidential candidates). While many would attribute this phenomenon to voters' conservatism, we believe it also reflects the absence of a labor movement as a factor in promoting wider voter participation, more pluralist politics, more serious inter-party competition, and less certain political outcomes.

Government regulation of the economy excites the interest of both managers and employees because of its potential impact on their circum-stances. In the absence of unions, employers have greater power to shape legislation to meet their perceived needs and to influence regulatory agencies. While safety and health regulation simultaneously serves employees and managers by reducing the cost of absence caused by illness and injury, powerful employer lobbies tend to focus only on the immediate cost burdens of regulation. Unions provide more balance in the debate.

American unions are relatively weak these days, with private sector union density dipping below 10 percent and vast regions of the country nearly union-free. It is difficult to determine if there is an optimal level of union density and political power. (The question itself derives from the certainty of the orthodox economist about a single point of equilibrium.) Contrary to Joseph Schumpeter (1947), who proclaimed the dangers of a "laborist capitalism," we submit that a more powerful labor movement is desirable. It would combat excessive economic inequality and enhance democratic pluralism across the nation. Reasonable (as yet unfulfilled) goals might be that employers recognize and bargain with unions where there is majority support, welcome their input where they have signifi-cant minority support, and invite dialog with unions on public policy issues (see Jacobs 1999). These developments would advance the "robust and diverse debate" (Levine 2001: 567) both within and outside the enterprise that many associate with civil society.

Union weakness, economic globalization, changing technology, and the virtualization of enterprise require the labor movement to rethink its structure and strategy. There is no single model for unionism, and con-tinuous adaptation to the environment is essential.

Many forms of labor organization

A survey of American labor history would reveal that workers have struggled in a variety of ways to secure representation as the economy has evolved. In doing so they have helped redeem the pluralist promise of American politics and society.

Workers pioneered labor parties advocating universal manhood suffrage and public education in the early 1800s. Local and national craft unions emerged as well. A lack of confidence in growing corporations stimulated the formation of the inclusive reform-oriented national bodies like the National Labor Union and Knights of Labor in the mid-1870s and 1880s. These organizations combined efforts to improve material conditions for workers with broader campaigns to democratize the economy.

The so-called "business unionism" of the American Federation of Labor, founded in 1886, de-emphasized larger reformist goals but refined the tools of collective bargaining for better wages and benefits. The industrial unions of the Congress for Industrial Organization brought previously unrepresented unskilled workers into the labor movement and enhanced labor's political activism. The New Deal led labor to focus on formal government-supervised representation campaigns in which workers would determine the union role by majority vote.

On the other hand, the Women's Trade Union League, the National Consumers League, the National Council of Senior Citizens, the contemporary Carolina Association for Fair Employment (extensively considered in Hoyt Wheeler's *The Future of the Labor Movement* (2002), and many other employee associations and lobbies, were created to serve as allies or adjuncts, if not affiliates, of organized labor. Just as the Webbs explained, workers may turn to collective bargaining, legal enactment, or mutual insurance to address their goals (Webb and Webb (1897); also see Jacobs (1987) for an analysis of "institutions of social unionism").

Region, nation, and globe

The emergence of multinational corporations (MNCs) as a dominant instrument in the world economy presents a complex context for labor activism. Regionalization and globalization are complementary. MNC managers seek opportunities to contain labor costs through the evasion of national labor standards. This is accomplished through migration to spaces characterized by maximum employer discretion, minimally constrained by law. Relative secrecy advances this cause, preventing illuminating comparisons in working conditions. The apparent turn to both states' rights and global free trade agreements favored by the Bush Administration (and US business allies) provides opportunities for lower labor standards domestically even as MNCs take advantage of global sweatshops.

The doctrine of states' rights shielded slavery from challenge for a time. The modern version of states rights erodes constraints on labor exploitation as states compete to attract business. Southern states in particular tend to offer the anti-union "business climate" that many employers desire. Labor standards regulation is lax and, in the case of "right to work laws," union rights available under federal law are expressly limited. Local labor practices are rendered a matter for local concern (until an unusually grim tale shocks the larger public, e.g., the 1990 fire at a North Carolina poultry processor that killed dozens of employees). Sweatshops occasionally attract the attention of activists but managers seek to preserve employment conditions as a more private matter. There is some danger of hardened caste systems in the unobserved dark corners in a world of intensified competition and compromised worker protection.

South Carolina is revealing as an exemplar of Southern anti-unionism. The official website of the state Department of Commerce announces the theme "Team South Carolina." The state's right to work law and low wages are key elements of South Carolina's strategy to recruit industry:

> Right-to-Work State
> Lowest unionization rate in US (1.8%)
> Work stoppage rate of 0.0002, significantly below national average of 0.02
> 1st in Southeast for productivity
> 3rd most productive workforce in US
> (South Carolina 2002)

The South Carolina workers' rights group, Carolina Alliance for Fair Employment, uses its website to proclaim the injustices visited upon labor:

> Business interests dominate our state legislature, and our labor laws are among the worst in the country. We're fighting for the views of workers to be heard and respected by lawmakers, so that our labor laws can be improved.
>
> (CAFE 2002)

Under the coupled phenomena of states' rights, labor abuses, and international sweatshops, Internet technology may be critical to the exposure of exploitation. It remains to be seen to what degree Internet communication has the capacity to limit the regression/deterioration of labor standards and to facilitate effective innovations in labor movements.

References

Boyer, G. and Smith, R. (2001) "The Development of the Neoclassical Tradition in Labor Economics," *Industrial and Labor Relations Review*, 54(2): 199–223.

CAFE (2002) "Cafe Mission." Online. Available HTTP: http://www.cafesc.org/mission.htm (accessed 18 October 2002).

Castells, M. (1996) *The Rise of the Network Society*, Oxford: Blackwell.

Commons, J. R. *et al.* (1966) *History of Labor in the United States*, vol. I, New York: Augustus M. Kelley.

Crandall, N. F. and Wallace, M. J. (1998) *Work and Rewards in the Virtual Workplace: A New Deal for Organizations and Employees*, New York: AMACOM.

Davidow, W. H. and Malone, M. S. (1992) *The Virtual Corporation*, New York: HarperCollins.

Doeringer, P. and Piore, M. (1971) *Internal Labor Markets and Manpower Analysis*, Lexington, MA: Heath.

duRivage, V. and Jacobs, D. (1989) "Home-based Work: Labor's Choices," in E. Boris and C. Daniels, *Homework: Historical and Contemporary Perspectives on Paid Labor at Home*, Urbana, Illinois: University of Illinois Press.

Freeman, R. and Medoff, J. (1985) *What Do Unions Do?* New York: Basic Books.

Jacobs, D. C. (1987) "The UAW and the Committee for National Health Insurance: The Contours of Social Unionism," in D. Lipsky, D. Lewin and D. Sockell (eds) *Advances in Industrial and Labor Relations*, vol. 4, Greenwich, CT: JAI Press.

Jacobs, D. C. D. (1999) *Business Lobbies and the Power Structure in America: Evidence and Arguments*, Westport, CT: Quorum Books.

Levine, P. (2001) "The Legitimacy of Labor Unions," *Hoftra Labor and Employment Journal*, 18: 529–573.

Lewis, B. (2001) "The Internet Has Prompted Many Things, Especially a Lot of Weird Business Decisions," *Infoworld* (5 February): 42.

Litan, R. E. and Niskanen, W. A. (1998) *Going Digital*, Washington, DC: Brookings Institution Press and Cato Institute.

Rogers, J. (1990) "Divide and Conquer: Further 'Reflections on the Distinctive Character of American Labor Laws.'" *Wisconsin Law Review*, 1990: 1–147.

Schattschneider, E. E. (1960) *The Semi-sovereign People: A Realist's View of Democracy in America*, New York: Holt, Rinehart, and Winston.

Schumpeter, J. A. (1947) *Capitalism, Socialism, and Democracy*, New York: Harper Torch Book.

Smith, J. H. (1998) "The Enduring Legacy of Elton Mayo," *Human Relations*, 51(3): 221–249.

South Carolina (2002) "Right to Work State," Online. Available HTTP: http://www.teamsc.com/workforce.html (accessed 18 October, 2002).

Webb, S. and Webb, B. (1897) *Industrial Democracy*, London: Longmans.

Wheeler, H. (2002) *The Future of the Labor Movement*, New York: Oxford University Press.

7

SOCIAL INTELLIGENCE, OPEN SOURCE, AND CRAFT

The development of software clearly illustrates that innovation has many authors. The multiple layers of machine language, operating system, and applications reveal the contributions of many individuals who could easily identify the code for which they were responsible.

The multiple authorship of software brings to mind John Dewey's concept of social intelligence. John Dewey is widely considered one of America's most important philosophers. He contributed to psychology, ethics, and educational theory during his long life spanning the nineteenth and twentieth centuries. Dewey contributed to the pragmatist tradition, of which Charles Peirce and William James were founding members. Contemporary exponents of pragmatism include Cornel West and Richard Rorty. Public figures as diverse as sociologist C. Wright Mill and New Left leader Tom Hayden were very much influenced by Dewey's work.

Dewey's pragmatism proceeds from the assumption that there is a world beyond the self, which humans share and attempt to understand. However, Dewey explicitly rejected the notion that there is any transcendent reality, or that there are underlying "forms" removed from experience or visible only to pure reason. He denied any division between mind and matter (which he classed as "different characters of natural events" (Dewey 1978: 74) or any mystery that limited the potential knowledge of ordinary humans. He appreciated the role of the scientist in discovery but found the scientific method, based on inquiry, experiment, and debate, to be within the capacity of citizens in general. The existence of a common reality makes communication and cooperation possible. These define the human experience and underlie business practice and Internet activism.

For Dewey and fellow pragmatists Charles Peirce and William James, truth is never absolute. Truth is provisional and instrumental; it is a useful view of the world. Useful truths may be superseded when new truths emerge from experience. Science represents a pattern of experimentation from which to infer causal relationships among events and to develop an understanding of the environment. Humans develop interpretations of these perceived causal relationships (Wicks and Freeman 1998: 126).

Deweyan pragmatism accords value to the perspectives of all participants in social inquiry, rather than merely deferring to the professional scientists or the putative experts. In doing so, Dewey disputed Charles Peirce's identification of pragmatism with the practices of expert scientists (Dewey 1920: 173). Dewey rejected the notion of intelligence as a property or asset of individuals. In his mind, human discovery was the result of a social process, of social intelligence in action, rather than of individual achievement.

Dewey noted with approval this comment by Henry George:

> There is nothing whatever to show that the men who build and navigate and use [the most advanced and speedy] ships are one whit superior in any physical or mental quality to their ancestors, whose best vessel was a coracle of wicker and hide. The enormous improvement which these ships show is ... an improvement of society.
>
> (Gouinlock 1976: 212)

Dewey had this explanation of the process by which technology is improved:

> The record would be an account of a vast multitude of cooperative efforts, in which one individual uses the results provided for him by a countless number of other individuals, and uses them so as to add to the common and public store.
>
> (ibid.: 213)

Dewey had enormous confidence in the ability of "ordinary" individuals to contribute to the social intelligence:

> Each of us knows, for example, some mechanic of ordinary native capacity who is intelligent within the matters of his calling ... Given a social medium in whose institutions the available knowledge, ideas, and art of humanity were incarnate, the average individual would rise to undreamed of heights of social and political intelligence.
>
> (ibid.: 213)

Dewey specifically disputed systems of human classification, whether by race, income, or other category, that set rigid limits on expectations of contributions to human knowledge. Whatever an individual's assumed intelligence, his or her perspective was valuable in the making of things or solving of problems.

142

Dewey believed scientific inquiry to be continuous with human experience, not removed. He saw in a baby's acquisition of language a process in which the baby's organically produced sounds represent an unconscious experimentation. The baby learns to choose among sounds from the responses of family members. From her experimenting, she acquires control over the making of speech as well as increasing her vocabulary. While the scientific method enhances rigor by stipulation of assumptions, sequenced hypotheses, and critical measures, the baby is also learning from experimental validation.

The Internet would appear to be a social medium in which an ordinary individual may discover new depths of intelligence. The Internet facilitates the assembly of information, allows the individual to associate ideas in new ways, and provides many means for the review of ideas, that is, multiple patterns of peer review. The links of hypertext bring multiple ideas into proximity for analysis and comparison. The web provides possible validation of models of the world. Distributed processing techniques permit the completion of complex calculations, including such enormous tasks as the search for extraterrestrial intelligence.

Consider a website that appears to present a consistent political perspective. For example, at this writing, www.commondreams.org provides left of center political commentary. Most of the content is culled from newspapers and magazines. One might assume that the reader would find his or her prejudices reinforced by the ideologically consistent essays. This is true but it is not the whole story. There are significant disagreements among the contributors. For example, some lean toward pacificism, others toward a more interventionist foreign policy. The variance in perspectives stimulates and enlarges the mind as the multiplicity of voices adds nuance and a higher order of resolution to argument. Not all ideological websites cultivate a universe of opinion, but hyperlinks and search engines leave few arguments unchallenged.

According to Dewey, the clear articulation of interests enhances understanding of social problems. Here the social intelligence approaches sociologizing. A website representing an interested organization and promulgating a specific conception of the public interest adds to the clarity of public debate.

Philip K. Dick's award-winning novel, *The Man in the High Castle* (1974), is a disturbing tale of layered illusion. The Axis powers have won World War II. There is a small subculture who consult the *I Ching* for enlightenment. They find an alternate reality in which the Allies were the victors. The Internet also has the capacity to invert conventional wisdom. Dissident perspectives are developed in web-logs and other on-line publications. Every epiphany and outlandish theory finds expression.

The Internet has extended the parameters of debate in the following significant way. The major newspapers revealed the outlines of the

143

controversy surrounding the 2000 elections in a fragmentary way. There was substantial coverage of the "chad" count and the divided Supreme Court. A consortium of newspapers undertook a full recount of the votes under various scenarios. Their conclusion, that Bush would likely have won a recount, did not answer the larger question of whom the majority of Florida voters chose. Among the many overlooked facets of the mystery was the substantial overvote in which voters punched their ballots for Gore and also wrote in his name. These ballots were discarded. It was a collection of dissident websites, not the major newspapers, that assessed the evidence of a campaign to prevent an accurate count of the vote.

Unfortunately, web commentaries on the right and left have played asymmetric roles. The Matt Drudge report and similar scandal sites on the right received attention in the "mainstream" press and provided ammunition for the Clinton impeachment in the 1990s while the 2000 election-related underground has largely been ignored by the mainstream media.

Jesuit thinker Teilard de Chardin (1955) predicted that human evolution would lead to a global consciousness, which he called the "noosphere." He argued that a world network of economic and social affiliations was emerging ever more rapidly. Chardin visualized the noosphere as a new membrane of mind linking all of human life. Internet enthusiasts have asserted that the Internet realizes the noosphere.

The concept of social intelligence provides a more apt way of understanding the Internet. Dewey was alert to the many ways in which philosophers dichotomized the individual and society. Neither individual nor society can truly be understood in isolation from the other. The term noosphere seems to invite reification of a collective mind when nothing in the Internet extinguishes the role of individuals or social groups as actors.

Open source software

"Open source software" would appear to be a particularly effective embodiment of social intelligence. Eric Raymond describes open source software as "the process of systematically harnessing open development and decentralized peer review to lower costs and improve software quality" (2001: 1). Open source software makes the underlying code available so that programmers can study and improve it. Users can report bugs so that they can be corrected.

Linux is an open source software operating system. What is illustrative about Linux and other open source software is that they are the products of many craftspeople collaborating over the Internet.

Open source software is not wholly the creation of isolated individuals. There are also workgroups who share the same physical space. While there is much done on a volunteer basis, Linux has been greatly advanced by commercial ventures that subsidize Linux development and provide a brick and mortar shopfloor. Contributors benefit from continuous employment and a shopfloor community.

Consider the documentation that accompanies this open source software for music, Modplug for Pocket PC:

Who are behind ModplugPC? We are:
- me - Eugene Rupakov <taurus_1@chat.ru>
I wrote simple ModplugPC front-end and have ported excellent MogPlug MOD-rendering library to PocketPC platform.
- Olivier Lapicque <olivierl@jps.net>
author of Modplug, which is arguably the best quality MOD-playing software available, has placed his sound rendering code in the public domain. Thanks a lot!
- Kenton Varda <temporal@gauge3d.org> (C interface wrapper). Thanks a lot!
- Markus Fick <marf@gmx.net>
Additional modifications, current Modplug library maintainer. Thanks a lot!
- Adam Goode adam@evdebs.org . . .
If you think you have found a bug, please, drop me a letter with full bug description, including: platform, device, memory status, what were you doing (playing) when a bug occurred, MOD-file title, Windows error message (if any), how to reproduce the bug, if you were able to resolve the bug, how did you do it

Legal stuff
~~~~~~~~~~~~
You can use this software FREE, without any obligations to its author(s). Although, any donation will be gratefully accepted (money, nice postcards, pizza vouchers etc. ;-)

BUT: if you use Modplug library in your own (free or commercial) projects, you MUST title the creators of the library in your product.
ModplugPC: Copyright (C) 2001–2002 Eugene B. Rupakov
ModplugPC and Modplug library are licensed under Artistic GPL.

Sources will be released as I cleanup and reformat them nicely :-)
Be good.
                    - Eugene

145

Note that the developer specifically requests assistance from users as well as inviting the participation of programmers.

The mod file format for music emerged from the collaboration of many programmers or "hackers" and has received impetus from the Internet. The mod was invented by Amiga computer users in the 1980s. It is a set of instructions directing the computer to send digitized samples of music instruments to multiple speakers and mix them according to a score. The score and the samples are contained within the file. The mod is processed by modplayer software, which is now available for computers running Windows, Linux, and other operating systems.

The mod community merges the subcultures of hacking and amateur music. Modfiles are ordinarily available without charge, as is modplayer software. The mod concept makes possible the transformation of a low-powered computer into a musical workshop. The individual computer user may assemble sounds collected from around the world in order to compose music (which then is available to others on the web). Composers may also improve the software. They have access to the underlying code and are encouraged by the broader community to contribute enhancements. For their composing and programming they receive recognition from their peers. They may simultaneously participate in the mod-based "gift" economy and earn money for music or software in other contexts. Mods have been critical to the development of "techno" and "ambient" music. (The MIDI and MP3 file formats have also provided new opportunities for independent musicians to compose, perform, and distribute their work without reliance upon major record labels.)

Sound synthesis experts have sought flexible means to generate instrumental sounds, maximizing the musician's creative possibilities. FM synthesis relied upon the simulation of instruments through the trial and error assembly and modulation of synthetic tones. Wavetable methods manipulated recorded samples of instruments. Physical modelling simulated the acoustic properties of instruments. Once the musical palette was devised, any amateur musician could play.

A font is the digital code for a typeface, but the term applies equally well to sound generation. The personal computer and the Internet reveal music to be a layered fabric, a cumulative project of many minds, a theme rendered with melodies and sound fonts, indeed, a creation of social intelligence.

Orthodox economists are not impressed by any claim that the open model fosters innovation and creativity. They contend that property rights are a necessary incentive to efficient productive activity, and that the absence of intellectual property rights in open source decreases the productivity of contributors. They insist that corporate control and ownership of ideas make self-interest the driver of innovation and efficiency. (In doing so, they seem to mistake corporations for individuals. Corporations demand loyalty as much as they embody self-interest.) Following the concept of social intelligence, a pragmatist would argue that free transfer of ideas is more critical for innovation and discovery than ownership of ideas.

The open source model by no means precludes personal profit from innovation, only limitations on the exchange of ideas. Loose and amorphous networks of individuals and groups, when they permit individual credit for achievement, seem to have great capacity for invention, or so academic research and much software suggest.

Given the potential for the creative recombination of information and the social process of software development, the Internet would appear to be an excellent medium for the social intelligence. The software upon which World Wide Web servers run and the browsers through which users search the Web are products of social intelligence in that they have emerged from the contributions of many programmers who are much like the weavers of a grand quilt.

Craft production

Craft is a network-oriented form of production that is rooted in social intelligence. (See Jacobs (1994) for another argument linking craft and social intelligence.) While a solitary individual may practice a craft, the necessary skills are passed from peer to peer. Each practitioner depends upon an evolving tradition of specialized knowledge. The boundaries of any workshop are less important than the patterns of learning, incorporating the contributions of many practitioners (accumulating knowledge as cooks collect recipes).

Craft is often practiced when quality and intelligent design are of paramount importance. Arts and crafts are produced in small batches, but they are thought to carry special value. Professional services are built around partnerships, however distorted by hierarchical adjuncts.

William Morris, the nineteenth-century British designer, artist, author, and activist, was among the foremost advocates of craft models of production. He favored democratic enterprises practicing art and craft in production and believed that a socialist revolution would be required to derail the capitalist model of industrialization. In the interim, Morris sought to practice business in a manner that was consistent with the moderately reformist ideas of John Ruskin. Ruskin had earlier in the century called for socially responsible business honoring craft and avoiding the perils of greed and traditional industrialism. Harvey and Press write that the pace of work in Morris' firm was humane, wages were somewhat above the norm, and that Morris himself joined the craftsmen in production (Harvey and Press 1995).

Morris set these desirable standards for business practice:

> It is right and necessary that all men should have work to do which shall be worth doing, and be of itself pleasant to do; and which should be done under such conditions as would be neither over-wearisome nor over-anxious.
>
> (Morris 1973: 111)

> Nothing should be made by man's labour which is not worth making; or which must be made by labour degrading to the makers.
>
> (ibid.: 123)

> No one who is willing to work should ever fear want of such employment as would earn for him all due necessaries of mind and body.
>
> (ibid.: 127)

In his *William Morris: Romantic to Revolutionary* (Thompson 1976: 99), E. P. Thompson stressed Morris' fidelity to Ruskin's vision of craft production in the former's business.

Morris paid homage to the medieval traditions of the guild and struck a chord with many skilled workers who could imagine or remember workplaces where they managed much of their work. Later, in 1906, A. J. Penty wrote *Restoration of the Guild System,* having been influenced by the ideas of Morris and Ruskin. He was a founder of the guild socialist movement, whose most prominent advocate was G. D. H. Cole.

Dewey was president of a group called the League for Industrial Democracy in the 1930s and was sympathetic to guild socialism in a non-doctrinaire way. Unlike Cole, Dewey believed that self-government in industry must be complemented by a larger democratic state, since democracy must stand prior to a specific economic form. Dewey stood with Ruskin and Morris in their insistence that everyday work incorporate elements of art and craft.

In the US, the concept of industrial democracy continued to carry associations with craft models of production. Steelworkers' union founder Clint Golden saw industrial democracy as the goal of collective bargaining, and Congress of Industrial Organizations President Philip Murray favored labor–employer co-management of industry through "industry councils" (Brooks 1978).

Lessem and Neubauer (1994) describe a "humanistic management" movement, preserving the craft tradition, in contemporary Europe. Humanistic management views the enterprise as a workplace community nestled in the neighborhood community. Lessem and Neubauer find this model best expressed in the Mondragon worker cooperatives of the Basque region of Spain and the small business networks of central and northeast Italy. In each case, employees find a measure of community in small, relatively democratic workshops within larger federations of enterprises. Basque priest Father Arizmendi is credited as the guiding spirit of Mondragon.

Action

Ruskin, Morris, and other advocates of craft clearly did not conceive of designing products as the prerogative of a special class of managers and entrepreneurs. Rather, they viewed their creative work as an arena for civic activism, for the building of community, for the resolution of social problems. Hannah Arendt, following Aristotle, termed this form of activism "praxis" or "action," as distinguished from "work" and "labor" (Arendt 1959).

Aristotle defined labor as the set of activities necessary for the subsistence of the household, as performed by slaves in ancient Greece. On the other hand, Aristotle called the making of useful and enduring objects (to be sold in the marketplace) "work." Finally, action is the process of creation, innovation, and self-expression that characterizes the life of the citizen, a small privileged minority in the Greek city state.

Action is the process of organizing social projects and revealing one's identity through creative initiatives in the public arena. Arendt argued that all humans may participate in action, not just a privileged few. Arendt wrote: "To act, in its most general sense, means to take an initiative, to begin ... to set something into motion ... Because they are ... newcomers and beginners by virtue of birth, men take initiative, are prompted into action" (1959: 177).

Action or praxis is a useful way to characterize the application of social intelligence in craft production. In fact, praxis is ordinarily defined as the unity of theory and practice. The craftsperson draws on and contributes to social intelligence and participates in the realm of action. We will later investigate praxis as it is evolving on the Internet.

Knowledge management

Employers are now addressing the problem of knowledge management, which focuses on the processes by which members of organizations share the information they need to perform their duties. It is a more practical, managerial view of information processing theory. One concern in knowledge management is the measurement of the value provided by intangible "assets" such as employee collaboration. Another is the creation of "cultural pockets," where employees may communicate and share knowledge more freely than is customary practice in a traditionally hierarchical organization (Perkmann 2002). What is revealing about knowledge management is that it amounts to a truncated view of social intelligence, trapped within the boundaries of a department or an organization. While a given unit in a firm will benefit from an informed and collaborative workforce, the other units and communities may suffer from the deprivation of information that might otherwise stimulate information and joint problem-solving.

Knowledge management inevitably involves the construction of boundaries to knowledge transfer, whether around "cultural pockets" or around the enterprise as a whole. The open source experience suggests that there are enterprise and social costs to limitations on information transfer. Proprietary information provides a temporary competitive advantage but may subtract from the sum total of possible innovation. (On the other hand, individuals and groups benefit from a realm of privacy and confidentiality; neither social intelligence nor the open source idea requires public disclosure of all that happens inside organizations.)

Total information awareness

While the Internet appears to be an excellent medium for the practice of social intelligence, computer networks may also be used for the purpose of employee and citizen surveillance. E-mail, web transactions, and every visit to a webpage can be monitored. While Internet users may rely on encryption algorithms to enhance the security of their communications, the federal government ordinarily has access to the keys to decoding. Nothing on the web is wholly secure; no firewall is impregnable.

Since the terrorist attacks of September 11, 2001, there has been considerable debate about the proper balance of liberty and security. The Pentagon's research arm, DARPA, has now launched the "Total Information Awareness" program to develop an information strategy to combat terrorism. The apparent goal is to assemble a massive database on individuals with information culled from web-based and other electronic transactions (DARPA 2002). Perhaps Total Information Awareness is the obverse of social intelligence. It generates information for the authorities (vertical information processing) rather than expanding the knowledge of the citizenry (horizontal information processing).

References

Arendt, H. (1959) *The Human Condition*, Garden City, New York: Doubleday.

Brooks, T. (1978) *Clint: Biography of a Labor Intellectual*, New York: Atheneum.

DARPA (2002) *Information Awareness: Proposer Information Pamphlet.* Online: http://www.darpa.mil/iao/BAA02-08.pdf (accessed 1 April 2003).

Dewey, J. (1920) *Reconstruction in Philosophy*, New York: Henry Holt and Company.

Dewey, J. (1963) *Liberalism and Social Action*, New York: Capricorn Books.

Dewey, J. (1978) "Ethics," Jo Ann Boydston (ed.) *The Middle Works, 1899–1924*, vol. 5, Carbondale and Edwardsville, IL: University of Southern Illinois Press.

Dewey, J. (1983) "Human Nature and Conduct," Jo Ann Boydston (ed.) *The Middle Works, 1899–1924*, vol. 14, Carbondale and Edwardsville, IL: University of Southern Illinois Press.

Dick, P. (1974) *The Man in the High Castle*, New York: Berkeley.

Gouinlock, J. (ed.) (1976) *The Moral Writings of John Dewey*, New York: Hafner Press.

Harvey, C. and Press, J. (1995) "John Ruskin and the Ethical Foundations of Morris and Company," *Journal of Business Ethics*, 14: 181–194.

Jacobs, D. (1994) *Collective Bargaining as an Instrument of Social Change*, Westport, CT: Quorum Books, 33–44.

Lessem, R. and Neubauer, F. (1994) *European Management Systems*, London: McGraw-Hill.

Morris, W. (1973) *Political Writings of William Morris* (edited by A. L. Morton), New York: International Publishers.

Perkmann, M. (2002) "Measuring Knowledge Value? Evaluating the Impact of Knowledge Projects," *KIN Brief* #7. Online. http://www.ki-network.org (accessed 21 October, 2002).

Raymond, E. (2001) *The Cathedral and the Bazaar*, Cambridge: O'Reilly.

Teilhard de Chardin, P. (1955) *The Phenomenon of Man*, New York: Harper and Row.

Thompson, E. P. (1976) *William Morris: Romantic to Revolutionary*, New York: Pantheon.

Wicks, T. and Freeman, E. R. (1998) "Organization Studies and the New Pragmatism: Positivism, Anti-Positivism, and the Search for Ethics," *Organization Science*, 9(2), 123–140.

8

INTERNET UNIONISM AND LABOR-FRIENDLY ENTERPRISE

Conservative employer interests have historically relied upon conceptions of "private" enterprise and the "free" market to resist social and state pressure to improve working conditions. Unionists have countered that the workplace is public and have sought to publicize instances of exploitation. E. E. Schattschneider explained, "Private conflicts are taken into the public arena precisely because someone wants to make certain that the power ratio among the private interests most immediately involved shall not prevail" (1960: 38).

The Internet potentially alters the debate as to the proper form of employee representation. It is an effective instrument for the illumination of worker abuse and solicitation of support. As early as 1972, Charles Levinson of the International Chemical Workers Federation (ICWF) suggested union use of computerized data banks through telex networks for the distribution of company information. Now unions are developing web-sites to more fully involve members in union business and better mobilize allies in labor struggles.

The Internet provides "free spaces," in the vocabulary of Harry Boyte (1989). Boyte describes free spaces as a realm of "voluntary associations ... that sustain an important measure of independence from large-scale systems and institutions of government, on the one hand, and that have public dimensions where a relational practice of power among different interests develops, on the other" (ibid.: 138). He provides the example of African-American beauty parlors, which helped sustain the energy and nerve of the civil rights movement in the American South.

Workers in anti-union employers have a similar need for space for organizing. Labor law circumscribes their opportunities for organizing in the workplace. While US factories, malls, and public spaces all have rules limiting the timing and character of protest, the Internet provides an alternative form of space in which at least some forms of protest can be effectively undertaken.

The Internet creates a plane that is less susceptible to employer control in which workers can assess the commonalities of their grievances. It provides a new forum for collective activity that is unlimited geographically. With the appropriate domain name, Internet activists may even contest the employer's claim on the company name.

Union leaders lack the ability to control Internet activism any more than employers do. While union leaders can control the content of an official web-site and moderate a discussion group, dissident union activists may establish their own Internet presence. There is no need for dissidents to rely upon either official union or employer hierarchies. Labor Notes and the Association for Union Democracy are two organizations which build lateral relations among reform groups across a variety of unions. (Labornotes is online at www.labornotes.org and represents militant "rank-and-file" groups across several unions. It has historically opposed concessionary bargaining and "union–management cooperation." Union Democracy in Action, another group which supports dissident unionists through legal action and other tactics, is online at www.uniondemocracy.com.)

Sociologist Arthur Shostak has provided these representative examples of labor's uses of the Internet: the Hotel, Restaurant, and Bartenders Union's use of a web-site for virtual picket lines; the Association for Flight Attendants web-site for collecting complaints from members about airplane equipment problems; the Allied Pilots Association use of e-mail to rally their troops; and a cyber-protest of Bridgestone-Firestone labor practices in the United States (Shostak 1999: 123).

The International Federation of Chemical, Energy, Mine, and General Workers Unions (ICEM: the successor to the ICWF) has undertaken several effective cybercampaigns on behalf of affiliates. ICEM's web-site (www.icem.org) helped win reinstatement for discharged strikers at two foreign-owned tire companies (1996, 1999), pressed a Russian employer to pay promised wages (1997), and secured changes in regressive labor and environmental policies at mining multinational Rio Tinto in Australia (1998). In the two tire company cases, Internet activism exposed to the world that Bridgestone-Firestone and Continental General denied US workers rights that these very corporations honored in their countries of origin (Walker 2001).

ICEM publications reveal a fundamental understanding of the value of network strategies. The federation seeks to build trade unionism with a "new power relationship to the real decision networks of the world economy – the transnational corporations" (ibid.).

Workingfamilies.com was inaugurated at the end of 1999 by the AFL-CIO. This web-based service offers low-cost Internet access, inexpensive computers, e-mail, chat rooms, news, and union-friendly shopping. Varied consumer products are available through the site, along with the names of the unions who represent the workers who make the products. This vastly simplifies the task of being a pro-union consumer.

Workingfamilies.com is designed to contribute to labor's broadly framed working families strategy, according to which existing union members and an unorganized but sympathetic public are jointly mobilized for issue campaigns (Workingfamilies.com 2002).

The Labourstart web page provides a portal for unionists around the world. There are links to country-specific labor news and resources for labor organizing. In fact, Labourstart offers an "Opera" brand browser preconfigured for union web-sites. It directs users to a unionized book-store for online purchases (Labourstart 2002). Labourstart's founder, Eric Lee has written extensively about Internet unionism. In an interview with a British union, he opined: "The Internet is as near to a classless society as you can get. Information is pooled, ideas exchanged, individuals become part of a global family."

He describes Internet goals for unionism in this way:

> the union objective should be to provide every member with a free e-mail number for life as part of union membership. Union members could then pick up and send their mail, and check the electronic equivalent of the office noticeboard for updated news on pay negotiations, health information, how to deal with sexual harassment or legal claims. Our aim is to communicate instantly with 260,000 members at no cost.
>
> (Quinn 1999)

Working Today (www.workingtoday.org) is a national non-profit membership (and union-like) organization for "independent" workers: freelancers, independent contractors, temps, part-timers, contingent workers, and people working from home. The web-site plays a critical role in informing members and allied workers of their rights. One new project is the development of a portable benefits plan. Founder Sarah Horowitz has won a MacArthur grant for her efforts. Working Today is one of the sponsors of www.NetproCWA.org, a union-oriented distance training initiative (Working Today 2002).

WashTech (www.washtech.org) has already been discussed. It is the web-site of the Washington Alliance of Technology Workers. WashTech is an initiative of temps and other workers at Microsoft and of pro-union employees at Amazon.com. WashTech was party to a successful suit challenging Microsoft's denial of benefits to temps. It has sought unsuccessfully to win formal bargaining rights at Amazon.com. WashTech is another sponsor of NetproCWA (WashTech 2002).

The IGC (www.IGC.org) is a federation of autonomous but progressive networks (e.g., labornet, peacenet) that predates the Internet (founded 1987). IGC affiliates helped spawn the Zapatistas movement in Mexico and a campaign for democracy in Burma. It is a project of Tides

Foundation, which contributes to a variety of socially responsible business and progressive Internet initiatives (IGC 2002).

As the work of the above union web-sites suggests, the Internet assists unions in a variety of ways. It plays an economizing role by providing low-cost international communications. There are great economies in postage and phone charges, thus facilitating international organizing and activism.

The Internet also ensures that union resource materials and databases are widely available to members, activists, and researchers. The results of corporate research can be assembled, dynamically linked to relevant resources, and distributed to the field.

The Internet provides an ongoing forum for internal deliberations (through listservers, chat rooms, and the like). The internal life of the organization is potentially enhanced. Union democracy, civil society within the labor movement, may be advanced (Diamond and Freeman 2001).

The Internet also provides an alternative to media that may be hostile to unions. It is readily apparent that the cable services, magazines, and newspapers that specialize in business news neglect many developments important to labor. The Labourstart web-site demonstrates how valuable a portal for labor news is to activists.

The pro-business *The Kiplinger Letter* reports describes this strategy for labor: "a new guild-like model, 21st-century version of the medieval groups, complete with virtual hiring halls" (Kiplinger 2000). This latter notion is not merely a means to enhance publicity of worker grievances. It is an effort to build a community of workers who are able to shape the contours of their industry through influence on the hiring process.

Diamond and Freeman (2001) describe a new model of "e-unionism." They argue that e-unions will provide individual representation, counseling, and customized services as well as collective bargaining to members and a broader constituency of supporters, serve employees on the web and in the workplace, and utilize artificial intelligence expert systems to inform members. They predict that the Internet will extend labor's reach by facilitating services to employees through "minority unions" where formal representation rights have not been won.

Freeman and Rogers (2002) expand on the e-unionism concept in their *WorkingUSA* essay entitled, "Open Source Unionism: Beyond Exclusive Collective Bargaining." Here they endorse the Internet as a platform for organizing and "open source" as a metaphor for the development of the new union model. The phrase "open source" indicates that Freeman and Rogers believe that effective union strategy will emerge from a process of experimentation in which activists devise models for union behavior, implement these approaches on-line, and invite participants and allied groups to evaluate the results:

> [o]pen source unionism would build a common collaborative platform, language, and practice among workers and union activists – often operating at some distance from one another, or at different work sites, or moving across multiple sites over their working lifetimes – as part of a more unified labor movement defined by shared values more than by present employment.
>
> ... an open source union movement would look for support anywhere it could find it ... Without European-style extension laws but with members in more workplaces than current unions, this new unionism would seek to moderate differences across work sites ...
>
> In contrast to the current union movement, based almost exclusively on workers in majority-member collective bargaining arrangements with employers, open source unionism would also include groups of workers who want union representation and advice but who fall shy of a majority at their workplace.

Understandably, some union advocates consider the idea of loose employee associations largely without traditional bargaining rights to be a pale imitation of unionism and possibly an obstacle to more traditional organizing. Chaison (2002) has several reservations about any such Internet-based unionism. He worries that web-site unionism will resemble a vending machine offering little of value for members and that employers will institute intranets, offering conference and complaint procedures but not effective representation, as an alternative they can control. It is clear that web-site activity can complement but cannot substitute for face-to-face organizing. Moreover, some argue that nothing short of bargaining representation offers durable gains to workers. (On the other hand, collective bargaining no longer guarantees durable gains either.)

While the Internet provides new opportunities for national and global unionism, it remains to be seen whether workers' access to computers and the Internet and trade unionists' sophistication with technology will be sufficient to permit the realization of these opportunities. Online protest is clearly insufficient as a labor strategy. A prerequisite for an effective model of unionism is that there be a continuing organization capable of preserving material gains for employees. The Industrial Workers of the World (IWW) demonstrated the inadequacy of protest-based unionism in their inability to protect wage gains for the textile workers of Lawrence, Massachusetts. The IWW abjured the negotiated contract, which appeared to represent capitulation to capitalism. They failed to build any form of power that would discourage employers from restoring the old terms of employment.

Wilson and Blain, active with WashTech, are persuaded that Internet unionism may have significant leverage with employers, at least in the high-tech sector. The key is providing training in technology and software as well as portable benefits to members so that organizing simultaneously satisfies some of the interests of employers and employees. Wilson and Blain (2002) use a "cut and paste" metaphor that resembles Freeman and Rogers' "open source" language as they explain the construction industry precedents for their conception of unionism.

> We also look around the labor movement and cut and paste ideas and concepts that could be applied to organizing IT workers. In particular, we look at the commercial building trades and we see a lot of parallels with the high-tech industry. Both industries revolve around many 6-month to two-year projects. In construction, a wide array of skilled trades people come together to build a building. In the software industry, a wide array of skilled trades people come together to build a computer program. We see that the building trades have built up an apprenticeship system that has put construction unions at the forefront of training, workforce development, and job placement issues in their industry, and we wonder why we can't develop a similar model for IT workers. In both industries, we see that the work is often project-based and cyclical ... union construction workers generally have portable benefits, administered through the union, that follow them from employer to employer. Many high-tech workers need and want such flexibility and portability of benefits and access to continuous training opportunities.

Of course, the construction union model depends upon the employer's willingness to rely on union members trained and referred by a union hiring hall. High-tech employers have the capacity to outsource work online to distant sites. If they can find competent and inexpensive help abroad, there is less incentive to engage with an organization like WashTech.

Internet unions perhaps can increase the likelihood of employer engagement through all the tools of corporate campaigns: publicizing workplace abuses, seeking support from consumers, litigation, and lobbying for helpful legislation. Moreover, union-sponsored training has the potential to produce a more broadly qualified workforce than employers are likely to do individually. Institutionalist economists have noted the "public good" character of training, which ensures that employers tend to underinvest in training. In the 1930s and 1940s, industrial unions proved their value to many employers as a means of promoting public purchasing power, upon which consumption and profits depended.

Wolfgang Streeck submits that today unions can demonstrate their continued relevance through their contribution to more valuable training (Wheeler 2002: 181).

Another approach that would enhance the value of an e-union model is the mandating of workers committees, as do Germany, the Scandinavian nations, and the European Community as a whole. If employers were obliged to consult with committees elected by their workers, e-unions could play a critical role assisting the works committees and improving their effectiveness.

One might characterize some of the above Internet benefits for workers (for example, offering training or illuminating worker abuses) as information effects. The neoclassical model stipulates that information is decisive in assuring rationality in market processes. One accepts or rejects a potential transaction based on available information about the value of the proffered commodity. Better access to information about an employer renders less likely an overvaluation of the terms of employment and the quality of the product. A corporate campaign on the Internet spreads useful information cheaply.

However, more perfect information would not by itself correct injustice in the workplace. At least as important is the impetus the Internet provides to the socialization of conflict (to sociologizing), which leads to employer concessions. To the degree that the Internet provides a new international plane for organizing, pressuring employers, and effecting change, Internet unionism will endure.

As should now be evident, effective labor activism on the net requires a willingness to engage constructively with employers and government. This depends upon a sustainable militancy that builds on incremental change. While the proper balance of adversarialism and cooperation is not a new problem for unionism, it may be elusive in the virtual mode. Cass Sunstein (2001) warns that the Internet exacerbates social polarization. He submits that identity group web-sites and dedicated listservers tend to reinforce the biases of participants, thereby heightening social division and limiting discourse and compromise. Anti-employer web-sites can broadcast damaging information without advancing solutions. Internet unionists must determine how to blend protest and responsibility.

Human communication ordinarily depends upon an interactive and iterative sequence of messages including both words and non-verbal cues. Traditional labor negotiations hinge at times on a rich pattern of communication that exceeds e-mail's capacity. Clearly unionism cannot take place exclusively online. Face-to-face interaction within unions and between unions and employers is a necessary supplement to virtual activism.

There may be another front for labor activism on the Internet, in devising a labor-friendly form of Internet enterprise. The dream of the National Labor Union and the Knights of Labor of an economy of small democratic workshops endures. The contemporary logic of democratic workshops depends on the social character of knowledge and innovation, the nature of craft as an expression of social intelligence, and the Internet's facilitating role.

Distributivism

The National Labor Union and Knights of Labor were nineteenth-century labor movements that protested the rise of powerful corporations. Leaders of these organizations considered corporations to be perversions of legitimate conceptions of enterprise and obstacles to broader opportunity. They counterposed a vision of small-scale internally democratic workshops to the corporate monoliths. They drew inspiration from Thomas Paine and other democrats who stressed the importance of widely distributed property to social justice. Their vision had much in common with the craft advocacy of Ruskin and Morris.

In the twentieth century, some have called the philosophy of widely distributed property "distributivism." Hillaire Belloc and G. K. Chesterton were well-known British distributivists, who based their ideas in part on Catholic social doctrine. (See Belloc's *The Servile State* (1912). Economist and US Senator Paul Douglas (1972) also embraced this philosophy.) Belloc and Chesterton opposed statist socialism and sought an alternative model of economic reform.

Distributivism endorses the redistribution of property in the interest of the many. Property is conceived more as a prerequisite for independence and economic security rather than as a vehicle for uneven accumulation. The gigantic modern corporation represents, in this view, an unjust consolidation of property.

The Internet may advance the distributivist vision. Internet technologies potentially flatten organizations by facilitating information processing (critical to production or distribution) and reducing the need for multiple levels of supervision. Similarly, Internet technologies increase the productive capacity of small groups, who may federate with others when additional competencies are needed. Networked computers enhance the potential for craft-based production. Desktop publishing and music provide examples. Computers replace fixed, dedicated tools with open-ended, configurable, systems (see Piore and Sabel (1984)). Individuals and groups can more efficiently produce in small quantities and respond rapidly to emerging needs.

In *The Second Industrial Divide: Possibilities for Prosperity*, Piore and Sabel (1984) present their vision of an economy in which communities of skilled craft workers play an increasingly important role. This future

they believe has been prefigured in the phenomenon of "flexible specialization":

> It is seen in the networks of technologically sophisticated, highly
> flexible manufacturing firms in central and northwestern Italy.
> Flexible specialization is a strategy of permanent innovation:
> accommodation to ceaseless change, rather than an effort to
> control it. This strategy is based on flexible "multi-use" equip-
> ment: skilled workers; and the creation, through politics, of an
> industrial community that restricts the forms of competition to
> those favoring innovation. For these reasons, the spread of flex-
> ible specialization amounts to a revival of craft forms of pro-
> duction.
>
> (ibid.: 17)

Piore and Sabel very provocatively argue that contemporary developments in the economy and technology make possible a revival of the
dream of artisanal democracy, of an economy based on craft communities embedded in a more democratic, egalitarian society. They submit that
computerized numerical control technology renders batch production in
small workshops an efficient alternative to traditional mass production:
"The effect of the computer [early engineering studies showed] would be
to lower the costs of such batch or job-shop production, as compared
with either one-of-a-kind customization or mass production" (ibid.: 259).
They also claim that batch production for niche markets is better suited
to succeed in an increasingly volatile global economy. Piore Writes:

> What might it be like to think of production as a form of action?
> It means that the production process becomes for the people
> who participate within it a public space like the political forum
> of ancient Greece, that they see that space as a realm in which
> they reveal themselves to each other as individuals.
>
> (Piore 1991: 22)

Piore has in mind Hannah Arendt's (1959) reconsideration of the Aris-
totelian categories of work, labor, and action. Piore interprets flexible
specialization and craft communities in the light of "action," which he
finds more relevant than traditional concepts of competition and commerce to the experience of craft networks.

Piore and Sabel were probably too sanguine about the potential of
flexible manufacturing networks to inspire a broad return to craft-style
production. The Italian small businesses which Piore and Sabel described
were not necessarily exemplars of good labor practices, nor have they
necessarily remained small and "democratic." They do, however,

demonstrate the relevance of computer technology to craft production, which remains viable in the contemporary era, if there is the will and power to sustain it.

The conventional wisdom is that the information economy has superseded the industrial age, and that information, rather than things, is the valuable commodity. This has always been true in that human participation in production is at base a processing of information. The individual reacts to complex stimuli and intervenes in mechanical operations so as to select a possible output. Desktop production lays out the detailed information in a way that permits direct manipulation of the variables (or language) of production by an individual.

For the sake of argument, let us assume that all production can be reduced to information edited on a computer and sent to a device that "prints" the desired product. This removes entire layers of work in traditional manufacturing, which otherwise consists of design, engineering, and execution. The design developed on a desktop can be transmitted directly to tools that cut and mold the product, or sent to a database, or shared with others for review and comment. Desktop production is reminiscent of historical craft technologies under which the worker has direct control over design and employs multi-purpose tools.

Open source software is one illustration of the possibility that skilled craftsmen might practice their skills on the Internet and reshape enterprise. While labor-anchored Internet enterprise may seem unrealistic in an era of corporate consolidation, a suggestive model is provided by the emerging Internet strategies of neighborhood enterprise. Stacy Mitchell of the Institute for Local Self-Reliance (Mitchell 2000) has been exploring the space on the Internet for local enterprise. Local bookstores and the like are deeply threatened by the vast economies, strategic alliances, superior capital, and wide publicity of the Internet superstores. However, neighborhood enterprises can build an Internet presence by collaborating through cooperatives and small business associations.

One leading example of this process is the American Booksellers Association and their Booksense.com web-site. The American Booksellers Association represents 3,500 local bookstores. Booksense.com will have a database of over one million titles. It will provide access to the sum total of all the books sold by member bookstores while informing consumers about the special identities of neighborhood stores (and reinforcing bonds with local communities). The American Booksellers Association is using political and legal means to contest the unfair advantages of superstores like Amazon.com, Borders, and Barnes and Noble.

Given the developments in batch production and industrial districts outlined by Piore and Sabel (1984), the mod/Linux experience, the Internet approaches of neighborhood enterprise, and scholars' development of online journals to bypass commercial publishers, it is possible to imagine a growing sector of small enterprises sustained by Internet economies and informational benefits. This outcome will not emerge automatically from market processes; it would require online activism, other pressure tactics, and government intervention to counteract the political and economic power of established corporations.

Conclusions about Internet unionism and labor-friendly enterprise

A modern version of the Knights of Labor dream of a more democratic economy would include brick and mortar and virtual workshops linked to one another and broader employee networks by the Internet. Trade unions would press for employer investment in workplace infrastructure, seek the implementation of labor standards and union contracts in and around these workshops (notifying the government and community of violations by e-mail), and enroll members on the shopfloor and online. They would shape the future of their industries through participating in training, counseling, research, and development, and by lobbying for supportive public policies.

The labor movement would consist of unions with formal representation rights on the job and allied employee associations. Both structures would utilize the web to communicate with members and supporters. Multi-party politics within unions would receive impetus from virtual "rank-and-file" organizations. As Hoyt Wheeler suggests in *The Future of the Labor Movement* (2002: 202), the labor movement should grow to incorporate a diversity of forms of employee representation to maximize numbers served as well as to facilitate experimentation.

Diffusion of these ideas first requires their implementation within a given industry or state. Networks of small craft-oriented workshops are likely be innovative as to product design, responsive to consumer preferences, and focused on quality. State governments can foster these networks by assisting with infrastructure, training, and Internet access, and by involving unions in economic policy-making. Unions can also take advantage of employer interest in divisionalization, decentralization, and outsourcing by building representation systems for all of these smaller workshops.

Unions can themselves find democratic enterprises to provide a model for progressive employment practices as well as to experiment with product design. Consider, for example, the TEAM X apparel enterprise (TEAM X 2002).

> We are pleased to introduce SweatX, a new line of casual active wear ... Designed and manufactured entirely within Los

Angeles, SweatX clothing is made by teamX inc., an employee owned, and unionized garment factory. At SweatX, we have assembled a highly experienced management group, and the fastest, most talented garment workers available, in one of the premiere centers of garment manufacturing. Utilizing the latest high-tech machinery in a brand-new factory space in the Los Angeles Garment District, there is a strong motivation on the part of both workers and management alike to take the apparel market by storm.

(TEAM X 2002)

On the one hand, TEAM X, Booksense, and WashTech provide the outlines of a more democratic economy propelled by sociologizing and praxis. On the other hand, the erosion of unionism continues, and it is the economizing mode that appears to be in ascendancy in public and private practice. It remains difficult to predict which Internet dynamics will prove more significant.

Toward social movement informatics

Contending with the perils and opportunities of the Internet requires a science of information systems that recognizes the social character of knowledge. The Internet is a new technology, but its challenge to hierarchy is merely a reaffirmation of the power of associated minds. The economizing, sociologizing, and praxis dynamics flow from the distinction between means and ends. When employees are only the means for profit-making, the Internet will economize at their expense. When employees are the ends of enterprise, the Internet facilitates sociologizing and supports praxis or action.

The Internet serves sociologizing and praxis best when it is democratic in framework. This entails the following.

First, the digital divide must be confronted. While the Internet is widely used, and a majority of Americans have access at schools, libraries, work, or home, the poor and lower working class have less opportunity to exercise their creative and organizational skills online. Computers are difficult to afford when food and shelter already strain family budgets. Continuous improvement in software based on increasing computer processing power requires frequent and expensive upgrades. Given the role of the Internet in employment and consumption, universal access to the Internet must be a public policy goal; the costs of basic service must be within the public's reach.

Second, the Internet should remain a commons built on open source software. Microsoft and America-On-Line have contrary plans. They would like to maximize their proprietary control. Web-sites should rely on protocols that are platform-independent without features that appear only in Internet Explorer or some other commercial browser. Open source software keeps the operations of the Internet transparent and susceptible to broad improvement.

Third, a labor and social movement practice should be developed. That is, activists and high-tech professionals should build institutions that support the progressive potential of the Internet. Such groups as the IGC, Computer Professionals for Social Responsibility, and the open source community are part of the solution. However, there is work that remains to be done.

One significant measure of progress will be whether a Social Movement Informatics discipline is born and prospers (Walker 2002). This would be reflected in a change in business schools and in the allied professions. There would be a growing community of scholars and practitioners who would devote their attention to the improvement of the Internet as a platform for social action, creative work, and production. We hope that this book contributes to the process.

References

Arendt, H. (1959) *The Human Condition*, Garden City, New York: Doubleday.

Belloc, H. (1912) *The Servile State*, London: T. N. Foulis.

Boyte, H. (1989) *CommonWealth: A Return to Citizen Politics*, New York: The Free Press.

Chaison, G. (2002) "Information Technology: The Threat to Unions," *Journal of Labor Research*, 23(2): 249–259.

Diamond, W. and Freeman, R. (2001) *Will Unionism Prosper in Cyber-space? The Promise of the Internet for Employee Organization*, National Bureau of Economic Research Working Paper 8483. Online. Available http://www.nber.org/papers/w8483 (accessed 24 November 2002).

Douglas, P. H. (1972) *In the Fullness of Time: The Memoirs of Paul H. Douglas*, New York: Harcourt Brace Jovanovich.

Freeman, R. and Rogers, J. (2002) "Open Source Unionism: Beyond Exclusive Collective Bargaining," *WorkingUSA*. Online. Available http://www.workingusa.org/2002sp/fulltext/osunionism.htm (accessed 24 November 2002).

IGC (2002) *Institute for Global Communications*. Online: http://www.igc.org (accessed 1 April 2003).

Kiplinger, K. (2000) *The Kiplinger Letter*, 28 July, p. 1.

Labourstart (2002) "Where Trade Unionists Start their Day on the Net," Online: http://www.labourstart.org (accessed 1 April 2003).

Lee, E. (1997) *Labour and the Internet: The New Internationalism*, London: Pluto Press.

Mitchell, S. (2000) *The Home Town Advantage: How to Defend Your Main Street Against Chain Stores and Why It Matters*, Minneapolis: ILSR Press.

Piore, M. J. (1991) "Work, Labor, and Action," unpublished MIT working paper.

Piore, M. J. and Sabel, C. (1984) *The Second Industrial Divide: Possibilities for Pros-perity*, New York: Basic Books.

Quinn, L. (1999) "Wizard of the Wire," *CWUVoice* (UK), (January 1999). Online: http://www.labourstart.org/cwuvoice.html (accessed 27 March 2003).

Rogers, J. (1990) "Divide and Conquer: Further 'Reflections on the Distinctive Character of American Labor Laws,'" *Wisconsin Law Review*, 1–147.

Schattschneider, E. E. (1960) *The Semi-Sovereign People: A Realist's View of Demo-cracy in America*, New York: Holt, Rinehart, and Winston.

Shostak, A. (1999) "CyberUnions: The Future of Labor," *WorkingUSA: The Journal of Labor and Society*, 3, 120–133.

Sunstein, C. R. (2001) *Republic.com*, Princeton, NJ: Princeton University Press.

TEAM X (2002) *What We Stand For*. Online. Available http://www.sweatx.net/stand/index.html) (accessed 22 November 2002).

Walker, S. (2001) *To Picket Just Click It: Social Netwar and Industrial Conflict in a Global Economy*, School of Information Management Working Paper, Leeds: Leeds Metropolitan University.

Walker, S. (2002) "Social Movement Informatics," e-mail (18 October 2002).

WashTech (2002) *A Voice for the Digital Workforce*. Online. Available http://www.washtech.org (accessed 24 November 2002).

Wheeler, H. (2002) *The Future of the American Labor Movement*, Cambridge: Cam-bridge University Press.

Wilson, G. and Blain, M. (2001) "Toward a More Inclusive Labor Movement. Organizing in the New Economy: The Amazon.com Campaign," *WorkingUSA: The Journal of Labour and Society*," Fall. Online: http://www.workingusa.org/2001fa/articles/wilsonblain.htm (accessed 1 April 2003).

Workingfamilies.com (2002) *The AFL-CIO Internet Community*. Online. Available http://www.workingfamilies.com (accessed 24 November 2002).

Working Today (2002) *Working Today*. Online. Available http://www.working today.org (accessed 24 November 2002).

NOTES

1 BETWEEN UTOPIA AND DYSTOPIA

1 Phone conversation with UAW official, *circa* March 2000.
2 Remarks of Secretary of Commerce William M. Daley, Digital Economy Conference, US Department of Commerce, May 25, 1999.
3 It is possible to extract other underlying mythical, if not biblical symbolism, as
well. For example, "Neo" (the Greek word for "new") plays out a savior role,
but he is also a superhero. The name of the leader of the rebellious group,
"Morpheus," comes from the Greek god of dreams. A futurist Moses, he is
trying to lead his people out of the "computer-generated dream world" known
as the Matrix. "Zion" is the surviving underground city of the remaining free
humans, but the word also connotes the notions of "homeland," "promised
land," and "ideal city," but also "utopia" and "heaven." Of course, "liberation"
is the main symbolic theme running through the movie, which can be interpreted as freedom from the limitations and depravations of modern technological society, and the freedom to realize ourselves separate from the
"programmed" traditional norms and standards imposed by that society.
Hence, it is possible to read in "countercultural" overtones that hark back to
the late 1960s and 1970s.

2 ONE, TWO, MANY INDUSTRIAL REVOLUTIONS

1 Although our primary focus is the Internet, most of the following discussion
refers to ICT. While the most visible manifestation of ICT growth during the
last half decade of the 1990s, the Internet's diffusion is largely tied to
performance improvements in microprocessors, telecommunications equipment, and software systems, which taken together have contributed to the
productivity acceleration during that period.
2 This includes labor productivity (measuring output per labor hour) and
multi-factor productivity (MFP; sometimes called total factor productivity, or
TFP), measuring increases in output generated by weighted inputs of labor,
capital, and sometimes materials, energy, and/or imports, and other factors.
3 Economists differ about whether ICT capital deepening – workers are given
more ICT equipment to work with – was mainly responsible for the dramatic
increase in service industries' labor productivity after 1995, or whether it was
increased MFP – reflecting the gains in labor productivity derived from
performance improvements in a production process. Triplett and Bosworth
attribute the gain primarily to MFP; their analysis shows that ICT capital

166

deepening was as prominent a source of services' productivity growth before 1995 as it was after (Triplett and Bosworth 2002: 25; see also Jorgenson *et al.* 2002).

4 Jorgenson *et al.* (2002) show that the acceleration was very concentrated in just three industries, wholesale trade, security brokers, and retail trade, while eighteen of the thirty-two service industries they examined showed negative MFP growth over the 1987–2000 period. Other analysts suggest that these negative results could be due to measurement problems. See Brookings Institution (2002).

5 Rosenberg (1982: 252) notes that reduced transportation costs also enabled greater degrees of regional specialization. He writes:

> As the costs of moving materials from one location to another decline, the productive activity undertaken in any particular area is less intimately linked to the resources found there. It becomes increasingly possible to base industrial activity upon raw materials transported over a considerable distance, especially where there is convenient access to water transport.

6 Most notably, three major innovations in ferrous metallurgy created the shift from iron to steel: Bessemer's converter, Siemens' open-hearth method, and the Gilchrist Thomas basic lining, making it possible to produce steel with high phosphorous ores (Mowery and Rosenberg 1989: 41).

7 Rosenberg (1982) reports that "Agriculture, Forestry, and Fishing" accounted for 35.9 percent of the working population in 1801, but declined to 8.7 percent by 1901. "Manufacturing, Mining, and Industry," which already accounted for 29.7 percent in 1801, jumped to 46.3 percent in 1901. "Trade and Transport" workers grew from 11.2 percent in 1801 to 21.4 percent in 1901.

8 Some of these firms are owned by large mass-production manufacturers, and many of the latter (DaimlerChrysler, Volkswagen, and even Ford) produce a line of very high end luxury cars (more than $85,000 and usually in the range of $100,000 or more, and some as high as $230,000), mixing the latest in new automotive technology with handcraftsmanship. See Miller and Lundegaard (2002).

9 Most of these inventions date from the last quarter of the nineteenth century, with the exception of the telegraph (1844) and television (1911).

10 Examples include water-controlled temple doors in ancient Rome, control devices in fourteenth-century clocks, a fully automatic grist mill built in 1784, and the Jacquard loom developed in the eighteenth century. Feedback was applied in seventeenth-century windmills, James Watt's flyball governors for automatically controlling steam engine speeds in 1788, and Charles Babbage's analytical machine built in 1840 (Buckingham 1970: 134).

11 Remington Rand sold the first commercially built computer, UNIVAC, to the government for processing the census, in 1950. General Electric was the first private firm to install a computer, for use in payroll processing, in 1954 (Greenbaum 1995: 46).

3 THE WIZARD OF OZ AND THE JOBS DILEMMA

1 Some care should be taken in interpreting these employment trends, however. It is probably impossible to isolate any single factor as causal, though some forces or events may be more determinant than others at any given time. For

example, manufacturing employment on the whole grew until the late 1970s, even though there were significant dips and rises along the way that can be attributed to events like war, recessions, and energy shocks. The sharp increase in manufacturing jobs in the mid-1960s followed by a sharp decline in 1970–1971 reflects in large part the build-up and subsequent slowdown of the Vietnam War, as also seen in the employment trend for the aircraft industry. The dips in the 1974–1975, 1980–1982, and 1990–1992 were recession-related. The drop in 1974–1975 was also probably exacerbated by the oil crisis. Higher energy costs affect producer costs, usually passed onto consumers in higher prices, which, in turn, can dampen the demand for manufactured goods.

2 Greenbaum traces the evolution of the computers that were progressively employed by large bureaucracies. A second generation of computers was introduced in 1959, using transistors rather than vacuum tubes, making them somewhat smaller (they were still huge by today's standards) and more reliable, using standard programming languages like FORTRAN and COBOL. The third generation of computers, introduced in 1965 used integrated circuits. "It was these machines that finally ushered in a more widespread use of mainframe computers and prompted computer manufacturers to develop standardized software tools to be used with them" (1995: 47).

3 The US goods trade deficit has continued to be high up through the present. The deficit jumped from $96.9 billion in 1992 to $191 billion in 1996, to $246.7 billion, in 1998 to $452.4 billion in 2000. It dropped a little in 2001, to $427.2 billion, but the deficits in 2000 and 2001 stand as the two largest in US history. Data Source: US Department of Commerce, Bureau of Economic Analysis.

4 See, for example, Congress of the United States (1989); Under-Secretary of Defense (Acquisition) (1998); Congress of the United States (1998).

5 Enabled by the 1984 National Cooperative Research Act of 1984, American firms joined advanced technology R&D consortia without fear of anti-trust actions, sometimes federally sponsored, to jointly support the development of next generation products in their sector. For example, the DARPA-supported Sematech consortium of major semiconductor firms in to strengthen the US position in the global semiconductor market. In 1988 Congress passed the Omnibus Trade and Competitiveness Act, which among other things, strengthened and created new federal agencies with a specific mandate to foster the competitiveness of US industry. The bill changed the name of the National Bureau of Standards to the National Institute for Standards and Technology (NIST), with the aim of making NIST the premier civilian agency responsible for supporting commercially important technology R&D. NIST also became home to two technology initiatives, the Advanced Technology Program (ATP) and what later became the Manufacturing Extension Partnership (MEP). ATP provides matching R&D grants to private firms to foster "pre-competitive," commercializable, cutting-edge technologies. MEP oversees a network of 400 centers spread throughout the nation which provide modernization and business assistance to small manufacturers. MEP supplies roughly one-third the funding for these centers; state grants and fees-for-service account for the other two-thirds.

6 According to Harrison (1994), for example:

> What is needed is a combined effort by a critical mass of representatives from farsighted companies, unions, and government to encourage new regulations and business practices that mute the distinction between insiders and outsiders – practices that promote both distributive justice and sustained economic growth.

Proposed measures include health insurance and pension benefits offered to contingent workers by amending the Employment Retirement Income Security Act, closer regulation of private temp agencies, stronger enforcement of the National Labor Relations Act, to include the right to form independent workplace organizations such as health and safety councils that also help improve the lives of both full- and part-time employees (ibid.: 45). Gordon (1996) recommended raising the minimum wage, enacting legislation that enhance workers' ability to achieve effective workplace representation, encourage flexible work conditions not disposable work, provide incentives for cooperative and democratic work organizations, and provide support for training assistance for cooperative enterprises (ibid.: 238–253).

4 E-BUSINESS AND THE VIRTUAL ORGANIZATION

1 When dispersed geographically such internal proprietary networks are called wide-area networks (WANs).
2 "E-Commerce Transforming Business," *Chemical and Engineering News* (12 July 1999), 11.
3 Blumenthal (1999: 7–8) provides a slightly more technical explanation of how these software protocol standards operate:

> The layers embody functions from connection to the physical means of communication to applications that represent tasks the user wants to accomplish via the Internet (e.g., send e-mail). This structure governs how the software system at a given layer relates to other software at adjacent layers on a given computer or other access device and how it relates to the software systems at the same layer on other computers with which communication is established.

4 Blumenthal (1999: 8–9) elaborates further:

> Information can be located and shared through the Web because the information is formatted and stored appropriately for http; actions associated with finding information take place via application software called "Web browsers" loaded onto the systems people use for access. HTTP is itself subject to frequent adaptation (via new standards) to support different kinds of access (e.g., by people with certain disabilities, or by people using wireless/mobile systems) and different kinds of activity (e.g., mechanisms to enhance the commercial value of Web sites, such as security features to protect financial transactions and information-gathering features to collect data about site use). Support for "text-only" browsing facilitates use by people with low-bandwidth access by avoiding communication of bandwidth intensive images.

5 The US Census Bureau (2002a) defines e-commerce sales as sales of goods and services where an order is placed by the buyer or price and terms of sales are negotiated over an Internet, extranet, EDI network, electronic mail, or other online system.
6 The US Census Bureau estimated that US e-commerce revenues for selected service industries reached $37 billion in 2000, an increase of 48 percent over 1999. These revenues accounted for 0.8 percent of total revenues in these sectors, versus 0.6 percent in 1999. Included in this data are online revenues

from newspaper, periodical, book and software publishers, online information services, couriers and messengers, and computer systems design and related services, many of which are business as well as consumer services (2002c).

7 According to Ernst, *supplier networks* are comprised of OEMs and their suppliers; *producer networks* include all co-production arrangements that enable producers to pool their production capacities, financial, and human resources; *customer networks* consist of the forward linkages of manufacturers with distributors, marketing channels, value-added resellers, and end users; *standard coalitions* are comprised of global standard setters with the purpose of locking in as many firms as possible into proprietary product or interface standards; and, *technology cooperation networks* support the acquisition of product design and production technology, enable joint process and production development, and allow scientific knowledge and R&D to be shared (cited in Castells 1996: 191).

8 Zysman relates CNPNs to Wintelism, which he considers a second major characteristic of the digital era. Wintelism, he explains, "reflects a shift in competition away from final assembly and vertical control of markets by final assemblers." In Wintelist competition, market power is located anywhere in the information technology value-chain including architectures, components, and software. The term Wintelism is derived from the dominant, strategic roles in computer and Internet value chains of software giant Microsoft (Windows) and microchip giant Intel, that have assumed greater influence over the evolution of these markets than final assemblers. He contrasts Wintelism with lean production, which "was about production innovation and the relationship amongst national production systems," while Wintelism "is about the integration of production systems across borders." CNPNs and contract services are the organizational counterparts of this shift (Zysman 2002: 28).

9 Quote taken from Borrus (1997).

10 Although Boeing's 777 was the first commercial airline created and put into production on a virtually paperless basis, using computer modeling almost exclusively, Northrop had pioneered the "paperless aircraft production" model at its El Segundo California plant in 1989. It replaced the 16,000 sheets of paper associated with the manufacturer of each F-18 fuselage with PC terminals at each assembly station, dropping costs 30 percent (Goldman *et al.* 1995: 138).

5 JOBS IN THE VIRTUAL ECONOMY

1 Earlier efforts to measure the economic impacts associated with digital (ICT and Internet) technologies (DOC 1998, 1999; OECD 1999) divided industry sectors into ICT-producing industries and ICT-using industries. ICT-producing industries include hardware, software/services, communications equipment, and communications services. Industries considered major users of IT equipment, include a large number of major services industries (telecommunications, legal services, FIRE, wholesale and retail trade, health services, legal services, business services), manufacturing (chemicals and allied products, electronic equipment, instruments and related), energy (pipelines, except natural gas, petroleum and coal products), and media (radio and TV, motion pictures). These industries were evaluated as among the top fifteen industries based on two measures: IT capital stock as a share of total equipment stock (net depreciation), or IT investment per employee.

2 These include computer software engineers, computer support specialists, computer software engineers (systems software), network and computer systems administrators, network systems and data communications analysts, desktop publishers, database administrators, and computer systems analysts. The other two fastest-growing occupations were personal and home care aides and medical assistants which are lower skilled and lower paid compared to the others (Hecker 2001b: 79).

3 Only public sector jobs have maintained a relatively strong union share. For example, in 2000, unions accounted for 32 percent of public administration jobs, 44 percent of elementary and secondary school jobs, and 70 percent of US Postal Service jobs. Bureau of National Affairs (2001: 58–67).

4 International Longshore and Warehouse Union, AFL-CIO "ILWU Hails Land-mark Agreement," press release, November 23, 2002 (http://www.ilwu.org/solidarityday/20021123/PressRelease.htm).

5 Appelbaum *et al.* (2000: 7) further note:

> Workers in an HPWS experience greater autonomy over their job tasks and methods of work and have higher levels of communication and work matters with other workers, managers, experts (e.g., engineers, account-ants, maintenance and repair personnel), and, in some instances, with vendors and customers.

INDEX

activism on the Internet 2, 5, 153–4
Aeppel, T. 98
aerospace/aircraft manufacturing
    31–2, 58, 95
AeroTech Service Group 96
agriculture 29
aid programs 57
Air Products & Chemicals 98
Airbus 62
aircraft/aerospace manufacturing
    31–2, 58, 95
Amazon.com 2–3, 85, 115, 132
America-On-Line 163
American Express 93
Appelbaum, E. 121
Apple 43
architecture of the Internet 82–4
Arendt, Hannah 149, 160
Aristotle 149
Aron, Ravi 93, 94
ARPANET 45
Arquila, J. 2
assembly lines 32–3
Aston Martin 34
AT&T 65
Atwood, R. 12
authority 135
auto industry 3, 12, 32–5, 40, 45–6, 58,
    72, 94–5; build-to-order model 107;
    Covisint trading platform 3, 88–9,
    110; efficiency and effectiveness
    improvements 80; and employment
    107, 110, 111; foreign competition 62;
    just-in-time delivery 46, 64; trade
    statistics 61
automation 12, 17–18, 35–41, 46, 47;
    computer-based 73–4;
    computer-integrated manufacturing

(CIM) 67–8; and employment 58–9,
    75–6, 103–4; and flexibility 64, 67;
    office automation 59;
    superautomation 74–5

banks 98
bar codes 24, 25
Bell, Daniel 3
Belloc, Hillaire 159
Bentley 34
Berman, D.K. 20
Bezos, Jeff 3
Birnbaum, J. 114
Black, M. 61, 62
Blain, M. 115, 156–7
Blumenthal, Marjorie S. 82, 83, 84
Boeing 58, 65, 88, 95
Bolton, A. 52
booksense.com 161
Borrus, Michael 61, 90
Bosworth, Barry P. 23, 25
Boyer, G. 133
Boyte, Harry 152
Braverman, Harry 6, 29, 30, 73
Bridgestone-Firestone 153
broadband communications 54
Buckingham, W. 38, 40
build-to-order model 79–80, 94, 107
Burns, T. 5
business intermediaries 88
business schools 1
business-to-business (B2B)
    e-commerce 85, 86–9, 109
business-to-consumer (B2C)
    e-commerce 85–6
Bylinsky, G. 96
Byrne, J.A. 65, 66